THE
NEW
MARKETING

THE NEW MARKETING

Transforming the corporate future

Malcolm McDonald and Hugh Wilson

OXFORD   AMSTERDAM   BOSTON   LONDON   NEW YORK   PARIS
SAN DIEGO   SAN FRANCISCO   SINGAPORE   SYDNEY   TOKYO

Butterworth-Heinemann
An imprint of Elsevier Science
Linacre House, Jordan Hill, Oxford OX2 8DP
225 Wildwood Avenue, Woburn, MA 01801-2041

First published 2002

British Library Cataloguing in Publication Data
A catalogue record for this book is available from the British Library

Library of Congress Cataloguing in Publication Data
A catalogue record for this book is available from the Library of Congress

ISBN 0 7506 5387 6

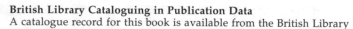

For information on all Butterworth-Heinemann publications, visit our
website at www.bh.com

Composition by Genesis Typesetting, Rochester, Kent
Printed and bound in Great Britain by MPG Books Ltd, Bodmin, Cornwall

Contents

Preface   vii

Chapter 1   **The new marketing: drive the digital market or it will drive you** 1
Marketing in crisis   2
But doesn't IT drive strategy now?   4
The argument for CRM systems   6
Marketing strategy and the Internet   8
A definition of new marketing   10
An overview of the new marketing process   12
The drivers of change   22
Marketing: the function and prerequisites for success   28
Summary   30
References   32

Chapter 2   **Building the future on solid foundations: defining markets and understanding value** 35
Introduction   36
Putting CRM in its proper context   36
Competitive forces analysis   42
Market definition and market segmentation   49
Conclusions   68
References   68

Chapter 3   **Planning for market transformation: determining the value proposition** 71
Introduction   72
Marketing planning   73
Planning and innovation   81
Future market mapping: analysing industry structure   83
Multi-channel integration: channel chains   91
Channel choice: the channel curve   93

The prioritization matrix: defining channel strategy   96
Determining channel tactics   102
Summary   103
References   104

Chapter 4   **Making the future happen: communicating and delivering value**   115
Introduction   116
The e-marketing mix   119
Towards the digital enterprise: a stage model   128
IT at the customer interface: front-office CRM   144
References   156

Chapter 5   **Staying on track: monitoring the value delivered**   159
Introduction   160
Monitoring the value received   161
Customer lifetime value   162
Monitoring the value delivered   164
Metrics for the sales process online   167
Analytical CRM   174
References   188

Chapter 6   **Avoiding pitfalls: implementation issues**   189
Introduction   190
Success factors in IT-enabled marketing projects   190
Managing for results: the benefits dependency network   204
Summary   207
References   208

Chapter 7   **Focusing on tomorrow's customer: future trends and the implications for marketing practice**   209
The changing customer   210
Styles of planning in the digital age   211
Marketing measurement and accountability   215
Organizational issues and the future of marketing   219
References   222

Index   223

Preface

Marketing is about the exchange of value between customer and supplier. However, the word 'value' has been much abused by business people in the last fifty years.

The overwhelming emphasis to date has been on value to the organizations themselves and their shareholders and, whilst it is obvious that long-term successful organizations have always created superior value for customers, such organizations have essentially been in truly free, competitive markets.

Compare this with those protected and cosseted markets in which the major players continue to thrive and prosper, in spite of treating their customers appallingly badly, and for whom value and electronic commerce mean little more than getting transaction costs down – in other words, cost cutting. The notion of using e-commerce to create superior customer value is still an alien concept!

Shining through the gloom, however, is a consumer-driven revolution, fuelled by information technology, in which customers know as much, if not more, about their suppliers, than they do about them. And they don't like what they are discovering and are voting with their feet in droves.

This new-found freedom is having a major impact on banking, airlines, financial services, former nationalized industries and many other erstwhile financially-driven markets, but in beginning to turn to traditional marketing, the move to a more market-driven orientation is being confounded by increasingly confusing patterns of consumer behaviour.

Consumers are alternating their identities between the extremes of cyber-consumer on the one hand and traditional buyer on the other. The new consumer is becoming something of an enigma, causing markets to fragment. Add to this an increasing proliferation of products, an endless stream of adverts and the fact that consumers have become more marketing literate (and in so doing are rejecting traditional make/promote/sell models) and we have a situation which demands a new, more proactive style of marketing.

The speed at which the commercial world moves today precludes the leisurely process of going out and asking consumers and customers what they

want and, in any case, no coherent answers would be forthcoming, for the simple reason that they don't know what is possible and are relying on suppliers to provide them with new, life-enriching experiences at reasonable prices. Those organizations who understand this and who take a more proactive, market-driving approach, will be the ones who succeed.

So, we have to take all that is best in traditional marketing, supplemented by some new techniques, and use it to drive markets by creating superior value propositions. These propositions need to be underpinned by an understanding of tomorrow's market structure, channels and customer needs, not just today's. Increasingly, we are called upon to bring about these changes in customer behaviour and the competitive environment, not just to predict them. We call this process 'New Marketing'. It involves a deeper understanding of the real role of marketing in transforming the corporate future and of how the e-revolution can be woven into the fabric of its processes to create a new garment that will delight customers and, in so doing, delight all other stakeholders.

This book isn't just for organizations struggling to understand the post-modern consumer. It is a book which is equally valid for business-to-business marketing. But it does need to be read most carefully, as it is not a trivial, gimmicky book.

We wish you well in using our version of new marketing.

Professor Malcolm McDonald and
Dr Hugh Wilson
Cranfield University School of Management

1

The new marketing

Drive the digital market or it will drive you

➡ Marketing in crisis

➡ IT and strategy

➡ The argument for CRM systems

➡ Marketing strategy and the Internet

➡ A definition of new marketing

➡ An overview of the new marketing process

➡ The drivers of change

➡ Marketing: the function and prerequisites for success

Marketing in crisis

After the best part of a century of marketing, at the dawn of the new millennium marketing was still perceived as being something to do with promotion and little else. Even more depressing, a study carried out at Cranfield University School of Management during 2001 and 2002 among senior non-marketers across a wide spectrum of organizations revealed that those in marketing are seen as 'expensive, unaccountable and slippery!'.[1]

All of this was first brought to a head in the now famous 1993 Brady and Davis *McKinsey Quarterly* article, in which they referred to the growing attention paid by chief executives to typically large marketing budgets and doubt about their value for money.[2] While this brought a crescendo of denial from the marketing community, the reality is that confusion still reigns about what marketing is and where it fits with other disciplines. The marketing community itself has many different names for different aspects of marketing, such as selling, advertising, direct marketing, market research and the like. Other major business functions, such as finance, also clearly define the different dimensions of their activities, such as auditor, cost and works accountant, management accountant and finance director. So, we don't blame the cost and works accountant for their company's failure owing to reckless business or financial strategy. Yet we tend to criticize the whole of marketing when, for example, the 'cost and works' marketer – perhaps a hotel marketing executive – fails to generate demand for a hotel built in the wrong place, with the wrong facilities, by operations management who felt they knew better then the marketplace and did not bother to consult it.

Table 1.1 gives just some of the hundreds of definitions of marketing that have appeared in books and journals over the years.

If you study the way the various definitions have been grouped, you will find that the essential difference between those in Group A and those in Group B is that *Group B definitions make an unambiguous reference to identifying and satisfying customer needs and building systems around this principle*. This is generally accepted as true marketing orientation, and is the stance taken throughout this book about marketing.

Group A definitions tend to focus far less on the customer (unless it is to *decide* what customers want, or to *exert influence* on the customer, i.e. to do things to the customer) and more on the company's own systems and profit motives.

Table 1.1 Some definitions of marketing

1 The planning and execution of all aspects and activities of a product so as to exert optimum influence on the consumer, to result in maximum consumption at the optimum price and thereby producing the maximum long-term profit.

2 Deciding what the customer wants; arranging to make it; distributing and selling it at a profit.

3 Marketing perceives consumption as a democratic process in which consumers have the right to select preferred candidates. They elect them by casting their money votes to those who supply the goods or services that satisfy their needs.

4 The planning, executing and evaluating of the external factors related to a company's profit objectives.

5 Adjusting the whole activity of a business to the needs of the customer or potential customer.

6 . . . marketing is concerned with the idea of satisfying the needs of customers by means of the product and a whole cluster of things associated with creating, delivering and, finally, consuming it.

7 The total system of interacting business activities designed to plan, price, promote and distribute products and services to present and potential customers.

8 (Marketing is) the world of business seen from the point of view of its final result, that is, from the customer's viewpoint. Concern and responsibility for marketing must therefore permeate all areas of the enterprise.

9 The activity that can keep in constant touch with an organization's consumers, read their needs and build a programme of communications to express the organization's purposes.

10 The management function which organizes and directs all those business activities involved in assessing and converting customer purchasing power into effective demand for a specified product or service and moving the product or service to the final customer or user so as to achieve the profit target or other objectives set by the company.

11 The marketing concept emphasizes the vital importance to effective corporate planning and control, of monitoring both the environment in which the offering is made and the needs of the customers, in order that the process may operate as effectively as is humanly possible.

12 The organization and performance of those business activities that facilitate the exchange of goods and services between maker and user.

13 The process of: (1) Identifying customer needs, (2) Conceptualizing these needs in terms of the organization's capacity to produce, (3) Communicating that conceptualization to the appropriate locus of power in the organization, (4) Conceptualizing the consequent output in terms of the customer needs earlier identified, (5) Communicating that conceptualization to the customer.

14 (In a marketing company) all activities – from finance to production to marketing – should be geared to profitable consumer satisfaction.

15 The performance of those business activities that direct the flow of goods from producer to consumer or user.

16 The skill of selecting and fulfilling consumer wants so as to maximize the profitability per unit of capital employed in the enterprise.

17 The economic process by means of which goods and services are exchanged and their values determined in terms of money prices.

18 The performance of business activities that direct the flow of goods and services from producer to consumer in order to accomplish the firm's objectives.

19 Marketing is concerned with preventing the accumulation of non-moving stocks.

20 The activity that can keep in constant touch with an organization's consumers, read their needs and build a programme of communications to express the organization's purposes . . . and means of satisfying them.

Group A	1	2	4	7	10	12	15	17	18	19
Group B	3	5	6	8	9	11	13	14	16	20

The problem with such definitions, however, is that none of them is sufficiently clear and unambiguous to remove the confusion surrounding this domain. One of the main purposes of this chapter is to define marketing in the clearest, most unequivocal way, in order that the function of marketing can take its rightful place at the heart of business management alongside finance, logistics, IS/IT, R&D, human resources, and operations.

Before we do this, however, let us begin by taking a look at the impact of IT on strategy and, in so doing, outline the main purpose of this book.

But doesn't IT drive strategy now?

The most distinctive feature of humans, although the least tangible and most mysterious, is our information processing ability. And yet it is only now that information-based products and services are accelerating past physical products as the dominant proportion of the economy. Information, increasingly encoded electronically, dominates growth industries such as entertainment and financial services, and its electronic version of transportation is at last fighting for market share with the physical transportation that formed the great growth industry of earlier parts of the last century.

The last century's dramatic increases in physical mobility are far from reaching a plateau – witness the continuing rise of global tourism. But the exponential increases in global communication of electronic information are sufficiently well established to justify speculation that the information revolution will be seen as a defining feature of our age.

It is widely recognized that information-based organizations are in the front line of this revolution. Newspapers find that their role in disseminating news is challenged by numerous search engines and content sites, and their job advertising is undermined by online recruitment. Universities are struggling to define what learning can viably occur at a distance and what requires the classroom and the live lecturer. Financial advisers are forming consortia to develop an online presence as consumers prefer to buy insurance products and simple investment products at home.

But however physical our needs, the information revolution is transforming industries. We need to be fed and clothed, but retailers face a major challenge from home shopping. We need to be housed, but the location of our housing in suburbs created by the physical transport revolution may be drastically modified with the increase in teleworking. We wish to stay healthy, but a health industry in which 25 per cent of costs are attributable to processing of information is increasingly global. Business-to-business sectors, led by the IT sector itself, are facing a restructuring just as radical due to information-enabled globalization and mass customization.

Two great trends in information technology are supporting this revolution. The first is the coming of age of database technology. Databases have evolved at the heart of the drives over the past 30 years to increase the efficiency of supply, production, distribution and finance. The costs have often outweighed the benefits as the computing industry has passed on the costs of its painful, disaster-ridden childhood since its birth a mere 40-odd years ago. Perhaps because of this, the realization is dawning that the more fundamental benefits of IT lie at the customer interface, through interactive exchange of information with the customer, leading to tailored, information-enhanced products offered to global niches or even markets of one. Databases that support the storage of intelligence about the customer, gathered and integrated from diverse sources, provide the engine that can realize this concept of information-based tailoring.

The second major trend in IT provides the road network, as it were, to enable the mobility of the new information-tailored products. As Adam Smith noted two centuries ago, mobility is essential if one wishes to access a large enough market to allow tailored specialization – without the cost disadvantages that caused the demise of the made-to-measure suit and, more recently, the hand-built motor-car. Computer networks have existed for decades, but rapidly decreasing tele-communication costs and gradual standardization have supported their recent prominence through the Internet in particular.

This book, then, cannot ignore the interface between marketing and IT – indeed, it forms one of our major themes. Although they have been historically placed in two separate departments, both have aspirations to lie at the heart of the organization. To quote Professor Kit Grindley of London Business School:

*I went to a talk shortly after the war where the chief executive of Hotpoint was talking. He said that marketing was now the central function. He said, 'We got here by making a good iron, which gets us into the white goods business. Now it doesn't matter what we produce, or even if we produce it, as our skill is marketing.' This was not the fashion in the 30s: everything was on the product, making it cheaply and well. Now there is no reason why one should not redraw his circle where he put marketing in the centre of the organization, and put IT there. There is nowhere that IT does not dominate your strategy today. It used to be the airlines and the banks, and all the

> The costs have often outweighed the benefits as the computing industry has passed on the costs of its disaster-ridden childhood

progammers wanted to work there because they got some kudos there. Now it is key to get the IT strategy right in any sector. Is that too confrontational for marketing people? I don't know. **"**

Professor Kit Grindley (author interview)

The truth is that neither function can achieve its aim of driving business strategy without the other. It is the new offering of information-tailored products to customers, through the medium of a location-independent marketspace as well as the physical marketplace, that is transforming every industry and placing IT-enabled marketing at the heart of every organization, whether it knows it or not.

One of the main terms used in connection with this IT-enabled marketing is Customer Relationship Management (CRM), which we will introduce briefly now, and return to frequently in this book.

The argument for CRM systems

Ever since the influential study in 1990 by Reichheld and Sasser,[3] which showed the large impact on profitability of small increases in customer retention rates, the marketing community has been more conscious of the need to manage customer relationships in the long term as well as prior to the first sale. The argument has been further strengthened by data on the low cost of better retention as compared with better acquisition, and the increasing profitability of customers the longer the relationship lasts. The term **'relationship marketing'** has come to represent this more balanced emphasis on continuing relationships rather than representing simply individual transactions.

Definition
'Relationship marketing': the cultivation of longer-term mutually beneficial relationships with a defined customer group

The popularity of this term has influenced the adoption of the expression 'customer relationship management' (CRM) over more recent years. Although some use this term as a synonym for relationship marketing – one definition for example being 'a management approach that enables organizations to identify, attract and increase retention of profitable customers by managing relationships with them' – a more typical definition is 'using Information Technology (IT) in implementing relationship marketing strategies'.

In addition to the inevitable supply-side push from the IT industry, the trend towards IT-enabled management of customer relationships has other influences:

One-to-one marketing. Segmentation can be seen as a simplification of the messy complexity of dealing with numerous individual customers, each with distinct needs and potential value. When customers are reached via mass media, it is helpful to have a simplified picture of a typical customer in a given segment. IT-enabled channels such as the Internet, though, allow (at least in theory) a one-to-one dialogue with a current or prospective customer, in which the product configuration, price and required service can be individually negotiated. Meanwhile, analysis tools attached to customer data warehouses can inform the supplier's side of this negotiation through analysis of customer lifetime value of the likelihood of purchasing a cross-sold product and so on. While segmentation theory is still essential, it needs supplementing with thinking about how to individualize relationships.

The pressure on marketing spend. As the very existence of a separate marketing department became questioned in the early 1990s' recession, marketing staff came under increasing pressure to justify expenditure. This has increased the attractiveness of IT-supported media such as direct mail and the telephone for reaching the customer, as compared to mass media or the sales force where effectiveness may be more difficult to measure.

Value chain management. Whether under the banner of value chain management, business process redesign, total quality or market focus, organizations are increasingly thinking across departmental boundaries in order to concentrate on adding value to the customer. Marketing has been ashamed that these initiatives have mainly originated elsewhere – in manufacturing, in the IT department, or from consultants brought in to manage a crisis. The need for marketing to act as an integrating function in co-ordinating the organization's interaction with the customer, always present in the textbooks, is now more widely recognized, and even in some cases practised. But attempts to enforce procedures representing marketing best practice on paper can easily be undercut by departments without a strong self-interest to comply – witness the sorry failure of many attempts to institute company-wide planning procedures, where the vital issue of 'buy-in' is often ignored. IT offers marketing staff the opportunity to embed their customer-informed notions of best practice in sales, logistics and customer service into the organization. To quote Kit Grindley again:

// IT can embed discipline because when a computer tells you to do something, you can't really avoid doing it. It's difficult for centralized marketing to impose an infrastructure. Certain things can be centralized, like branding, and marketing strategy. But attempts to impose procedures can easily be ignored: it's easy for human

> While segmentation theory is still essential, it needs supplementing with fresh thinking about how to individualize relationships

> Organizations are increasingly thinking across departmental boundaries in order to add value. Marketing has been ashamed that these initiatives have mainly originated elsewhere

beings to duck and weave. In the days when you could shoot people for disobedience it was different. **"**

Professor Kit Grindley (author interview)

Trends in customer behaviour. Marketing has also been subject to consumer pull. Today's first-world consumer is more highly educated, under higher stress, more specialized, living longer, and more influenced by global culture than those of the 1960s and 1970s when our view of marketing was formed. This is resulting in various changes to consumer behaviour, such as: an increased pressure on shopping time; a trend towards outsourcing by consumers, as in the increase in ready meals; increased consumer rationality; a fragmentation of consumer markets; and, as we have already discussed, an increase in the consumer's power relative to the producer's. Nor are these trends specific to consumers. Customer expertise, sophistication and power is increasing likewise in industrial goods and services markets. This power shift stems partly from the concentration of buying into fewer hands, evident in many industries, and partly from the development of buyer groups, networks and alliances, all recent phenomena which have swung market control away from manufacturers. These trends in customer behaviour collectively put considerable demands on the organization's information systems as higher service levels are demanded.

The need for a CRM strategy, then, is widely perceived by practitioners. This could cynically be regarded as simply a rebranding of marketing strategy. But it can be argued that the various forces we have described, such as the power of individualization and the need to concentrate on the whole relationship, require at least a re-emphasis in the theory of marketing.

We will now consider whether the Internet similarly leads to any need to rethink the nature of marketing.

Marketing strategy and the Internet

Strategic planning and the processes which underpin it have long been open to the charge of maintaining the status quo and stifling innovation. An early study of marketing planning effectiveness in 1968 reported that:

"We were surprised to see how many planners had tunnel vision in thinking about how the business should be run. In fact, so many plans were based on nothing more than straight-line extrapolation of the past. **"** [4]

Not much had changed a decade later, according to a 1981 study:

" A common worry is that managers may follow planning instructions to the letter, and yet fail to show evidence of the special kind of thinking, both analytical and innovative, that the instructions are supposed to engender. *"* [5]

In similar vein, Piercy and Morgan found in 1994 that a myopic focus on projecting current trends was negatively associated with plan credibility.[6]

Given this record, can we blame the early e-commerce innovators, who extolled a 'just do it' mentality with a disregard for planning procedures, arguing that all was now changed and that immediate action was the only answer? Maybe not, but the disadvantages of such an approach have become more obvious with time. We have seen clothes retailers such as Gap steadily and quietly make progress online, based on careful market research which led to its hybrid clicks-and-mortar model, while an online counterpart Boo foundered with – among its many other mistakes – a proposition which ran counter to known consumer buying patterns. A consumer may buy their second pair of khakis online, but they will buy their first from a store; and while they may buy their first Gap shirt online, it won't be their first purchase from Gap. We have seen First Direct cut costs, improve cross-selling and reduce churn by converting 30 per cent of customer contacts to the Web on a proposition based on customer service rather than price, while Egg have been forced to backtrack from their initial price-driven strategy.

Those with a sound existing business to lose at least have a renewed interest in thinking through their e-commerce strategy before plunging in. They wish to answer such questions as: Will customers switch to an online service if we offer it? Should we bypass our distributors – or are we ourselves in danger of being disintermediated? And how can we prioritize between the numerous opportunities presented to us by the Internet?

While standard marketing and strategy books might be expected to address these questions, in practice they tend to have several gaps, which tend towards maintaining the status quo. Consider the relationship between market segmentation and industry structure. The best contemporary approaches to segmentation start with a map of the industry structure. Segmentation then proceeds at the points of greatest 'leverage' in this map, where the buying decisions are being made, these points being divided into groups with similar buying behaviour. But even with this method, there is a major problem due to the assumption that industry structure remains fixed, whereas channel innovations such as those offered by the Internet can radically affect the external value chain by which a product is assembled and distributed to its end customers.

A second, related gap is the assumption that channel choice is automatic – indeed, often an undeclared assumption made by managers, who state that 'In our industry selling is done via a sales force', or 'We work through independent financial advisers'. An exception is the work of authors on integrated marketing communications,[7][8][9] who recognize the need to make explicit choice of the most appropriate channel for a given communication, but who provide only limited guidance about how to do so.

In this book, we have endeavoured to reduce at least some of these gaps in existing planning processes. We present a tool for choosing which channel to use for which job (the 'channel curve'); a tool for deciding how channels will combine together ('channel chains'); a discussion of how to predict the future shape of the industry ('future market mapping'); a variant on traditional prioritization matrices better suited to planning in times of change; and a tool for deciding how the new features of IT-enabled media can best be used (the 'e-marketing mix'). Appropriate planning processes will not of themselves ensure innovative thinking; but if the process allows the definition of strategies which are market driving rather than simply market driven,[10] then at least the process will not become part of the problem. We also include guidance on the numerous IT-related implementation issues which marketers must now be conversant with.

But we also believe that the baby should not be thrown out with the bathwater. Marketing needs to be holistic if practitioners are to have a hope of managing its complexities in a way which is credible to colleagues in other functions. And practitioners tell us they need a sense of how to order the tasks in their overflowing in-trays, at least as much as help with the minutiae of their decision-making. Hence we will describe our new tools within the context of a holistic map of marketing, which includes updated versions of essential well-established elements such as segmentation theory as well as these new techniques.

A definition of new marketing

Marketing is a specialist function, just like HR, or logistics, or IT, or finance, or manufacturing and business schools and marketing practitioners really must stop the trend towards aggrandizing what is, in effect, a relatively simple, if vital role.

> Appropriate planning processes will not of themselves ensure innovative thinking; but if the process allows the definition of strategies which are market driving rather than simply market driven, then at least the process will not become part of the problem

The need to define marketing more tightly arose from a Cranfield research club, Improving Marketing Effectiveness through IT. Clearly, if managers were to understand what kind of marketing tasks needed to be supported by what kind of IT applications, a tight definition and a map were needed to help them navigate this domain.

Surprisingly, in spite of literally hundreds of definitions of marketing, most of them hopelessly wrong, we couldn't find such a map anywhere, so we started with our *own* definition of marketing. But, before giving it, let us stress once again that, wherever the function of marketing is located in the organization and no matter what it is called, it will be ineffective unless the whole company is market driven ('customer driven', 'customer-needs driven', 'demand driven' are other expressions for the same thing). This market-driven philosophy has to be led from the board downwards.

On the assumption that this is in place – a mega assumption indeed! – let us consider our definition of marketing, shown in the box.

Marketing is a process for:

➡ defining markets

➡ quantifying the needs of the customer groups (segments) within these markets

➡ determining the value propositions to meet these needs

➡ communicating these value propositions to all those people in the organization responsible for delivering them and getting their buy-in to their role

➡ playing an appropriate part in delivering these value propositions to the chosen market segments

➡ monitoring the value actually delivered.

As we have already stated, marketing never has, nor ever will be, responsible for *delivering* customer value, for this is the responsibility of everyone in the organization, but particularly those who come into contact with customers.

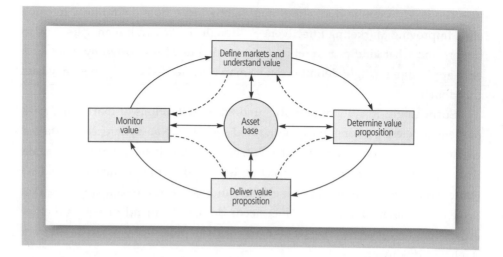

Figure 1.1
Overview of
marketing map

An overview of the new marketing process

With this in mind, we can now examine a map of this process – see Figure 1.1.

This process is clearly cyclical, in that monitoring the value delivered will update the organization's understanding of the value that is required by its customers. The cycle may be predominantly an annual one, with a marketing plan documenting the output from the 'Understand value' and 'Determine value proposition' processes, but, equally, changes throughout the year may involve fast iterations around the cycle to respond to particular opportunities or problems.

We have used the term 'Determine value proposition', to make plain that we are here referring to the decision-making process of deciding what the offering to the customer is to be – what value the customer will receive, and what value (typically the purchase price and ongoing revenues) the organization will receive in return. The process of delivering this value, such as by making and delivering a physical product or by delivering a service, is covered by 'Deliver value proposition'.

Thus, it can be seen that the first two boxes are concerned with strategic planning processes (in other words, developing market strategies), while the third and fourth boxes are concerned with the actual delivery in the market of what was planned and then measuring the effect. Throughout we use the word 'proposition' to indicate the nature of the offer from the organization to the market.

It is well known that not all of the value proposition delivering processes will be under the control of the marketing department, whose role varies considerably

Not all of the
value proposition
delivering
processes will be
under the control
of the marketing
department

between organizations. The marketing department is likely to be responsible for the first two processes, 'Understand value' and 'Determine value proposition', although even these need to involve numerous functions, albeit co-ordinated by specialist marketing personnel. The 'Deliver value' process is the role of the whole company, including for example product development, manufacturing, purchasing, sales promotion, direct mail, distribution, sales and customer service.

The various choices made during this marketing process are constrained and informed not just by the outside world, but also by the organization's asset base. Whereas an efficient new factory with much spare capacity might underpin a growth strategy in a particular market, a factory running at full capacity would cause more reflection on whether price should be used to control demand, unless the potential demand warranted further capital investment. As well as physical assets, choices may be influenced by financial, human resources, brand and information technology assets, to name just a few.

We will be using this process as a structure for the rest of this book, with a chapter on each of the four boxes. First, though, we will introduce each box in more detail.

Define markets and understand value

Inputs to this process will commonly include:

➡ the corporate mission and objectives, which will determine which markets are of interest;

➡ external data such as market research;

➡ internal data which flows from ongoing operations.

The process involves four major sub-processes, shown in Figure 1.2.

First, it is necessary to define the markets the organization is in, or wishes to be in, and how these divide into segments of customers with similar needs. The choice of markets will be influenced by the corporate objectives as well as the asset base. Information will be collected about the markets, such as each market's size and growth, with estimates for the future.

Once each market or segment has been defined, it is necessary to understand what value the customers within the segment want or need. This value is most simply thought of as the benefits gained from the product or service, but it can also encompass the value to the customer of surrounding services such as maintenance or information. This step also encompasses what the customer is

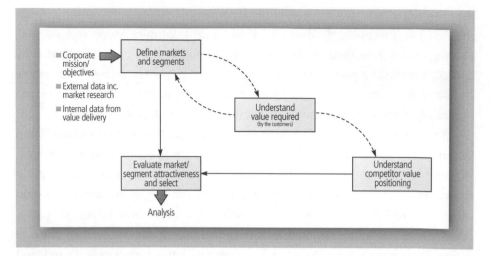

Figure 1.2
Define markets
and understand
value

prepared to give in exchange, in terms of price and other criteria, such as lifetime running cost or convenience of purchase. One way of expressing customer value requirements is via a **critical success factor** analysis, which might list such criteria as product specification, quality or reliability, the quality and range of services, price and the ease of purchase, and which might also include weights to illustrate their relative importance to the customer in the buying decision. This step of 'Understand value required' also includes predicting the value which will be required in the future.

In performing this step, it may emerge that subsets of the customers within a market have very different requirements. In this case, the market may need to be further segmented to represent these subsets. Hence there is an important feedback loop from this step to the 'Define markets' step.

'Understand competitor value positioning' refers to the process of establishing how well the organization and its competitors currently deliver the value that the customers seek. To illustrate in terms of critical success factors, this process would correspond to scoring the organization and its competitors on each of the customers' success factors. (We will show an example of this analysis later in the book.) Again it involves looking into the future to predict how competitors might improve, clearly a factor in planning how the organization is to respond. **SWOT analysis** is one tool used here.

From these three processes, the relative attractiveness of the different markets or segments can be evaluated. One tool of relevance here is Porter's five forces model, showing the forces which shape industry competition and hence the

Definition

Critical success factor: One of the few things which any competitor must get right in order to succeed in a market or segment

Definition

SWOT analysis: a listing of the organization's strengths, weaknesses, opportunities and threats in a particular market

attractiveness of a given market.[11] We will discuss its relevance in today's rapidly changing industry structures in Chapter 2.

The output will be some form of analysis, such as a 'marketing audit'. One way of summing up much of the key information is a portfolio matrix such as a Boston matrix or directional policy matrix. Such a matrix provides a sensible basis for prioritization among the many possible product/market combinations which the organization could address. We will see in Chapter 3, though, that the portfolio matrix needs adapting in the Internet age.

While this stage can be aided by IT tools, these are far from sufficient on their own, as we will discuss in Chapter 2.

Determine value proposition

The definition of the value proposition to the customer contains five sub-processes, shown in Figure 1.3 (more commonly referred to by us as strategic marketing planning). The key input to this process is the prioritization of target markets, based on an analysis of customer needs and the relative attractiveness of different customer segments, which was produced by the previous process.

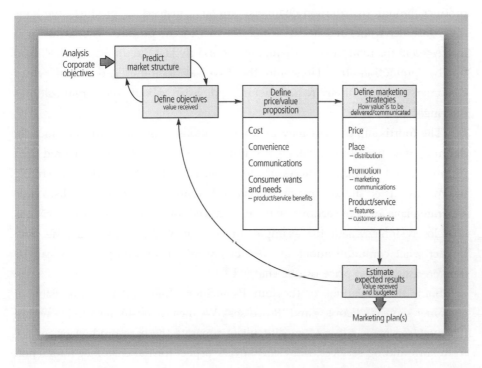

Figure 1.3
Determine value proposition

There is an important sub-process which is normally missing: 'Predict market structure'. This deals with the vital issue of how the industry structure might change, irrespective of any actions which we might take

The four Cs translate the four Ps of marketing from what the organization does to what the customer cares about

Before we can begin to plan our value proposition for each market, though, there is an important sub-process which is normally missing from planning methodologies: 'Predict market structure'. This deals with the vital issue of how the industry structure might change, irrespective of any actions which we might take, as a result of channel innovations. Clearly if we are to be bypassed by our suppliers, or if our customers are likely to wish to buy via an e-hub rather than directly from us, we need to know about it. A technique for predicting future market structure is a major part of Chapter 3.

The next two sub-processes define the core of the value proposition to the customer. While they can occur in either order, organizations typically start by defining the value they hope to receive from the segment: 'Define objectives'. This involves defining marketing objectives in terms, for example, of market share, volume, value or contribution by segment.

The other half of the equation is defining the value to be delivered to the customer in return. This price/value proposition can be thought of using the four Cs: 'Cost', 'Convenience', 'Communications' and 'Consumer wants and needs'.[8] These translate the four Ps of marketing from what the organization does to what the customer cares about. For example, the customer is concerned with 'convenience' of purchase, which influences how the organization will 'place' the product through distribution channels. Similarly, instead of 'product', we have the 'consumer wants and needs' which are met by the product. The customer is interested in the total 'cost' to them, not necessarily just the up-front 'price'. And finally, 'promotion' translates into the two-way 'communications' in which customers declare their requirements and learn about the organization's offerings.

The fourth sub-process may involve iterations with the third one since, in defining the marketing strategies – how the value is to be delivered and communicated – it may be necessary to reconsider what that value can actually be. We have listed the four major aspects of this process using the four Ps. While separate plans, or plan sections, may be produced for each of these, the decisions are closely intertwined: for example, the choice of distribution channel will impact what communications are feasible, what surrounding services can be delivered, and what price can be charged.

Some reformulations of the four Ps include others such as 'Provision of customer service', 'People'; and 'Processes'. We include customer service within 'Product/service', as it is often difficult to separate the core product or service from surrounding services, but clearly every aspect for the customer interaction needs to be planned for. 'People' and 'Processes' represent dimensions that certainly need to be planned, but we view them as arising from the consideration of the customer-focused four Ps, by asking what changes to people or processes are necessary in order to achieve the desired product offering, price, place or promotions.

Once these issues have been resolved, an estimate of the expected results of the marketing strategies can be made, in terms of the costs to the organization and the impact of the price/value proposition on sales. This final step closes the loop from the original setting of objectives, as it may be that iteration is required if it is considered that the strategies that have been defined are not sufficient to meet the financial objectives.

The output from the 'Determine value proposition' process is typically a strategic marketing plan, or plans, covering a period of at least three years. In some cases, specific plans are produced for aspects of the four Ps, such as a pricing plan, a distribution plan, a customer service plan or a promotions plan. However, even when no plans are produced, the organization is implicitly taking decisions on the offer to the customer and how this offer is to be communicated and delivered. The content of these plans has to be communicated to and agreed with all departments or functions responsible for delivering the customer value spelled out in the plans.

Integrated marketing communications

Before considering the delivery of value, we will give some further attention to promotion. Promotion is changing in a number of respects. New channels such as the Internet are emphasizing an already growing trend from mass media such as advertising through addressable media such as direct mail to interactive media such as call centres and the Web. Integrating these channels within a coherent strategy is not an easy task. As we have mentioned, writers on the new field of integrated marketing communications emphasize that before engaging on detailed planning for each medium – writing sales plans or promotions plans, for example – it is necessary to choose which medium to use for which customer interactions.[7] This is illustrated in Figure 1.4.

The choice of channel/medium is generally a complex one, involving different media for different communications with the same customer. The organization will also frequently wish to leave some options in the hands of the customer. For example, a Dell customer may find out about Dell from colleagues

> The Internet is emphasizing an already growing trend from mass media through addressable media to interactive media

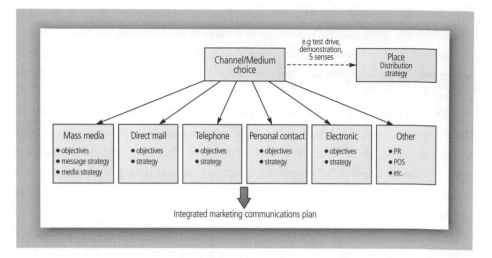

Figure 1.4
Define marketing
strategy –
promotion

or from press advertising; investigate which product to buy, what the price is and what configuration is required using the Web; print out order details and pass them to the purchasing department to place the order via fax; check on the delivery time via telephone; take delivery via a parcels service; and obtain customer service using e-mail. Customers are no longer content to have the medium dictated by the supplier.

We will describe new tools for choosing the right channel for the right task, the 'channel curve' and 'channel chains', in Chapter 3.

Having chosen the most appropriate medium for given customer contacts with particular segments, the traditional planning by medium can then be conducted.

The choice of medium is clearly closely intertwined with the distribution strategy. Distribution channels often have a mix of purposes, providing both a means of conveying a physical product to the customer, and a medium for information exchange. A garage, for example, provides information on the model, an opportunity for a test drive, a location where price negotiations can occur, and a step in the physical delivery of the car to the customer. A clothes shop provides a location where the information exchange of trying on a garment and feeling it can occur, in a way which is difficult to replicate using direct marketing approaches. So the focus of promotion on information exchange is closely linked to the physical issues of distribution. However, considering the two separately can result in new solutions, such as direct banking, Web shopping for CDs (which may need to be sampled but will not need to be felt physically), and

Distribution channels often have a mix of purposes, providing both a means of conveying a physical product to the customer, and a medium for information exchange

However, considering the two separately can result in new market-driving solutions

complementing the sales force with telemarketing and websites for minor transactions or less important customers in business-to-business markets.

As we have mentioned, it is crucial to predict these kinds of changes to distribution channels, such as the increasing prevalence of the 'direct' model. In Chapter 3, which expands on this stage, we will discuss how to predict the future shape of the chain from producers to the eventual consumer.

Deliver value proposition

The third major process is to deliver the value proposition. This is illustrated in Figure 1.5.

The major input to this process is the strategic marketing plan(s) derived from the previous stage.

The starting point for our analysis of this process was Porter's **value chain.** This is reflected in the tasks we have listed within 'Deliver the product/service' in the top half of the figure: research and development, leading to inbound logistics, then through operations to outbound logistics and finally to service.

● **Definition**
Value chain: the sequence of activities by which an organization transforms its inputs in order to produce outputs of greater value

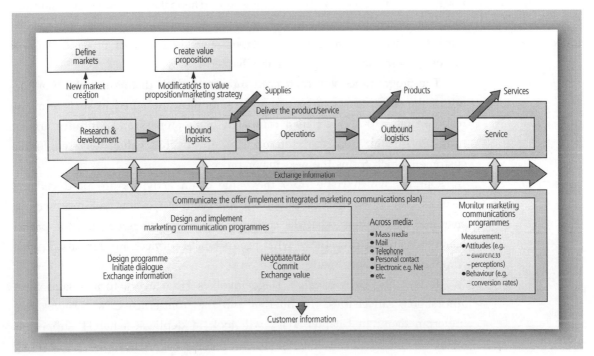

Figure 1.5 Deliver value proposition

However, we suggest that there are a number of marketing activities which shadow these value chain activities, under the general heading of 'Communicating the offer'. Porter placed 'Marketing' after 'Operations' in the value chain, but in today's one-to-one world, these communications can occur in parallel with all the tasks involved in value delivery. One might, for example, check a product with customers at the R&D stage. The product may be tailored by the customer, resulting in different components being bought in, assembled and delivered. And so on.

Communicating the offer is typically managed by designing, implementing and monitoring a number of marketing communications programmes. A communication programme could be, for example, a direct mail campaign; an advertising campaign; a series of sales seminars; an in-store promotion; and so on. We have also stretched the term 'marketing communication programmes' to include management of such media as the sales force, which may be managed in a more continuous way, with annual targets broken down by quarter or month.

In order to represent the interactive, one-to-one nature of today's marketing, we have renamed the classic steps in the sales process

Whatever the medium, the campaign will be aiming to contribute to one or more of the tasks listed in Figure 1.5 within the 'Design and implement marketing communication programmes' box. The tasks may have an unfamiliar look: in order to represent the interactive, one-to-one nature of today's marketing, we have renamed the classic steps in the sales process. We will discuss this revised sales process in Chapter 4.

The programmes will then need monitoring. We distinguish the monitoring of the effectiveness of particular programmes, measured in such terms as response rates to a direct mail campaign or awareness and attitudes arising from advertising, from the monitoring of the overall value delivered to the customer, which forms the next major process.

Outputs which come from the value chain activities are products and services. An important output from the communication sub-processes is customer information: what the customer's problems or issues are, the particular needs arising from these, what products and services are purchased, what complaints have been made, and so on.

Today, this 'Deliver value' stage involves IT at every turn – sales force automation, call centres, the Internet and the front-office CRM systems that underpin them. In Chapter 4 we will look in depth at what IT support is available, and how to decide what to use, using what we term the 'e-marketing mix'.

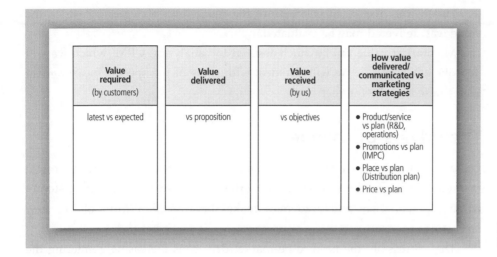

Figure 1.6
Monitor value

Monitor value

Monitoring the value delivered to the customer, and received from the customer, is the purpose of 'Monitor value', illustrated in Figure 1.6.

There are four main areas where monitoring can occur, corresponding to the main types of information dealt with in the planning processes of 'Understand value' and 'Determine value proposition'.

First, the organization can monitor whether the value the customers actually require corresponds to the previous analysis of customer requirements carried out as part of 'Understand value'. The information for this may be gained partly from the information gained in the 'Deliver value proposition' process, or it may require special activity such as market research.

Second, the value delivered can be monitored against the value proposition which was defined during the 'Determine value proposition' process. As all aspects of value are as measured by the customer's perception, this will again involve asking the customer by some means.

The organization will also wish to monitor the value it receives against the marketing objectives defined during 'Develop value proposition'. This is the area that most organizations are best at, through monthly analysis of sales by product, channel and so on (though analysis by segment or customer is often poorer than analysis by product, with customer profitability or lifetime value generally difficult to obtain). But as the financial results are a result of customer satisfaction, monitoring the value delivered to the customer is equally important, and, for many organizations, one of the simplest ways of improving performance.

As financial results are a result of customer satisfaction, monitoring the value delivered to the customer is one of the simplest ways of improving performance

Finally, the overall effectiveness of the marketing strategies by which the value was delivered may be evaluated.

Monitoring value can be much assisted by 'analytical CRM' which we will describe in Chapter 5. We will also deal with some of the specific measurement issues raised by the Internet.

The drivers of change

Let us conclude this chapter by explaining why there is so much interest in marketing in the modern world and why this book is such an important step in helping practitioners and academics make the transition from old to new marketing.

The expression 'the need to be market driven' is increasingly entering the lexicon of chief executives and boards, whose old behaviours no longer work in a world driven by overcapacity and customer choice, hence customer power. In order to explain this, let us turn to a piece of well-established management theory – the diffusion of innovation, first discovered by Everett Rogers in 1962.[12]

Diffusion is:

1 The adoption

2 of new products or services

3 over time

4 by customers

5 within social systems

6 as encouraged by marketing.

Diffusion refers to the cumulative percentage of potential adopters of a new product or service over time. Everett Rogers examined some of the social forces that explain the product life cycle. The body of knowledge often referred to as 'reference theory' (which incorporates work on group norms, group pressures, etc.) helps explain the snowball effect of diffusion. Rogers found that the actual rate of diffusion is a function of a product's:

1 relative advantage (over existing products)

2 compatibility (with lifestyles, values, etc.)

3 communicability (is it easy to communicate?)

4 complexity (is it complicated?)

5 divisibility (can it be tried out on a small scale before commitment?)

The rate of diffusion is also a function of the newness of the product itself, which can be classified broadly under three headings:

➡ continuous innovation (e.g. the new miracle ingredient)

➡ dynamically continuous innovation (e.g. disposable lighter)

➡ discontinuous (e.g. microwave oven)

However, Rogers found that, for all new products, not everyone adopts them at the same time, and that a universal pattern emerges as shown in Figure 1.7.

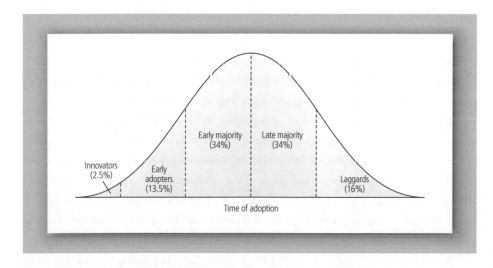

Figure 1.7
The diffusion of innovation curve

In general, the innovators think for themselves and try new things (where relevant); the early adopters, who have status in society, are opinion leaders and they adopt successful products, making them acceptable and respectable; the early majority, who are more conservative and who have slightly above-average status, are more deliberate and only adopt products that have social approbation; the late majority, who are below average status and sceptical, adopt products much later; the laggards, with low status, income, etc., view life through the rear mirror and are the last to adopt products.

Figure 1.8 shows the diffusion of innovation curve and the resulting 'product/market life cycle' curve and helps to explain the dynamics of markets.

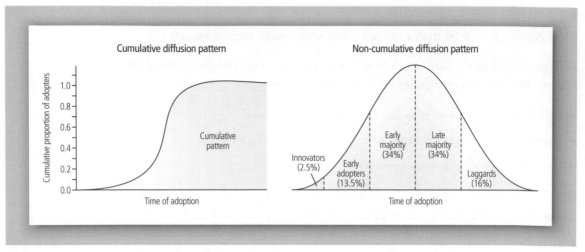

Figure 1.8 Diffusion of innovation and the product life cycle

It illustrates, for example, that when everyone who could use a product or service is using it, the market becomes a 'replacement market' and is subject totally to gross domestic product changes, demographic changes and the like.

Most organizations today, but particularly those in the West, face three major challenges: market maturity, globalization, and customer power. Market maturity is the result of the 'diffusion of innovation' effect described above. So, most people in developed countries have TVs, dishwashers, washing machines, calculators, phones, cars, etc. This makes marketing much more important than it has ever been, because growth has to be based on an even deeper understanding of consumer needs.

> The car industry and the accountancy industry are but two examples of concentration and fragmentation. Being 'stuck in the middle' is not an option any more

Market maturity has, in turn, led to globalization, as leading companies have grown bigger and turned to international markets for their growth. The result in many sectors is that there are a few very large global companies and a very large number of smaller, niche companies. The car industry and the accountancy industry are but two examples of such concentration and fragmentation. The point is that being 'stuck in the middle' is not an option any more. Figure 1.9 shows the natural process of most markets over time.

All of this has led to an unprecedented increase in customer power.

For now, however, let us consider what happens to organizations at each stage of market development in the diffusion of innovation curve (Figure 1.8).

In the early stage, *technology* is paramount: if we do not have a boat we cannot go to the island.

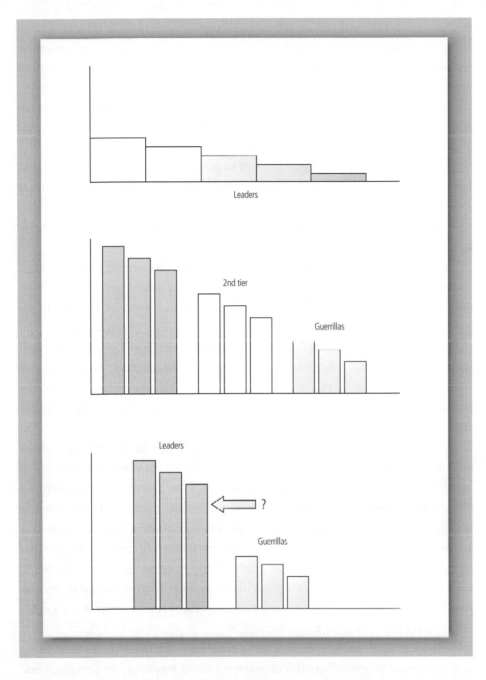

Figure 1.9
The evolution of markets over time

By stage 2, demand tends to outstrip supply, so *production* becomes the overriding consideration, as the race is on to meet demand. During this phase the barons of the organization are the technical people, whether they be production engineers, lawyers, architects, chemists or whatever.

In stage 3, the market is established and new entrants join to take advantage of the high sales and profits growth. Consequently, markets begin to fragment, or segment, and the response is *promotion*, which now becomes a priority, often in the form of advertising and proactive selling.

By the time stages 4 and 5 are reached, there is still growth, as new users are still entering the market, but there are fewer of them, so the rate of growth begins to decline, often leading to overcapacity and price wars.

It is usually at this stage that *financial husbandry* takes over: costs are cut and ratio management is introduced. The trouble with this is that it tends to create delusions of success and often leads to what the UK journalist Andrew Lorenz has described as 'anorexia industrialosa' – an excessive desire to be leaner and fitter, leading to emaciation and, eventually, death.

It is interesting to note that, of Peters and Waterman's 43 so-called 'excellent' companies cited in *In Search of Excellence: Lessons from America's Best-Run Companies* in 1982 (Warner Books), there were only six that could be considered excellent just eight years later, according to Richard Pascale.[13]

Financial husbandry on its own can have disastrous consequences, and success today, unless anchored in real customer satisfaction, is likely to be transitory. You have only to look at the problems that have been dogging the once blue-chip UK retailer Marks & Spencer (M & S) to see the price of ignoring the customer.

M & S's profits were slashed and its confidence dashed in the biggest shock in its 118-year history. The official story was that it got its fashion line wrong, but in fact the company's problems had been accruing over many years. For example, it was only recently that customers could use debit and credit cards in the stores. If a food line was out of stock, the story goes that customers blamed themselves for arriving too late! Until recently customers could not try on clothes, and changing-booths were introduced very reluctantly. Such arrogance was bound to have detrimental consequences – particularly as other high street stores such as Gap and Next were offering attractive, high-quality merchandise at reasonable prices, together with good customer service.

Marks & Spencer's experience, of course, begs the question as to whether long-term market leadership and domination leads inevitably to arrogance and complacency, and whether this militates against new ideas, products, processes and regeneration. Virgin's 'tracker' funds, Yahoo!, Amazon.com and the like are forcing well-established leaders to re-examine traditional management models and outmoded formulae for success.

> Financial husbandry on its own can have disastrous consequences, and success today, unless anchored in real customer satisfaction, is likely to be transitory

But during the past ten years, many companies have sought a remedy for their declining fortunes by retreating into faddism, hungrily adopting one fad after another as they were peddled by eager consultants. In most cases these initiatives have failed, as organizations have treated them as a quick-fix bolt-on without addressing their underlying problems. The International Standards Organization's ISO 9000 quality initiative, for example, very laudable when used sensibly, has, in the main, only been a guarantee that organizations can produce rubbish perfectly and consistently. We use the word 'rubbish' judiciously, because there is a little point in producing perfectly something that people do not buy.

Another fad has been Business Process Re-engineering (BPR). This has been an outstanding success in those companies which have used it to redesign their processes to create value for customers. But in those organizations which have not grasped the nettle of customer satisfaction, it has achieved merely cosmetic productivity improvements. Yet another fad has been balanced scorecards. This too, for CEOs who understand the need to balance the requirements of all stakeholders in a company delivering customer value, has been very successful. But for those CEOs who do not understand the importance of being market driven, it has proved to be just another fad. Yet another initiative is knowledge management.

Of course, all of these initiatives are fabulous and do work, but only when they are seen in the context of providing superior customer value as a means to providing superior shareholder value. Alas, even in those organizations committed to 'relationship' and 'one-to-one' marketing, too often customers remain the Cinderellas. As Harvard Business School's Susan Fournier has pointed out, rapid development of relationship techniques in the USA has been accompanied by growing customer dissatisfaction. The much vaunted relationship that companies were so eager to forge with their customers involved not so much delighting them as abusing them, suggested Fournier.

The problem is that companies have become so internally focused that they have got carried away with supply-side issues and taken their eye off the customer ball. Until organizations make a serious effort to lift their heads above the parapet and understand their markets and their customers better, all the great initiatives referred to above will amount to expensive, time-consuming mistakes. Most boards are spending too much of their valuable time on internal operational efficiency (doing things right) at the expense of external operational effectiveness (doing the right things).

> During the past ten years, many companies have sought a remedy for their declining fortunes by retreating into faddism

In many cases managerial attitudes and corporate cultures became ingrained during the heady years of success, so companies persevere with the old tried-and-tested formulae, usually with disastrous results.

We will now turn our attention to what being market driven means, and to an explanation of how 'marketing' – a word which, as we have said, causes a lot of confusion – fits into the market-driven, customer-focused approach. The term 'marketing' is frequently used to describe a customer-driven organization's philosophy. The Marketing Council has coined the expression 'pan-company marketing' to describe its philosophy of making the entire organization, not just the marketing department, focus on the customer. But the word 'marketing' is most frequently used to describe the function of marketing.

Marketing: the function and prerequisites for success

The marketing function (or department) never has been and never will be effective in an organization with a technical, production, operations or financial orientation. Such enterprises adopted the vocabulary of marketing a long time ago and applied a veneer of marketing techniques.

Many of the high street banks have spent fortunes on hiring marketing people, often from Fast-Moving Consumer Goods (FMCG) companies, producing expensive television commercials and creating a multiplicity of products, brochures and leaflets. But most customers still cannot distinguish between the major players, so what competitive advantage have any of these organizations gained? Is this marketing in the sense of understanding and meeting customers' needs better than the competition, or is it old-fashioned selling with the name changed, where we try to persuade customers to buy what we want to sell them, how, when and where we want to sell it?

The computer industry provides even clearer examples. For years IT companies used the word 'marketing' indiscriminately as they tried to persuade customers to buy the ever more complex outpourings of their technology. Racked by recession, decline and huge losses, the industry was transformed by new customer-oriented entrants like Microsoft and Dell, which forced it to change root and branch the way it went about its business.

Generally, marketing departments never have, nor ever will, actually *do* marketing. The reasons are obvious. If the term 'marketing' embraces all those

Generally, marketing departments never have, nor ever will, actually *do* marketing

activities related to creating and satisfying demand and the associated intelligence, then it is clear that most marketing takes place during the delivery of the
service and during contact with customers. While marketing supports and reflects
this process, it is not the sole preserve of those people in the organization who
happen to work in the marketing department.

It is equally absurd to suggest that personnel issues are the sole preserve of
the HR department, as though nobody else in the organization need concern
themselves with people. The same could be said for finance and information
systems. Indeed, it is such myopic functional separation that got many
organizations into the mess they are in today. In our experience organizations that
have always been focused on the market rather than preoccupied with their own
functional hierarchies have few of the problems referred to in the 1993 Coopers &
Lybrand report that severely criticized marketing and judged it to be going
through a 'mid-life crisis'.[14]

Again, the banks provide a good example. Most people hold banks in
contempt, and any organization that believes that marketing is something people
'do' on the sixth floor in London's Lombard Street deserves to fail. It is not the
fault of the marketing department if an organization is not commercially
successful, and to believe it is is to misunderstand and misappropriate the role of
marketing.

Such organizations themselves may be at the crossroads, but until they really
come to understand what a marketing orientation or culture is and create an
environment in which marketing professionals can operate effectively, all we are
really witnessing are the growing pains or, in some cases, the birth pangs of
marketing. It may not look like this to the casual observer, but as we have already
indicated, most companies have adopted a superficial marketing veneer.

> It is such myopic functional separation that got many organizations into the mess they are in today

Understanding what marketing really is

We are not trying to exonerate the marketing community from all blame for
corporate failure. Words can get in the way of meaningful communication and
action. This, perhaps, is the most valid criticism of marketers. They have failed to
define effectively what marketing is, what it can achieve, and how it must be
supported in order to stand any chance of fulfilling its mission of leading the
corporation in understanding and satisfying the needs of all of its consumers and
customers – through innovation, R&D, production, purchasing, logistics and so
on – to create competitive advantage.

For marketing to work it must flourish at three different levels in the enterprise.

1 The board of directors must understand and enthusiastically embrace the notion that creating and maintaining customer satisfaction is the only route to long-term profitable success. Only when the top management team share this common vision is there any chance of inculcating an organization-wide marketing culture where everyone, including the telephonists, van drivers, order clerks and so on, believes in and practises the concepts of superior customer service. This corporate top-down driven vision of what marketing is can create significant and sustainable success, as companies like General Electric, 3M and Unilever have demonstrated.

2 The business strategies of the company must start with and be evaluated against what the market wants. Unless marketing has a strategic input in order to ensure that the future of the company is planned from the marketplace inwards, any subsequent marketing activity is likely to be unsuccessful.

3 Tactical marketing activities must be implemented within the context of the market-led strategies. They must meet high professional standards across the spectrum of functions such as market research, product development, pricing, distribution, advertising, promotion and selling.

Summary

We have presented an outline process map of the marketing process. Some relevant features of the map are:

➡ *The map is inherently cross-functional.* 'Deliver value proposition', for example, involves every aspect of the organization, from new product development through inbound logistics and production to outbound logistics and customer service. Hence marketers must be adept in managing cross-functional processes and relationships, while IT-enabled marketing projects can develop a daunting scale and complexity, requiring extensive cross-functional commitment.

➡ *The map represents best practice, not common practice.* Many aspects of the map are not explicitly addressed by well-embedded processes in even sophisticated companies. This may be a surprise to colleagues in other functions such as IT, who meekly come asking what are the management processes which are to be

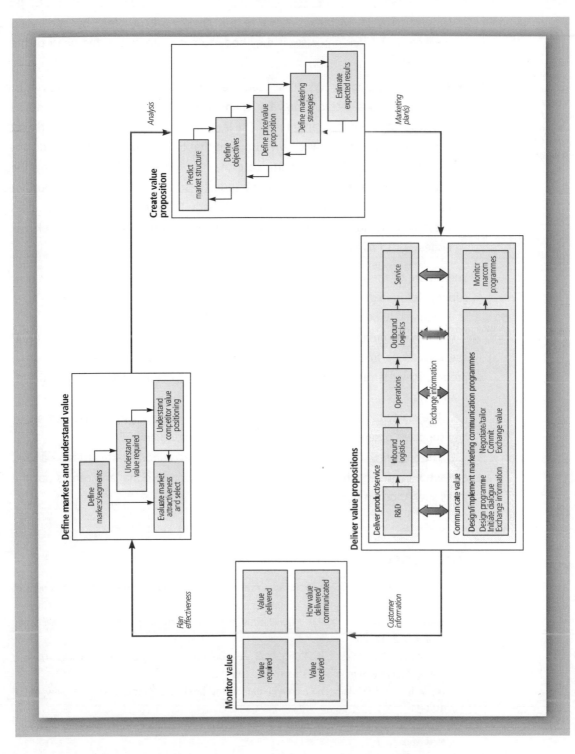

Figure 1.10 Summary of the map of marketing

Marketers need to put their house in order by addressing weaknesses in their own processes if they hope to put customers at the heart of the organization

supported by IT. Marketers need to put their work in order by addressing weaknesses in their processes if they hope to put customers at the heart of the organization.

➡ *The map is changing.* We have seen that, today, the marketing process must include conscious decisions on what channels to use for what customer contacts – we cannot take it for granted that 'The Internet doesn't affect us, as our industry uses a direct sales force'. We have also seen that the supply chain from producers to consumers in which we participate may be restructured around us by the actions of others, so predicting future industry structure becomes an important part of distribution and communications strategy. Marketers need tools to address these areas to supplement their existing toolset – a need which this book will endeavour to fill.

The nature of the marketing map, then, has some important implications for how support for marketing should be provided by organizations.

Figure 1.10 summarizes and consolidates all of the above.

Surely, this map is far superior as a method for organizing the functions and specialist departments in any organization to support customers than some predetermined arrangement that puts all kinds of functions within the control of marketing?

The reality today, though, is that the customer is agog with indifference about any supplier's organization, which is bound to be wrong anyway!

The authors of this book do not care how the marketing department is organized and who reports to whom, just so long as it is fully professional and carries out the tasks spelled out in our definition of marketing.

References

(1) Baker, S. (2001 ongoing) Unpublished, Cranfield study of senior non-marketers' perceptions of marketers.

(2) Brady, J. and Davis, I. (1993) 'Marketing in transition: Marketing's mid-life crisis', *McKinsey Quarterly*, **2**, 17–28.

(3) Reichheld, F. F. and Sasser, W. E. Jr (2000) 'Zero defections: quality comes to services', *Harvard Business Review*, September–October, **68**, 105–11.

(4) Ames, B.C. (1968) 'Marketing planning for industrial products', *Harvard Business Review*, **46**(5), 100–11.

(5) Hopkins, D.S. (1981) 'The marketing plan', The Conference Board, Research Report No. 801, New York.

(6) Piercy, N.F. and Morgan, N.A. (1994) 'The marketing planning process: behavioural problems compared with analytical techniques in explaining marketing plan credibility', *Journal of Business Research*, **29**, 167–78.

(7) Belch, G.E. and Belch, M.A. (1993) *Introduction to Advertising and Promotion: An Integrated Marketing Communications Perspective*. Homewood, IL: Irwin.

(8) Schultz, D.E., Tannenbaum, S. and Lauterborn, R.F. (1993) *Integrated Marketing Communications*. Chicago: NTC Business Books.

(9) Fill, C. (1995) *Marketing Communications: Frameworks, Theories and Applications*, Hemel Hempstead: Prentice Hall.

(10) Kumar, N., Scheer, L. and Kotler, P. (2000) 'From market driven to market driving', *European Management Journal*, **18**(2), 129–42.

(11) Porter, M.E. (1980) *Competitive Strategy: Techniques for Analysing Industries and Competitors*. New York: Free Press.

(12) Rogers, E. (1962) *The Diffusion of Innovations*, New York: Free Press.

(13) Pascale, R.T. (1990) *Managing on the Edge: How Successful Companies Use Conflict to Stay Ahead*. London: Viking.

(14) Coopers & Lybrand (1993) *Marketing at the Crossroads: A Survey of the Role of Marketing*, London: Coopers & Lybrand.

2

Building the future on solid foundations

Defining markets and understanding value

➡ Putting CRM in its proper context

➡ Competitive forces; competitive dimensions

➡ Market definition and market segmentation

Introduction

In Chapter 1 we outlined a market map for our definition of marketing (Figure 1.1). The first box was entitled 'Define markets and understand value'. The purpose of this chapter is principally to expand on the brief outline provided in Chapter 1 and to provide robust processes for readers to implement. We have chosen Customer Relationship Management (CRM) as a vehicle for this, as CRM is often confused with market segmentation, as we will explain later.

Putting CRM in its proper context*

As this book is being written, billions of dollars are literally being wasted on what has come to be known as customer relationship management – CRM.

It will, however, be blindingly obvious that, no matter what particular definition is given for CRM, and no matter how much money is spent on databases and on systems for accessing and promulgating such data, unless there exists a deep understanding of the market and of the needs of customers within market segments, CRM will become merely the latest fad and will soon wane in importance.

In Chapter 1 we berated organizations which embraced TQM, BPR, balanced scorecards, knowledge management and whichever latest acronym-promoted fad emerged from consultants and business schools. Precisely the same reasoning as we applied in Chapter 1 can and should be used in the case of CRM. CRM is the latest must-have management fad, not, we stress, because there is anything wrong with either the process or with the underlying technology that supports it, but because the fundamental preconditions we outline in Chapter 1 are not being met in most organizations. We will expand on these conditions later. For now, let us look a little more closely at the latest acronym, CRM.

What is CRM?

Well, it depends. CRM is really too young to be fully formed yet and what it is rather depends on who you happen to be talking to – or who is trying to sell it to you. Definitions of CRM are everywhere, and different. We offer a selection in the box.

---

* The authors are grateful to the contributions of Ian Dunbar, Professor John Ward and Paul Fifield to these views on CRM and market segmentation.

'A continuous performance initiative to increase a company's knowledge of its customers'.

'CRM comprises the organization, processes and systems through which an organization manages its relationships with its customers'.

'Consistent high quality customer support across all communications channels and business functions, based on common information shared by employees, their customers and business partners'.

'A methodology, based on new information technology, that helps companies reach their long-held goals for improved customer satisfaction'.

'An integrated, multiple delivery channel strategy that allows companies to capture profitable new customers and improve service'.

'ERP is from Mars, CRM is from Venus'.

The quicker-witted among you will have noted that the IT/systems backbone of CRM keeps peeking through the skin. This is not automatically a bad thing, but we need to recognize CRM, at least as it currently stands, for what it is.

At the moment, CRM is being delivered as a method of combining one or more of the IT systems that exist or can be placed into an organization relating to the customer interface. Depending on the source of reference, the following are usually mentioned:

➡ data warehouses

➡ customer service systems

➡ call centres

➡ e-commerce

➡ Web marketing

➡ operational systems (order entry, invoicing, payments, point-of-sale, etc.)

➡ sales systems (mobile representative communications, appointment making, etc.)

The basic idea, then, is to integrate these systems, thus enabling the organization to manage its customers flawlessly. It goes without saying that having different

The fact that
marketing doesn't
talk to finance or
sales is no excuse
for the systems to
act as badly as the
humans

systems in the same organization that do not and cannot talk to each other is not conducive to efficiency. The fact that marketing doesn't talk to finance or sales is obviously no excuse for the systems to act as badly as the humans. The process of integrating/cleansing/unifying/presenting the diverse data is obviously a 'good thing', no doubt about that, but does it all add up to 'customer relationship management'?

The promised benefits of CRM

Depending on who you are talking to, the benefits of a CRM project might include everything you have ever wanted. Certainly nothing less than the answer to who buys what and why. At last, the marketing Holy Grail – unpredictable customers reduced to numbers that can be analysed, plotted, planned and categorized. The question is, however, will CRM deliver?

If the answer is '*I don't care, let's give it a go*', do you remember the last time you felt like this? When was it, about the time of business process re-engineering, benchmarking, customer service, investors in people, knowledge management? Or was it even about the time of total quality management or 'excellence'? None of these initiatives was a bad idea, but very few got anywhere near delivering the benefits that were promised.

Table 2.1 CRM – the features

➡ Customer analysis
➡ Market segmentation
➡ Manage target marketing activities
➡ Model customer behaviour (predictive)
➡ Customer service history
➡ Access self-service patterns
➡ Customer marketing history
➡ Measure customer retention
➡ Measure customer loyalty
➡ 'Single view' of the customer
➡ Revenue analysis
➡ Customer information (demographics and life cycle/lifestyle)
➡ Score customer responsiveness to different forms of communication and service
➡ Identify different forms of product/service in use

Of course, executives hope CRM will be different, as the features listed in Table 2.1 promise. The problem is, this time we don't just risk messing up the back-office processes, now we are playing with customer relationships and if we get CRM wrong, customers leave, never to return.

What Is CRM all about?

Ultimately CRM has to be about *competitive advantage*. This is what organizations want and what the consultants can sell. There is also no doubt that CRM can be a major factor in achieving competitive advantage. Whether CRM is the whole answer is quite another question.

There are three legs to the CRM 'stool': strategy, marketing and IT. Take just one of the legs away and the stool will fall over. Try to build CRM on just one leg alone and you won't even get your organization off the floor.

The simple truth is, CRM projects will spill out enormous amounts of customer data. Whether your organization is able to make that data meaningful and turn it into 'information', then knowledge, depends on whether you know what you want to do with it. Imagine (and this is a real example) that you discover the most important fact (correlation) about the heaviest users of your communication service is that they are likely to be cat owners. Then what? Joint promotions between telecoms and cat food? Too many companies believe that all they have to do is collect large amounts of similarly pointless data and they will finally be able to meet those (ludicrous) cross-selling objectives. The power to annoy more customers, faster and at greater cost is a distinct danger.

> The power to annoy more customers, faster and at greater cost is a distinct danger

Making the small print big print

All of the CRM literature that we have seen does (more or less clearly) state that the success of any CRM project depends on key strategic issues being agreed before any work is done. And, to be fair, those organizations currently marketing CRM solutions do mention the other things that need to be in place before (their version of) CRM will work. Unfortunately, these 'things' are neither small nor particularly easy to put in place. Of course, nobody writes this in red, or inserts health warnings at this point, but it needs to be done.

Perhaps it's time to learn from the pioneers of a previous technological age. Imagine CRM as the railway track. Lay the lines and it will get the train to its destination quickly and efficiently – you may have to knock down a few buildings standing in the way, but that is surely a small price to pay. The nineteenth-century entrepreneurs soon learned (sometimes the hard way) that success existed less in knowing how to lay the lines and more in knowing where people wanted the trains to go. Simple, isn't it?

Pushing the image as far as (or even beyond where) it will go, imagine the company trying to build the first fastest and best line to, well, anywhere really. Customers are taken along for the ride and arrive where none of them ever wanted to be. Exit the customers and exit the business – faster than if it had done nothing in the first place – yet there are many potential benefits, as shown in Table 2.2.

Table 2.2 CRM – the potential benefits

➡ Identify most profitable customers
➡ Serve most profitable customers better
➡ Manage less profitable situations better
➡ Identify the lifetime value of customers
➡ Reduce customer 'churn'
➡ Find profitable prospects
➡ Market the right products
➡ Reduce selling and marketing costs
➡ Improve effectiveness of marketing communications and direct marketing
➡ Improve customer service
➡ Focus e-commerce to the right customers
➡ Focus marketing to the right customers
➡ Refine marketing strategy
➡ Obtain competitive advantage
➡ Win!

So, do you know where your customers want to go?

Find out where you need to be and then you will begin to understand how CRM might help you get there.

No new technology or TLAs (three letter acronyms) here, just the same old difficult questions that nobody wants to answer. But with CRM looming, there really is no longer a choice. Tomorrow's battle will not be won by the best CRM system, but by the organizations with the clearest idea of where they are going and how they are going to get there. Simple, maybe, but not easy.

What questions need to be answered?

Where are we now?

Ever since Theodore Levitt wrote 'Marketing Myopia' in 1960,[1] the question of 'What business are we in?' has vexed marketers to the point of forcing them to ignore this most fundamental of all strategic questions. Defining the industry and market within which your organization is going to operate is central to any practical strategy. This is a question all world-class companies are currently asking themselves. Until it is properly answered, none of the tools and techniques of marketing work. Certainly CRM won't. This is an issue we will expand on later in this chapter to show how it should be done.

What do our customers want?

Identifying the critical difference between what you are making/selling and what your customers are buying/using identifies your organization's strengths and weaknesses and its real competition – the old features–benefits argument. Be very careful. Your customers really do pay good money for the benefits rather than the technical features.

What will our customers want tomorrow?

The objective: where do we want to be in the future? Not expressed in financial terms; this should describe the ambitions of the organization and the role it expects to be playing in its customers' lives.

Do different customers want different things?

All the CRM vendors make a great play on segmentation as being the key to today's fragmenting and competitive markets. Absolutely true. The big problem in all this is that very few are talking about segmentation, preferring to spend more time talking about classifying customers by the data that can be collected from data warehouses. Segmentation is less about which customers do what and more about why they do it. More meaningful customer data will reduce communications and sales wastage and create competitive advantage. Later in this chapter we explain a straightforward process for doing proper segmentation.

Segmentation is less about which customers do what and more about why they do it

Which customers should we be targeting?

Spotting and serving the most profitable customer has to be the name of the game. Applying segmentation strategically will allow the organization to decide where it needs to focus its activities for greater returns. The time when we could be all things to all people has largely passed. Tomorrow belongs to the credible specialist. An effective CRM process will enable the organization to focus on the customers it wants to retain over the longer term and will allow the business to develop just those offers that appeal to its target markets.

How do we differentiate our company/brand(s)?

We know a few things about customers – not as much as some would like – but something. We know for example that, in every developed market (consumer and business-to-business), nine out of ten customers would prefer to buy on non-price criteria. That means the secret to success lies in being different from the rest, not the same – and for 90 per cent, not the cheapest! Differentiation and owning a unique market position is critical. Do you know how you want to differentiate your offer from the rest? Because if you don't, you might end up with a CRM that only allows you to do the same as everybody else. The inevitable result – commodity status, price competition and death.

The secret, of course, is careful market segmentation before embarking on expensive and time-consuming CRM projects. However, even before we embark on this journey, there are some fundamental steps that need to be taken as part of a CRM readiness audit. These involve answering the following questions:

➡ What are the forces driving our industry?

➡ What are our fundamental competences?

Competitive forces analysis

The purpose of this part of the audit is to analyse the forces affecting competition in your industry.

Five forces which affect industry competition are: the threat of new entrants; the threat of substitute products or services; the bargaining power of buyers; the bargaining power of suppliers; and rivalry of existing competitors (see Figure 2.1). As part of business strategy development, it is valuable to

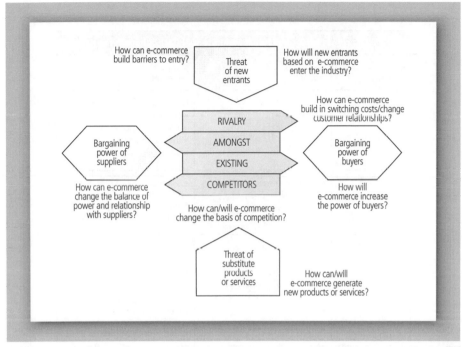

Figure 2.1
Competitive forces in an industry and e-commerce

Source: Adapted from Porter by Ward[2][3]

assess the impacts of each force (high, medium and low, for instance) and then to describe the nature of the impact where it is high, in order to identify ways of counteracting that force.

For example, many organizations are considering the impact of e-commerce on their industry. One way to do this is to answer the questions in Figure 2.1 about the impact of e-commerce of these five areas.

In thinking about IT in general, rather than just CRM, Figure 2.2 summarizes some of the key implications of this analysis, and gives examples of ways in which IT investments can influence the situation. Again, e-commerce provides many current examples. New entrants in the form of intermediaries between existing competitors and their customers, while not a new phenomenon, are particularly important in the e-commerce context, as the information-processing advantages of the medium are well suited to intermediaries, while the fast-moving nature of the field makes new entrants difficult to predict. Other impacts on the industry structure arise from 'e-hubs' which increase the buying leverage of groups of people with similar interests, and switch industries towards a different way of trading, such as auctions rather than fixed pricing. Potential

Impact of competitive forces and potential IS/IT opportunities		
Key force impacting the industry	Business implications	Potential IS/IT effects
Threat of new entrants	• Additional capacity • Reduced prices • New basis for competition	Provide entry barriers/reduce access by: • exploiting existing economies of scale • differentiating products/services • controlling distribution channels • segmenting markets
Buyer power high	• Forces prices down • Demands higher quality • Requires service flexibility • Encourages competition	• Differentiate products/services and improve price/performance • Increase switching costs of buyers • Facilitate buyer product selection
Supplier power high	• Raises prices/costs • Reduced quality of supply • Reduced availability	• Supplier sourcing systems • Extended quality control into suppliers • Forward planning with supplier
Substitute products threatened	• Limits potential market and profit • Price ceilings	• Improve price/performance • Redefine products and services to increase value • Redefine market segments
Intense competition from rivals	• Price competition • Product development • Distribution and service critical • Customer loyalty required	• Improve price/performance • Differentiate products and services in distribution channel and to consumer • Get closer to the end consumer – understand the requirements

Figure 2.2
Competitive
forces and IS/IT

Source: Adapted from Cash by Ward[4][3]

changes to industry structure identified using this tool are explored in more detail in the next chapter.

Worksheet 2.1 at the end of this chapter can be used for performing this analysis.

Dimensions of competence

The purpose of this part of the audit is to balance the external view of competitive forces analysis with an internal view which considers what aspects of business performance the organization has the skills to excel in as a basis for achieving market leadership.

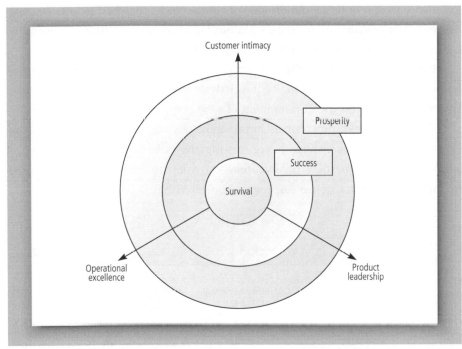

Figure 2.3
Dimensions of
competence

Source: Adapted from Treacy and Wiersema[5]

This tool suggests that there are three paths to market leadership (see Figure 2.3).

➡ *Operational excellence:* enabling products and services to be obtained reliably, easily and cost effectively by customers, implying a focus on business processes to outperform others, delivering both low costs and consistent quality of customer satisfaction, e.g. Dell Computer, Wal-Mart, Federal Express.

➡ *Customer intimacy:* targeting markets precisely and tailoring products and services to the needs of particular customer groups, exceeding expectations and building loyalty. IBM's recent success in services has been based on such a strategy.

➡ *Product leadership:* continuing product innovation that meets customers' needs. This implies not only creativity in developing new products and enhancing existing ones, but also astute market knowledge to ensure they sell. Johnson & Johnson, for example, pioneered the introduction of disposable contact lenses.

Excellence in one of these 'dimensions of competence', matched by a reasonable degree of performance on the others (i.e. not falling below the 'success' line in the future), can lead to a strong competitive position.

Understanding one's skills in existing product-markets can help to position one's offering in new ones. Equally, the analysis may suggest that a new business environment requires the development of new competencies.

For example, e-commerce may improve the position of all competitors on one or more of these dimensions, hence 'raising the bar for everyone'. Figure 2.4 suggests some key questions organizations can ask in relation to how e-commerce might affect their strategy in each of these dimensions.

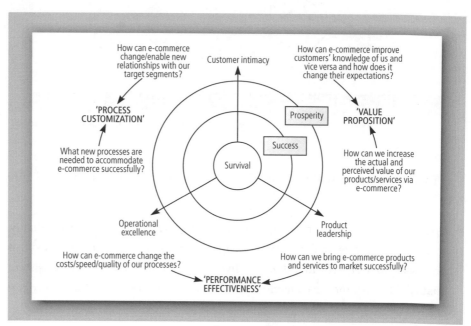

Figure 2.4
The impact of e-commerce on the dimensions of competence

Source: Adapted from Treacy and Wiersema by Ward[5][3]

Worksheet 2.2 at the end of this chapter can be used for performing this analysis on your own organization.

Completing the competitive forces analysis and the dimensions of competence analysis should give all organizations a better understanding of their competitive position in their markets prior to conducting a more specific CRM audit, which we turn to now. Table 2.3 lists the content of a CRM audit.

Table 2.3 CRM – the audit

➡ Identification of the market being served; answering 'What business are we in?'

➡ A quantification of the customer/process dynamics within this market

➡ An understanding of the competitive environment including competitor positions and competitive dynamics

➡ An unbiased (NOT a priori!) segmentation of the market we are interested in serving

➡ An understanding of customer needs in each segment

➡ A realistic assessment of the organizational implications of introducing CRM

➡ An outline plan for the introduction of CRM

➡ An assessment of the likely costs and benefits of CRM for the organization

➡ An outline brief for CRM suppliers, especially IT

How do we create a CRM process that will work *for* us, not against us?

The investment involved in agreeing your organization's longer-term ambitions (and therefore the objectives for a CRM project) will be minute compared to the cost of the CRM project itself. If past experience is anything to go by, the IT and organizational costs of CRM are likely to run to many millions – and that is without the potential business costs of getting it wrong. Surely it must make sense to stop and think through these fundamental questions before committing the organization to an uncertain future.

Very few companies would embark on a major capital project without a feasibility study, or an acquisition without 'due diligence'. So, why set out to spend millions on something that could cause irreparable harm without a CRM audit? But what is a CRM audit? As the name implies, it is an unbiased assessment of your organization's current customer position and requirements from any CRM process. An audit such as this represents an investment that pays off in two directions: it reduces the downside risks of disaster and increases the upside benefits from success.

The conclusion is probably best summed up by adapting Benjamin Franklin's famous quote, 'Drive your CRM or it will drive thee'.

CRM – some important questions

Before plunging into CRM without agreeing where you want it to take you, think about the following:

Customers

Customers are the name of the game. Without customers there is no business. Levitt said, '*The purpose of a business is to create and keep customers*'. Achieving that is not easy, especially as most customers make emotional rather than rational buying decisions and, more often than not, have no idea what they want.

Relationships

How many 'relationships' do you have? How many of those are with commercial organizations? You need to be clear about what is required here. If all you are trying to do is to retain more customers longer to make more money, you can probably do that by making fewer mistakes, so giving fewer excuses for your customers to leave. Building a 'relationship' is quite another matter. But are you sure that your customers want a 'relationship' in the first place? 'Please stop sending me birthday cards, just answer the phone when I ring' is a frequent complaint that we hear. Supplier delusions about the state of customer relationships have reached alarming proportions. Also, don't forget that, just as in our own personal lives the capacity to build close relationships with *all* our friends is limited, so it is with major customers.

> Are you sure that your customers want a 'relationship' in the first place?

Management

Almost everything we read about CRM either talks about or implies the organization managing its customers/relationships. Much as it might be the preferred route, it just doesn't work like that. You don't manage the customer, your customer manages you. At least that is the impression you should be trying to create. Most customers like to feel in control, so help them. Information flows, systems and processes designed from the customer's perspective might give you a better chance of achieving the results you really want; happy customers spending more and more often. Now, the CRM process that allows customers to manage the organization better to get more of what they want from it certainly would be worth having.

> You don't manage the customer, your customer manages you

Is CRM just another dangerous management fad or the answer to everyone's prayers? It doesn't just depend on the CRM providers, but on you and how well you apply the concepts.

Don't be duped into thinking that massaging your own databases will produce the results you want. Remember what most of the real management gurus have said world-class marketing is over the years. In order of most frequent mention, these are:

→ a deep understanding of the market

→ market segmentation

→ differentiation, positioning and branding

→ integrated marketing (marketing planning)

Note the order and note the expression 'market segmentation', *not* 'your own database segmentation', since your own database segmentation is often a reflection of historical accidents or your own cleverness – in other words, it's what someone sold to someone at some point in time. And since many sales are of products which are the easiest to sell, bought by customers who are the easiest to sell to, this isn't really very promising.

So, before investing in CRM, think about devoting some of the funds set aside for CRM to an audit, or you will waste millions and CRM will join all the other fads.

Market definition and market segmentation

By now, we hope we have convinced you about the preconditions for CRM, so we will proceed to explain how these steps can be carried out professionally and effectively. In effect, we are exploring in more detail the first of the four boxes in the map of marketing, shown below in Figure 2.5.

The first of these boxes is shown in more detail in Figure 2.6.

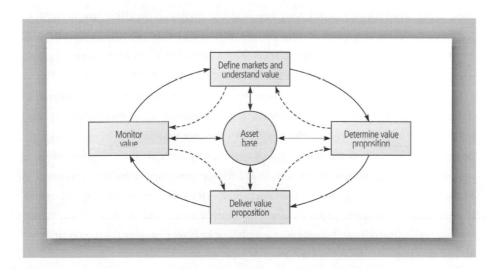

Figure 2.5
'Understand value' and the marketing map

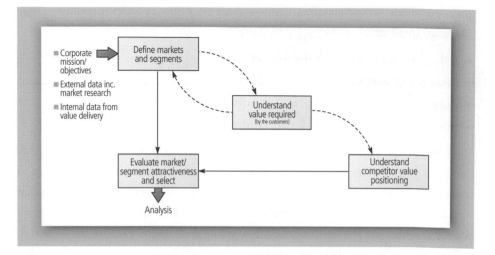

Figure 2.6
Define markets
and understand
value

Surely marketing has moved on – segmentation?

As we have stressed earlier, whatever the latest management idea sweeping through organizations, it will only deliver its promised benefits if it is implemented (or perhaps even rejected!) when a customer perspective is included in its equation. Few businesses in the world, however, can truly regard each customer as an individual market for which they design a specific product, service, distribution channel and so on. The economics of true one-to-one marketing just don't stack up for the majority of businesses. At the same time, the days of being able to treat all customers as if they were a single entity looking for the same offer have long since disappeared into the history books. Note that the advent of e-commerce does not rescind this simple truth. There is no single e-commerce formula that will work across the market. Not all customers want e-commerce, and even those that do don't all want the same e-commerce formula.

To be successful, businesses have to view their markets as consisting of distinct customer groups, each with their own distinct set of requirements, and then deliver targeted offers to the customer groups they elect to serve. It may not be the latest idea to sweep the world of commerce, but customer segmentation is essential to commercial success, and that includes the successful implementation of today's latest management ideas and those ideas that may emerge tomorrow. If segmentation is done properly and thoroughly every fad, matrix, guru, paper, course and initiative can be assessed according to how it improves the company's ability to satisfy its selected customer segments.

> The economics of true one-to-one marketing just don't stack up for the majority of businesses

It can be pictured as a bridge across a river, with the latest business idea being constructed by a company on one bank of the river and the customer segments constructing their part of the bridge on the other bank of the river. Both are reaching out to each other with the hope that somewhere on the way they will meet. Unfortunately, the customers have the upper hand because they will build their side of the bridge irrespective of how the company is building its side of the bridge. Now if the two sides don't exactly meet in the middle, the customers will just keep building until they find the right supplier. In the meantime, in order to satisfy their demands in the short term, the customers may add a temporary link to the company's bridge, but the customers will break it once their true needs are satisfied. This is why market **segmentation** is one of the oldest and most long-standing of all marketing processes.

True customer segmentation has such a profound impact on a business that getting it right cannot be left to chance. But what is 'right'? During the last fifty years, however, there have been a substantial number of different bases for segmentation proposed by the academic and practitioner community.

The basic premise of market segmentation is that a heterogeneous group of customers can be grouped into homogeneous clusters or segments, each requiring different applications of the marketing mix to service their needs. The focus of research and discussion has therefore been concerned with the analytical approaches by which homogeneous clusters can be established from a heterogeneous sample.

If 'segmentation', however, represents the customers in a market it clearly has to have a customer-centric focus. So it's no longer how the *company* segments its market, it's how the *customers* segment in *their* market. And there is only one way customers segment, and that is according to how they maximize their purchase value. Therefore, a process that builds this picture from a customer standpoint is required, but before deciding what such a process should look like, it is appropriate first to list what is required from segmentation:

➡ There has to be a reasonable amount of certainty that the decision-makers have been segmented.

➡ There has to be a way of identifying which customers fall into which segment.

➡ It is essential to understand what it is the customers in each segment are looking for.

> ● **Definition**
> A **segment** is a group of customers sharing the same or similar needs

> There is only one way customers segment, and that is according to how they maximize their purchase value

➡ It is important to be sure that there is sufficient business in each segment to justify putting together a distinct marketing strategy for each of the segments chosen to serve.

➡ It is necessary to track how customers segment over time to ensure that changes in the market are captured.

This may sound straightforward, but to do it properly takes time, and money. So instead of investing heavily in the latest business idea, it would seem prudent to go back to basics and examine the marketplace in order to understand its behaviour better.

Methodology for developing a structured system and process for segmentation

The following structured approach is the result of a painstaking process of research into the practical difficulties that organizations experience in segmenting their markets. It is tried and tested and has been successfully implemented in hundreds of organizations across the world.

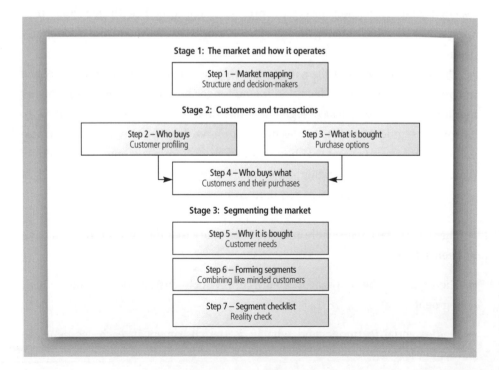

Figure 2.7
The market segmentation process

The process consists of seven steps contained within three distinct but related stages and is summarized in Figure 2.7.

It should be noted at this stage that the process is presented primarily in a format designed to utilize information already held by or accessible to a company, and this is the approach it is appropriate to adopt initially.

Segmentation step by step

Stage 1 – the market and how it operates

Step 1 – market mapping

This part of the process tackles the first requirement of segmentation, which is to determine who are the decision-makers. A prerequisite is, however, to define clearly the market about to be segmented.

The general rule developed for 'market' definition is that it should be described in terms of a *customer need* in a way which covers the aggregation of all the alternative products or services *customers* regard as being capable of satisfying that need. For example, lunch-time hunger can be satisfied not only by the in-company caterer, but also by external restaurants, public houses, fast food specialists and sandwich bars. The in-company caterer must therefore consider these alternatives in understanding the market they are in rather than putting on the blinkers and deciding that their market is 'company catering'.

> The market definition should be described in terms of a customer need

Once the definition is clear, it is essential that the market is mapped out in a way which illustrates where the decision-makers are to be found, as it is these individuals whose needs must be understood and around whom the segments will be built.

It is useful to start a market map by plotting the various stages that occur along the distribution and value-added chain between the companies that supply products/services into the market and the final users. At the same time, the particular routes to market the products go down should be indicated as not all of them will necessarily pass through all of these stages. An example of this starting point for market mapping is shown in Figure 2.8.

This market map consists of five stages, one each for suppliers, distributors, retailers, contractors and final users. This map illustrates that products are also acquired by the final users directly from the suppliers and the distributors, as well as from retailers and contractors. Some retailers also bypass distributors and acquire their stocks directly from the suppliers.

These transaction stages (represented by the cubes in Figure 2.8) are referred to as *junctions*, with each junction on a market map positioned hierarchically according to how close it is to the final user. The last junction along the market map would, therefore, be the final user.

Ensuring the market map continues right the way through to the final user is also appropriate in those situations where final users have their products/ services purchased for them, for example, by their company's purchasing department. In such instances, the market map would track products/services

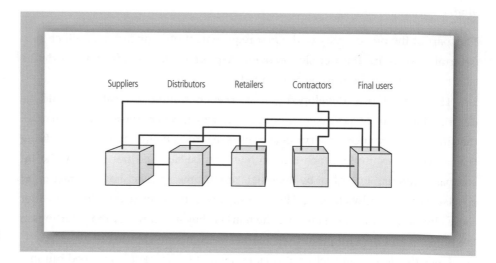

Figure 2.8
Starting a market map

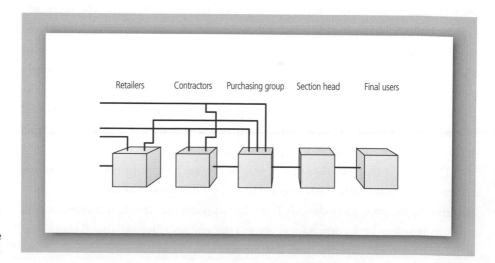

Figure 2.9
Market map with final users 'hidden' from the suppliers

down the corridors of the business clients and continue beyond the purchasing department to the department(s) in which the final user(s) were found. This is illustrated in Figure 2.9.

A further refinement of the market map, particularly in business-to-business markets, could be the inclusion of purchasing procedures as a distinct junction to capture the fact that there is yet another hurdle to be surmounted between the suppliers and the final user. In Figure 2.9 this would most likely be located between the purchasing group and the section heads, the purchasing group simply carrying out instructions, though they may, of course, be involved in the purchasing procedure.

With quantification playing an important part later on in the segmentation process, it is useful to mark at each junction and along each route the volumes or values dealt with by each of them. In most cases the annual figures for the market would be used. Where figures are not available guesstimates should be made in order to convey the appropriate relative importance of different routes. Also note the company's market share (again, guesstimate if necessary). This is illustrated in Figure 2.10.

Note that the number of units entering a market usually equate to the number of units 'consumed' by the final users. Therefore, rather like the work of an accountant, it all 'balances'. In some markets, however, it is possible for intermediaries both to take product from suppliers and to put together the product themselves. In these circumstances, the number of units in the market will increase along the distribution/value-added chain.

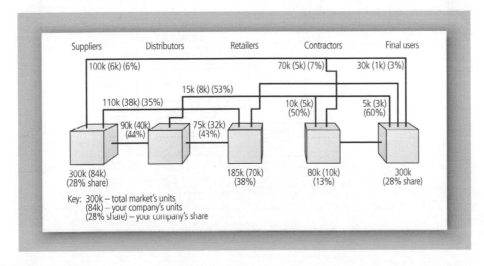

Figure 2.10
Initial quantification of a market map

Now that the market map is complete, the decision-makers can be identified by highlighting on the market map the junctions where they are to be found. These are referred to as market leverage points and are where the next stages of the segmentation process will focus.

Figure 2.11 shows a completed market map for a business-to-business market served by a particular range of specialized technical equipment. The importance of tracking products/services down the corridors of business clients proved to be particularly important in this market. This map not only highlights the five groups of decision-makers (highlighted by the arrows), it also attempts to illustrate what amount of the market their decisions control.

As an example of the value of this approach, it can be seen in Figure 2.11 that if a segmentation study were to focus entirely on the final users decision-making for nearly two-thirds of the market would be overlooked. It also illustrates at a very early stage in the study that a single approach to this market is unlikely to work. For example, decision-making by Technicians is unlikely to be along the same lines as decision-making by Administrators. Other useful insights can be obtained by presenting markets along these lines. For example, the company undertaking this project can now see that it is totally excluded from nearly a

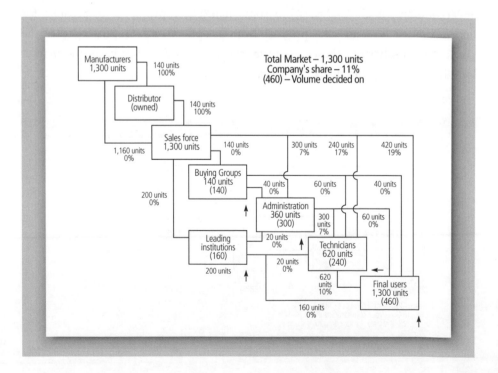

Figure 2.11
Market map example – specialized technical equipment

quarter of the decision-making due to its complete lack of presence in the Buying Groups and Leading Institutions. In addition, by projecting this market map forward by five years the company in question realized that decision-making was moving away from those with whom the company had a good share towards those with whom the company had a poor share.

Stage 2 – customers and transactions

Step 2 – who buys

A further essential requirement for successful segmentation is to be able to identify which customers fall into each of the concluding segments. Unfortunately, however, it is not until the segmentation project has been concluded that it is possible to uncover what information about the customers helps distinguish one segment from another. This means that as much information about the decision-makers in the selected market should be gathered as early as possible, but with one proviso: selecting the information to record should be governed by its practical use in enabling the identification of the members of each concluding segment.

It is recorded at this early stage of the process because it may be possible to link it to information put together in later steps. For example, certain features identified in the next step and taken through to the subsequent step may be associated with specific types of customers.

Step 2 is also the opportunity to introduce into the process any current segmentation structures believed to exist in the market. This could well be the different decision types appearing on the market map. The nature of the process being followed, however, ensures that these pre-defined segments do not form a mould out of which emerge the concluding segments. So, although Figure 2.11 shows that the market it represents is seen to be structured around five different decision groups, adopting these groups as preliminary segments will not force the conclusion in any way.

Step 3 – what is bought, where, when and how

The third item in the list of what is required from segmentation referred to the need to understand what it is the customers in each segment are looking for. The particular step in the process being described, along with the next two steps, will progress towards this goal.

Customers express their requirements by the features on which they focus their decision-making. The name we give to these is **Key Discriminating Features** (KDFs). These features could be found in what it is the customer is buying, in the channel through which they buy it, by when they want it or even by the different methods of payment they prefer. In most instances, the first two, namely what and where, are accountable for the bulk of a customer's decision-making. By carefully understanding the KDFs of a market, the segmentation project is progressing in two ways:

➡ It provides the framework for the most crucial stage in the market segmentation process, namely, identifying the range of benefits being sought by the market (described later). Given that segments are based on groups of customers with similar requirements satisfied by a distinct marketing mix, this information is critical to the segmentation process.

➡ It enables the building of a model of the market based on all the different purchase combinations that are known to take place within it, any of which could be reflecting a different customer requirement.

It is important to emphasize here that as this step provides the link with the needs-based buying requirements sought by the market (the benefits), it is essential that it is approached from the customer's perspective.

For some markets, the lists of different what, where, when and how factors can be quite extensive, but some simple rules can restrict these lists so that they do not lose their contribution to the segmentation process. A guiding principle is to maintain the customer's perspective, as customers tend to look at complex offers in far simpler terms than those of the suppliers.

The first 'rule' for restricting these lists is to remove from them all those features which are basic entry requirements to the nominated market for any supplier, sometimes referred to as 'market qualifiers' or 'hygiene factors'. These are the features which the users expect to have as a matter of course. However, once one company introduces improvements to these features, the entry level requirement moves up to this higher level. For example, in the market for PCs the constant improvement in processor speeds simply moves the market up a further notch in terms of the customer's standard level of expectation. For a segmentation study, listing processor speeds for such a market is unnecessary.

A second 'rule' for restricting these lists is to focus only on those groups of features that have an important influence on the choice of product or service for

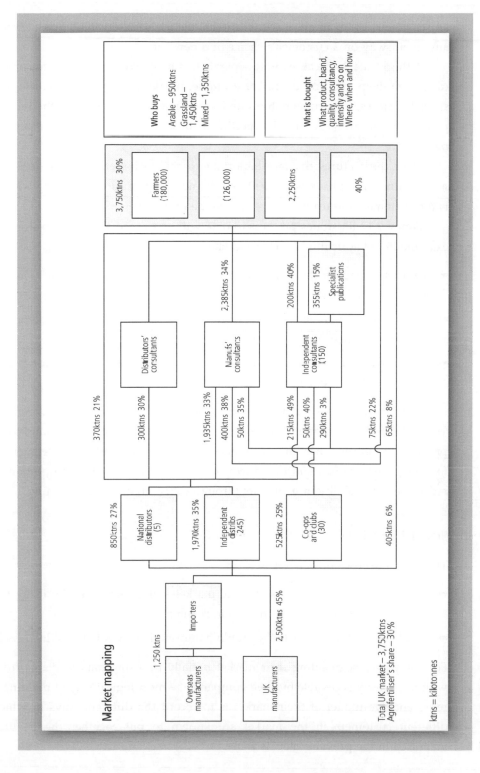

Figure 2.12 The process of segmentation – Steps 1 to 3

any customer. For example, it is unlikely that the radio cassette built into a car has any great sway on a customer's choice of a new car.

A third 'rule' looks at merging separate features according to how customers categorize them and buy them, For example, breaking down retail outlets into specialist stores, department stores and so on may be irrelevant to the buying process if 'local store' is the pertinent description from the customer's perspective.

Once the features that are important to the customers in their decision-making (the KDFs) have been identified the next stage of understanding what it is the customers are really looking for can be undertaken.

Figure 2.12 illustrates progress to date with the process. It is taken from an example in the agricultural sector and shows:

➡ the market map for this particular project with the final users, farmers in this case, identified as the decision-makers – Step 1;

➡ an initial segmentation structure for farmers which the company undertaking the project wanted to test – Step 2;

➡ an overview of the features decision-makers regarded as important when deciding between one supplier and another – Step 3.

It is interesting to note that the specific product for this project, fertilizers, was 'officially' declared to be a commodity. This 'commodity' status was found to be profoundly untrue once the customers in its market had been segmented following this process, and this discovery enabled the company in question to rediscover profitability in its market through differentiation and targeting.

Step 4 – who buys what

The main purposes of this step are:

➡ to construct a customer base for the market being segmented by using the information put together in the previous step;

➡ to link this customer base to the profiling information recorded in 'Who buys'.

For companies segmenting their market initially by using data available from within, or easily accessible by, their company, the most logical way of building a representative model of their market is to record the different ways in which different customers in the market are known to put together the features identified in the previous step as KDFs.

As an example, take a company looking at segmenting the market served by the provision of temporary accommodation for workers at building sites. Some of the market's customers require just the basic shells, others require them to be fully furnished but with only basic furniture. Others in this market for temporary buildings want them to be furnished to a high specification and yet others want them not only to be furnished, but also serviced. By following this basic logic, a model of any market can be put together quite easily.

At the extreme, each of the KDF combinations could be reflecting a different requirement and, therefore, a different segment. The reality is, however, that these different combinations tend to focus upon satisfying a smaller range of core requirements. It is just that different customers often satisfy these core requirements with different features. Therefore, in order to arrive at a segmentation structure for the market, it is an important step in the process to list the different combinations known to occur in the market and then to understand them.

It is worth noting that in practical exercises it is usual to arrive at between 30 and 50 different purchase combinations, referred to as micro-segments in the process. When the number of micro-segments appears to be getting out of hand, the simplest check, and the one that tends to return the project to manageable proportions, is to conduct a reality check to ensure that each micro-segment truly represents a customer's actual behaviour in the market.

While putting together micro-segments, it is essential to add profiling information to each of them. This is first approached by seeing if any specific features can be linked as a whole to any particular profiling characteristic. This is then followed by attaching to each micro-segment profiling characteristics known to be associated with the buyer(s) identified as depicting that micro-segment.

For the segmentation projects which turn to market research in order to obtain a statistically sound sample of customers for their market, this process would regard each completed interview as a 'micro-segment'.

An example of micro-segments for an agricultural supplier is given in Figure 2.13.

Stage 3 – segmenting the market

Step 5 – why it is bought

So far, the decision-makers in the defined market have been focused on, the key features they use to differentiate between one offer and another have been

Feature groups	Features	Micro-segments				
		G1	G2	G3	G4	G5
'What' - product	AN and manufacturer blends / AN and bespoke blends / Urea and bespoke blends	✓	✓	✓	✓	✓
'What' - brand	Well established / Any brand	✓	✓	✓	✓	✓
'What' - quality	High / Any quality	✓	✓	✓	✓	✓
'Where' - channel	Local distributor / Importer	✓	✓	✓	✓	✓
'What' - intensity	High nitrogen level	✓	✓			
	Low nitrogen level			✓	✓	✓
'What' - consultant	Manufacturer's	✓		✓		✓
	Distributor's				✓	
	Independent		✓			
	Not purchased					

Key: 'G1', 'G2' and so on are the individual identifiers for the micro-segments, the 'G' indicating that they come from the 'grassland' preliminary segment. Each feature associated with a particular micro-segment is indicated by a ✓

Figure 2.13
A selection of micro-segments for a preliminary segment in the case study

identified, a picture of the market based on the different purchase combinations the decision-makers put together has been built and information about who they are (their profile) has been attached to these micro-segments. It is now necessary to understand what are the real drivers for the micro-segments in their choice between different offers, in other words, their needs-based buying requirements. This will then satisfy the third requirement of a segmentation project.

The essential clues for understanding the real needs of the market have already been covered. Customers only seek out features regarded as key because of the benefit(s) these features are seen to offer them. The benefits linked to each KDF should, therefore, be listed. In addition, for some customers it is only by combining certain KDFs that they obtain the benefit(s) they seek. Benefits should also be looked at from this perspective.

In theory, arriving at the benefits should be straightforward, as selling the benefits, not the features has been a rallying call for decades. In practice, however, some companies are unclear about the benefits their customers are looking for and stick rigidly to espousing the features as opposed to the benefits. To move forward in customer-based segmentation, it is clearly essential to uncover the benefits. It is important to spend as much time as necessary in compiling these benefit lists as they will be used to determine the segmentation structure of the market.

Past research and talking with representatives of the customer contact staff can be a useful first assessment of benefits. If the company also follows the practice of putting together lost sales reports, a review of these could also prove to be a useful source of information. It may, however, be necessary to commission some research specifically to uncover the real benefits being sought by the market.

Once the list of benefits has been drawn up for the market, this can be used as a common framework against which one micro-segment can be compared with another. The principle is to determine for each micro-segment how important each of the benefits are to them. An example appears in Table 2.4. It is once again taken from the agricultural project referred to earlier. This example has used the procedure of distributing a total score of 100 between the list of benefits for each micro-segment.

Table 2.4 Benefits scores for a selection of micro-segments

Market Benefits	Micro-segments				
	G1	G2	G3	G4	G5
Innovative/new	9	11	–	–	20
Proven/traditional (reassurance)	5	4	21	20	–
Healthy looking crop (*includes grass*)	27	24	–	–	–
Healthy looking animal stock	–	–	26	25	–
Sophisticated	–	–	–	–	5
Maximum crop growth and output	18	22	–	–	10
Easy to handle (quality)	16	15	9	8	–
Service (qualified help from manufacturer)	11	9	–	–	–
Distributor – convenient local supply	11	8	39	42	–
Price	3	7	5	5	65
Total	**100**	**100**	**100**	**100**	**100**

Key: 'G1', G2' and so on are the individual identifiers for the micro-segments, the 'G' indicating that they come from the 'Grassland' preliminary segment.

Step 6 – forming segments

With a representative picture of the market, and each customer now comparable with every other customer because they have all been assessed against a common framework, like-minded customers can be brought together to form clusters.

With a manageable number of micro-segments it is possible to carry this out manually. However, in most instances the assistance of a suitable computer-based support package is required. It should be stressed, however, that progressing the segmentation project does not depend on the use of a PC-based support package. It is possible to carry out this key step manually, although a knowledge of statistical techniques would be essential.

Referring back to Table 2.4, it is possible to see how this very small selection of micro-segments would cluster. Micro-segments 1 and 2 are clearly very similar to each other and would therefore form one cluster. Micro-segments 3 and 4 are similar to each other, but different from the other three. Micro-segments 3 and 4 would therefore form another cluster. The final micro-segment in Table 2.4, micro-segment 5, is unlike any other in this small selection, and would therefore form a cluster on its own.

It is worth noting that most markets split into between five and eight segments, though on some occasions they have concluded with nine or ten segments. Not all of these segments will, of course, be suited to the company carrying out the segmentation study and its particular strengths in the market, so it is not necessary to serve every segment that exists.

An example of a completed segmentation initiative is given in Figure 2.14 for a company called Global Tech. Before the segmentation study, this company gave the same after-sales service to the whole market and, not surprisingly, were losing market share because they weren't giving the appropriate service to the different segments.

Step 7 – segment checklist

The fourth requirement from a segmentation project is that:

➡ It is necessary to be sure that there is sufficient business in each segment to justify putting together a distinct marketing strategy for each of the segments selected to be served.

This is the first check for the concluding segments. It means, however, that each of the preceding steps will need to have been quantified during progress through the project.

Koala Bears	Uses and extended warranty to give them cover. Won't do anything themselves, prefer to curl up and wait for someone to come and fix it.	
	Small offices (in small and big companies)	*28% of market*
Teddy Bears	Lots of account management and love required from a single preferred supplier. Will pay a premium for training and attention. If multi-site, will require supplier to effectively cover these sites (protect me).	
	Larger companies	*17% of market*
Polar Bears	Like Teddy Bears except colder! Will shop around for cheapest service supplier, whoever that may be. Full third-party approach. Train me but don't expect to be paid. Will review annually (seriously). If multi-site will require supplier to effectively cover these sites.	
	Larger companies	*29% of market*
Yogi Bears	A 'wise' Teddy or Polar Bear working long hours. Will use trained staff to fix if possible. Needs skilled product specialist at end of phone, not a bookings clerk. Wants different service levels to match the criticality of the product to their business process.	
	Large and small companies	*11% of market*
Grizzly Bears	Trash them! Cheaper to replace than maintain. Besides, they're so reliable that they are probably obsolete when they bust. Expensive items will be fixed on a pay-as-when basis – if worth it. Won't pay for training.	
	Not small companies	*6% of market*
Andropov Big Bears	My business is totally dependent on your products. I know more about your products than you do! You will do as you are told. You will be here now! I will pay for the extra cover but you will…!	
	Not small or very large companies	*9% of market*

Figure 2.14
Global Tech

Size is not everything however, and other possible items suggested in the checklist process are as follows:

➡ *Differentiated:* Is the offer required by each segment sufficiently different from that required by the other segments? This is where the marketing strategies appropriate for one segment are checked to ensure they are distinguishable from the marketing strategies developed for the other segments.

➡ *Reachable:* This is where the different marketing strategies are checked to ensure that they can be directed towards their applicable segments. Each segment must therefore have a distinctive profile, for example:

- distinct television viewing, radio listening, newspaper or magazine reading profiles; and/or
- distinct characteristics which can classify them by who or what they are, such as socio-economic group, type of company; and/or
- distinct characteristics which can classify them by a geographic area, such as postcodes; and/or
- distinct characteristics which can classify them by their purchasing preferences, such as purchasing patterns, distribution channels, distinct benefits sought, distinct response to prices.

This requirement was first mentioned in Step 2.

Once these items have been checked off there is one more test before launching the company into one or more segment-based strategies. It is probably the most testing item on the checklist: i.e. compatibility.

➡ *Compatibility:* This is where the organization rigorously checks its own ability to focus on the new segments by structuring itself around them organizationally, culturally, in its management information systems and in its decision-making processes. Such changes may not be possible immediately, therefore the organization's ability to evolve to the required structure should be tested.

Any organization rigorously applying this process to arrive at segments is now ready to adopt any initiative such as CRM.

Time

Segments, however, do not stand still. They change, grow and decline over time and even new ones emerge. Segmentation is not something done today in the hope that it will remain the same forever. Hence the fifth and final requirement from segmentation:

➡ It is necessary to track how customers segment over time to ensure changes in the market are captured.

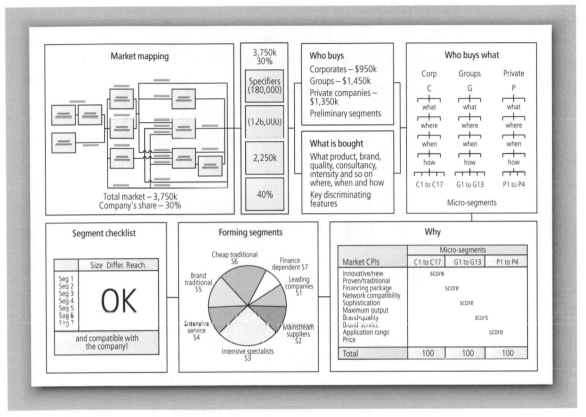

Figure 2.15 The market segmentation process

Every two years is recommended. If the company wants to deliver shareholder value consistently, and shareholder value after all only comes from retaining and acquiring profitable customers, then repeating segmentation projects in order to keep in touch with the market is essential.

A structured process for segmentation is essential, as it is not the easiest of marketing issues to address. It is also essential for any company wishing to succeed in its market and to remain successful.

There is, however, only one way in which a market segments, and that is according to how the customers in that market obtain value. Any process of segmentation must, therefore, ensure it builds itself around this essential requirement and the process outlined above, and presented again in Figure 2.15.

Conclusions

In conclusion, let us stress that, whether or not we call it 'new marketing', certain fundamentals have to be in place. These include:

➡ understanding the forces which are driving our industry

➡ understanding our own distinctive competences in this market;

➡ carrying out an audit to ensure that we fully understand the market we are in, the segments that form the market, and the needs of the customers who inhabit each segment.

When these prerequisites have been completed, CRM systems have some chance of succeeding. If not, CRM is destined to become yet another management fad.

References

(1) Levitt, T. (1960) 'Marketing myopia', *Harvard Business Review*, July/August, 45–56.

(2) Porter, M.E. (1980) *Competitive strategy*, New York: Free Press.

(3) Ward, J.M. (1999) *Value Chain Analysis and Electronic Commerce: An Overview*, Working Paper, Bedford: Cranfield University School of Management.

(4) Cash, J.I. (1988) 'Inter-organizational systems: an information society, opportunity or threat?' *The Information Society*, **3**(3).

(5) Treacy, M. and Wiersema, F. (1993) 'Customer intimacy and other value disciplines', *Harvard Business Review*, January/February.

Worksheet 2.1 Internal competence dimensions

Customer intimacy

Targeting markets precisely and tailoring products and service to the needs of specific customer groups, exceeding expectations and building loyalty (e.g. First Direct)

Product leadership

Continuing product innovation which meets customer needs. This implies not only creativity in developing new products and enhancing existing ones, but also astute market knowledge to ensure they sell (e.g. Johnson and Johnson, 3M)

Operational excellence

Enabling products and services to be obtained reliably, easily and cost-effectively by customers, implying focus on business processes to outperform others, delivering low costs and consistent customer satisfaction. (e.g. Dell, Wal-Mart, Federal Express)

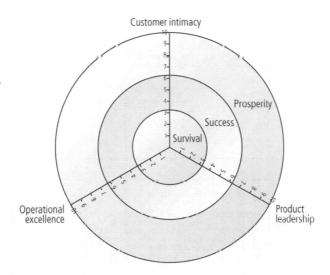

1 Score your company out of 10 on your current position against each of these three dimensions and join the lines up. N.B.
   - ➡ Score yourself 1–3 if you are currently below the minimum level required in your market
   - ➡ Score yourself 4–6 if you are currently as good as the average in your sector
   - ➡ Score yourself 7–10 if you currently exceed the average in your sector.

2 Score your company out of 10 on the position you would need to attain in, say, 3 years' time against each of their dimensions in order to ensure your continuing prosperity.

3 On a separate sheet, list some of the main strategies you will need to implement to achieve the desired positions.

Worksheet 2.2 New media and industry competition

How might the Internet (or other new channels) change the basis of competition?		WHERE DOES MY COMPANY STAND?		
		THREATS	OPPORTUNITIES	
			Cost reduction	Customer value creating
1 THREAT OF NEW ENTRANTS *Can we use e-commerce to build barriers to entry?*	a) Market share/size/brand/service b) Leverage physical assets c) Provide dominant exchanges d) Cost/price e) Remote delivery of bitware f) Others			
2 BARGAINING POWER OF SUPPLIERS *How will e-commerce change the balance of power and relationships with suppliers?*	a) E-commerce-enabled forward integration or disintermediation b) Lock-in (EDI) c) Others			
3 BARGAINING POWER OF BUYERS *How can e-commerce build in switching costs or change customer relationships?*	a) Price transparency b) Systems integration c) Aggregation of demand d) Others			
4 THREAT OF SUBSTITUTE PRODUCTS/ SERVICES *Will e-commerce generate new ways of satisfying customer needs?*	a) Remote delivery of bitware b) Others			

3

Planning for market transformation

Determining the value proposition

- ➡ Marketing planning
- ➡ Planning and innovation
- ➡ Future market mapping
- ➡ Multi-channel integration: channel chains
- ➡ Channel choice: the channel curve
- ➡ Prioritizing opportunities
- ➡ Channel tactics

Introduction

In the last chapter, we explored in greater detail the first of the four boxes in the map of marketing that we have used as the basis for this book (see Figure 3.1). The purpose of this chapter is to explore in more detail the second box, 'Determine value proposition', which is expanded on in Figure 3.2.

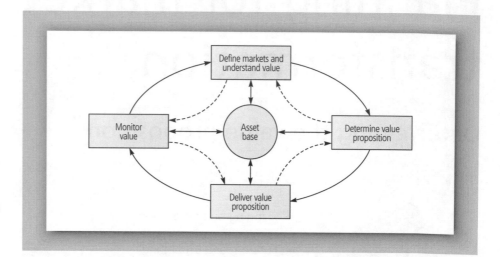

Figure 3.1
'Determine value proposition' and the marketing map

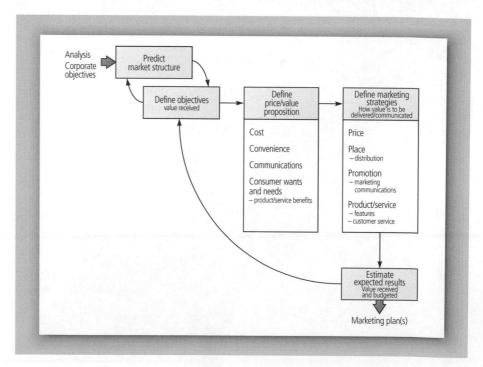

Figure 3.2
Determine the value proposition

Marketing planning

The authors are privileged to be given the opportunity to work with the operating boards of many companies in the service, industrial and not-for-profit sectors in many countries of the world. In initiating discussions, we set what one would consider to be a relatively simple 'test' in order to focus minds on the task in hand. The first question is.

➡ *Please list your key target markets in order of priority.*

This is a question which often elicits the response, 'What do you mean by markets?' Many directors write down words like 'Pensions', 'Middleware' and 'Micro-computers', even though it is clear that these are products, not markets. On explaining the difference, they still experience great difficulty in reaching agreement on what these markets are and how relatively important each one is.

The second question is:

➡ *In each market, what is your organization's differential advantage?*

Already you will begin to understand that, if the operating directors cannot answer these relatively simple, but crucially important questions, it is highly unlikely that the organization will have much chance of organizing its scarce resources around the needs of its core customers. In other words, such an organization is unlikely to be market driven, or, to put it a different way, is unlikely to be focused on satisfying customer needs as a source of differential advantage.

Having said this, marketing as a process and as a function will not stand any chance of being effective unless all the other essential ingredients of business success are also in place. Figure 3.3 shows how all the core functions of a business must work together in order to create sustainable competitive advantage.

From this it can be seen that organizations need to benchmark best practice in all their operations, including manufacturing, logistics, information technology, human resource management and so on, because inefficiencies in any of these areas could lead to unacceptably high relative costs, which could negate excellence in other business areas. Likewise, the basic financials of the organization need to be under control, as unacceptably high break-even points, too much debt (gearing) and so on could also negate excellence in other areas. The well-documented problems of British Telecom are testimony to this truth. In building up debts of £30 billion, their excellence in other areas was compromised and their share value fell dramatically as a result.

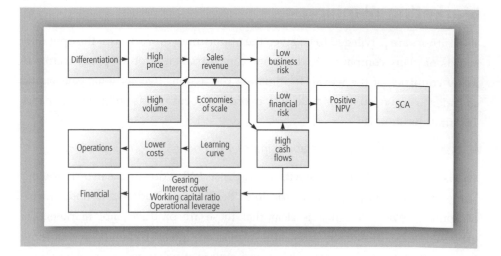

Figure 3.3
The route to
sustainable
competitive
advantage

The point is that marketing will not be effective if other parts of the organization are inefficient and, as a result, ineffective.

The top line refers to 'differentiation', which invariably leads to relatively high prices and high volumes. It is no accident that most readers will have in their homes products by Heinz, Mars, Kellogg's, Proctor & Gamble and Unilever. In the same way, consumers cannot 'taste the difference' (as it were) between Castrol GTX and any other oil, but the moment it is put in a can with this name on it, it gives Castrol massive global market shares. The same can be said for SKF bearings, Tetralaval machinery, Intel microchips and the like. So, there is clearly something to be said for 'differentiation'. It is no accident that balance sheets don't actually mean much in the real world. 'Assets' consist of items like plant, buildings, offices, vehicles, etc. 'Liabilities' consist of sources of finance, such as shares, loans, overdrafts, etc. and, of course, they always balance! It is strange, then, that most acquisitions are made at over five times the so-called value of the tangible assets. The resulting consolidated balance sheet of the acquiring organization then has to include a balancing item on the 'assets' side of the balance sheet known as 'goodwill'. An uncharitable commentator would say that this is the first time in the history of the company that the size of the error made by accountants in valuing the company comes to light and that it takes an acquisition, or the threat of an acquisition, to work out how big the mistake is!

There are, of course, perfectly good reasons why professional accountants do not recommend goodwill to be included in balance sheets as a matter of course and the authors agree with such reasoning. Nonetheless, it is obvious that this

> Consumers cannot 'taste the difference' between Castrol GTX and any other oil, but the moment it is put in a can with this name on it, it gives Castrol massive global market shares

'goodwill' is the only real asset that any company has and that its value resides in intangibles such as brand names, organizational reputation, relationships with distribution channels, the trust of customers and consumers, etc. All of these quintessential elements are what marketing as a function and as a process is there for. So, having spelled out the vital importance of correct market definition and segmentation, we can now proceed to expand on how strategies can be developed for these defined segments which explain why customers would prefer to buy from us rather than from any other competitor who happens to be around. In popular terms, this is more commonly known as 'strategic marketing planning'.

The desired outcomes of strategic marketing planning

There are some 40 years of research into the topic of strategic marketing planning, an area that overlaps with and is sometimes indistinguishable from strategic planning and corporate planning. The topic is generally seen as beginning with Levitt,[1] with major landmarks in the work of Chandler,[2] Ansoff[3] and Andrews.[4] A thorough review of this vast amount of work shows two striking features:

1 *A bias to process at the expense of outputs:* Most of the published work in the area concentrates on the process of planning with relatively little attention paid to the desired outcomes or outputs of that process. Although widely seen as leading to a plan, the implementation of which will lead to sustainable competitive advantage, there is a distinct lack of definition about what the precursors or contributory components of sustainable competitive advantage might be.

2 *A set of useful tests for strategy quality:* The more advanced work in the field does attempt to identify generic properties of a good strategy that might be used as quality tests for the outputs of the strategic planning process. While this work is clouded by lack of agreement on terms and unevenness of approach between different thought leaders, it is possible to discern and explicate a list of these generic qualities of a good marketing strategy. These are described in Table 3.1.

This part of this chapter, therefore, makes clear the intent and goals of strategic marketing planning. The next part seeks to understand the processes by which these goals are attempted and the degree to which formal strategic marketing planning processes are used.

Table 3.1 The nine generic properties of a good marketing strategy*

Generic Property of Strategy	Description
Clarity of scope	Good marketing strategy clearly defines the scope of activity of the organization both positively (e.g. what product/market combinations will have resource allocated to them) and negatively (what product/market combinations will not have resource allocated to them)
Definition of intended competitive advantage	Good marketing strategy clearly defines the nature of competitive advantage in terms recognizable to the customer (e.g. lower price, better performance with respect to some customer needs)
Internal consistency and synergy	Good marketing strategy minimizes conflict and contradictions and maximizes synergies between the different elements of the marketing mix
Degree of uniqueness	Good marketing strategy is to a degree unique (compared to the competition) in a way recognizable to the customer
Congruence with the external environment	Good marketing strategy recognizes the implications of the external environment and aligns the organization's resources towards those implications
Consistency with the organization's objectives	Good marketing strategy is compatible, in both scale and direction, with the quantitative and qualitative goals of the organization
Acceptability of risk level	Good marketing strategy proposes a broad course of action that limits risks within the boundaries acceptable to the organization
Feasibility within the organization's resources	Good marketing strategy is implementable within the resources available or accessible to the organization without contradicting its goals or risk acceptability boundaries
Provision of a level of guidance to tactical activity	Good marketing strategy makes clear the direction and scale of tactical activity both positively (what is to be done) and negatively (what is not to be done)

Summary: Any marketing strategy has two core components: a statement of the target market(s) and a statement of the intended basis of competitive advantage. Good marketing strategies define these in such a way as to optimize strategic fit, synergy, risk etc.

*This list owes much to the original work of Brian Smith, Managing Director of PragMedic.

The process and practice of strategic marketing planning

Marketing planning

All organizations operate in a complex environment, in which hundreds of external and internal factors interact to affect their ability to achieve their objectives. Managers need some understanding, or view, about how all these variables interact and they must try to be rational about their decisions, no matter how important intuition, feel and experience are as contributory factors in this process of rationality. Most managers accept that some kind of formalized procedure for planning the organization's marketing helps to sharpen this rationality so as to reduce the complexity of business operations and add a dimension of realism to the organization's hopes for the future.

The essence of marketing planning

The contribution of marketing planning to organizational success, whatever its area of activity, lies in its commitment to detailed analysis of future opportunities to meet customer needs and a wholly professional approach to selling to well-defined market segments those products or services that deliver the sought-after benefits. Such commitment and activities, however, must not be mistaken for budgets and forecasts. These have always been a commercial necessity. The process of marketing planning is a more sophisticated approach which is concerned with identifying what, and to whom, sales are going to be made in the longer term to give revenue budgets and sales forecasts any chance of being achieved.

In essence, marketing planning is a managerial process, the output of which is a marketing plan. As such, it is a logical sequence and a series of activities leading to the setting of marketing objectives and the formulation of plans for achieving them. Conceptually, the process is very simple and is achieved by means of a planning system. The system is little more than a structured way of identifying a range of options for the organization, of making them explicit in writing, of formulating marketing objectives which are consistent with the company's overall objectives and of scheduling and costing the specific activities most likely to bring about the achievement of the objectives. It is the systemization of this process which lies at the heart of the theory of marketing planning.

Types of marketing plan

There are two principal kinds of marketing plan:

➡ the strategic marketing plan

➡ the tactical marketing plan

The **strategic marketing plan** is a plan for three or more years. It is the written document which outlines how managers perceive their own position in their markets relative to their competitors (with competitive advantage accurately defined), what objectives they want to achieve, how they intend to achieve them (strategies), what resources are required, and with what results (budget). Three years is the most frequent planning period for the strategic marketing plan. Five years is the longest period and this is becoming less common as a result of the speed of technological and environmental change. The exceptions here are the very long-range plans formulated by a number of Japanese companies which may often have planning horizons of between 50 and 200 years!

The **tactical marketing plan** is the detailed scheduling and costing of the specific actions necessary for the achievement of the first year of the strategic marketing plan. The tactical plan is thus usually for one year.

Research into the marketing planning practices of organizations shows that successful ones complete the strategic plan before the tactical plan. Unsuccessful organizations frequently do not bother with a strategic marketing plan at all, relying largely on sales forecasts and the associated budgets. The problem with this approach is that many managers sell the products and services they find easiest to sell to those customers who offer the least line of resistance. By developing short-term, tactical marketing plans first and then extrapolating them, managers merely succeed in extrapolating their own shortcomings. Preoccupation with preparing a detailed marketing plan first is typical of those companies that confuse sales forecasting and budgeting with strategic marketing planning.

> By developing short-term, tactical marketing plans first and then extrapolating them, managers merely succeed in extrapolating their own shortcomings

The contents of a strategic marketing plan

The contents of a strategic marketing plan are as follows:

➡ *Mission statement* – This sets out the *raison d'être* of the organization and covers its role, business definition, distinctive competence, and future indications.

➡ *Financial summary* – This summarizes the financial implications over the full planning period.

➡ *Market overview* – This provides a brief picture of the market and includes: market structure; market trends; key market segments; and (sometimes) gap analysis.

➡ *SWOT analyses* – These are the strengths and weaknesses of the organization compared with competitors against key customer success factors plus the organization's opportunities and threats; they are normally completed for each key product, or segment.

➡ *Issues to be addressed* – These are derived from the SWOT analyses and are usually specific to each product or segment.

➡ *Portfolio summary* – This is a pictorial summary of the SWOT analyses that makes it easy to see, at a glance, the relative importance of each; it is often a two-dimensional matrix in which the horizontal axis measures the organization's comparative strengths and the vertical axis measures its relative attractiveness.

➡ *Assumptions* – These are the assumptions which are critical to the planned marketing objectives and strategies.

➡ *Marketing objectives* – These are usually quantitative statements, in terms of profit, volume, value and market share, of what the organization wishes to achieve. They are usually stated by product, by segment, and overall.

➡ *Marketing strategies* – These state how the objectives are to be achieved and often involve the four Ps of marketing: product, price, place, and promotion.

➡ *Resource requirements and budget* – This is the full planning period budget, showing in detail, for each year, the revenues and associated costs.

The contents of a tactical marketing plan

The contents of a tactical marketing plan are very similar, except that this plan often omits the mission statement, the market overview and SWOT analyses, and goes into much more detailed quantification by product and segment of marketing objectives and associated strategies. An additional feature is a much more detailed scheduling and costing of the tactics necessary to the achievement of the first year of the plan.

The marketing planning timetable

Figure 3.4 depicts the relationship between the marketing planning process and the output of that process: the strategic and tactical marketing plans. Figure 3.5

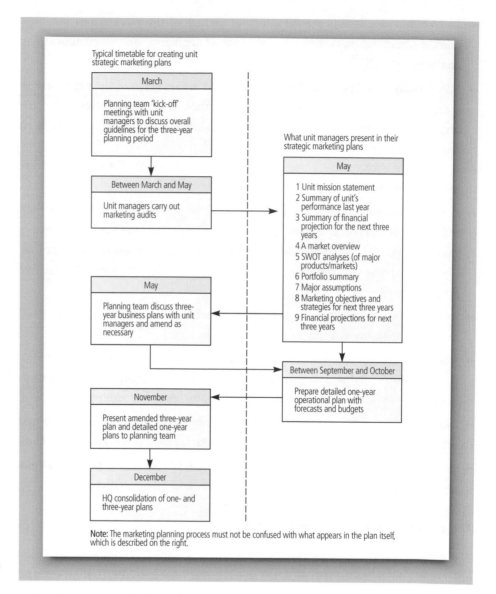

Figure 3.4
Strategic and
tactical marketing
plans

shows the same process in a circular form, as this indicates more realistically the ongoing nature of the marketing planning process and the link between strategic and tactical marketing plans.

As we indicated in Chapter 1, it is important to be clear about the difference between our (the company's) objectives, which are usually to do with profit, volume, value and market share, the strategies we put together (the four Ps) to

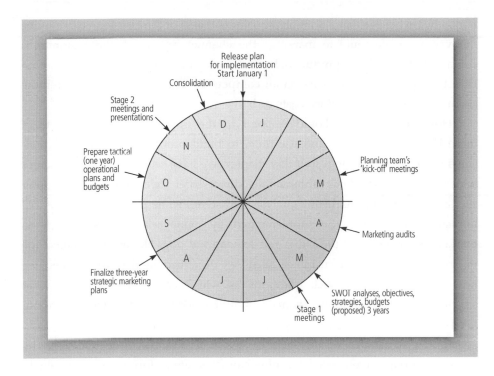

Figure 3.5
Strategic and
operational
planning cycle

deliver to our customers, and the benefits our customers receive (the four Cs) which make them want to buy from us and stay loyal to us.

Having explained the essence of best practice in marketing planning, we will now turn our attention to how the established tools of marketing planning need supplementing in today's multi-channel environment.

Planning and innovation*

We live in a time of rapid innovation. The FMCG companies which have long been held up as examples of marketing excellence are themselves privately admitting that they have yet to learn how to move beyond the continuous, minor innovations at which they are expert towards the step-change innovations now demanded by the business environment.

While product innovation continues apace, with the Internet giving many opportunities for providing digitizable products and surrounding services

> While product innovation continues apace, we believe that a dominant business theme of the next ten years will be innovation in the route to market

---

* The authors are grateful for the substantial contributions of Dr Liz Daniel, Professor John Ward and Professor Adrian Payne to this thinking on planning for IT-enabled channels.

remotely, we believe that a dominant business theme of the next ten years will be innovation in the route to market – the channels by which the customer is communicated with the product delivered. Companies such as Direct Line, First Direct, easyJet, eBay and Amazon all compete by exploiting IT-enabled remote channels to add value, reduce costs or both.

How organizations should respond to the opportunities and threats of these IT-enabled channels and use them to build profitable customer relationships is the subject of the rest of this chapter. We have seen that the IT packages which enable sales force automation, direct mail, telemarketing, customer service, e-commerce, marketing analysis and so on, while providing an essential infrastructure, need to be supplemented by managerial processes such as market segmentation if the tail is not to wag the dog. Having segmented the market and understood customer needs as described in the last chapter, we now need to consider such questions as which channels to use for what segments, and how different channels should work together to meet customer needs.

In the remainder of the chapter, we will address these questions by working through a process for multi-channel strategy formulation, shown in Figure 3.6. This really expands on certain parts of Figure 3.2 with which we began this chapter: the Ps of 'place' and 'promotion', as well as the 'Predict market structure' box. The following sections describe each stage in the process, and present diagnostic tools for performing the stage.

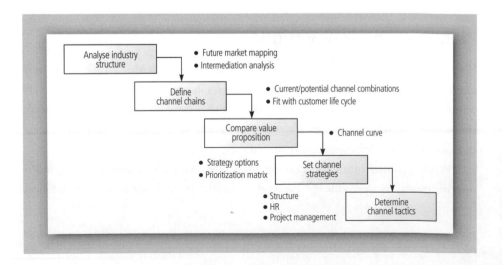

Figure 3.6
A process for multi-channel strategy formulation

Future market mapping: analysing industry structure

There is clearly little point in making decisions on what channels to use until the future shape of the whole industry has been considered. Therefore, once a market map of the current market structure has been developed as we described in Chapter 2, it is necessary to consider what factors are likely to change the flow of goods and services through this map. E-commerce is clearly one such major factor.

There is little point in making decisions on what channels to use until the future shape of the whole industry has been considered

The analysis of forces affecting industry competition, which we described in Chapter 2, often proves very useful for generating ideas on what changes might occur. These ideas can be fed into a redrawn future market map.

We saw in the last chapter how to annotate a current market map with flows of money and goods. Given that channels are also used to convey information, though, it is useful for our purposes also to annotate how information is flowing. As Evans and Wurster pointed out, physical and information flows together represent the value added by each step in the chain [5] One can then consider whether these components of value can be better provided by a different configuration of the map.

One possible way in which the car dealer's role might become unbundled in future, for example, is shown in Figure 3.7. Recent innovations such as direct car sales by manufacturers, or sales via Web-based intermediaries like Auto-By-Tel, have begun to experiment with these kinds of changes. Which of these

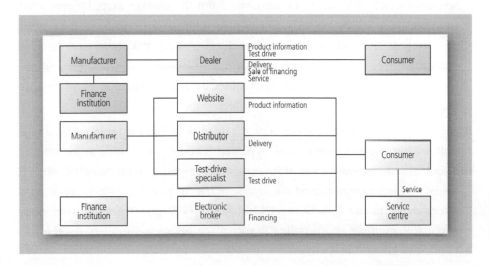

Figure 3.7
Current and potential market maps: car retailing

experiments proves permanent is, of course, another issue; but drawing maps of this sort can help a management team to flesh out the possible options and identify the relevant opportunities and threats.

There are five main ways in which the market map can be reconfigured:

1 *Substitute/reconfigured products.* A new channel may enable the underlying customer need to be satisfied in a different way ('substitute products'). E-mail, for example, can substitute for physical post, providing a threat to paper manufacturers, while online distance learning provides a challenge to book publishers. Or customer needs may be bundled into different product configurations ('reconfigured products'). To illustrate, the newspaper is a bundled product providing job advertisements, weather information, news, consumer-to-consumer advertisements and so on for a bundled price. It is now competing with Internet services which either simply offer one of these components – such as consumer auction sites – or in other cases, combine some aspect of the value provided by newspapers with other types of value – an example being portals. A portal such as Yahoo! meets some of the needs met by a newspaper, such as the day's news, and acts as a gateway to others, such as weather and auction sites, while also satisfying further needs not covered by the newspaper through the ability to search the Web. It can be seen that reconfigured products add complexity to the planning process, as two market maps from different industries may 'collide' and need to be considered together.

Definition

Disintermediation is the bypassing of an agent, distributor or other intermediary with a direct sales channel

2 *Disintermediation.* IT-enabled channels such as call centres and the Internet can sometimes enable a link to be removed from the market map, by removing intermediaries whose primary function of information transfer can be more effectively performed by other means. Examples are telephone and Internet banking; direct purchase from clothes manufacturers via websites; and the bypassing of sales agents and distributors by some consumer goods manufacturers who are selling direct to retailers.

Definition

Reintermediation is the introduction of an electronic marketplace or other intermediary between customers and suppliers who previously traded directly

3 *Reintermediation.* In some cases, a previous intermediary is replaced by a new online intermediary, rather than bypassed. Online sites which automatically search for the cheapest car insurance are competing with telephone-based brokers, which in turn caused the demise of the Automobile Association's high-street shops in the UK. General Electric's TPN Register provided an early successful example of an online marketplace between suppliers on the one hand, and GE and its partners on the other.

4 *Partial channel substitution.* This forms a halfway house towards disinter-mediation, in which an intermediary's role is reduced but not eliminated, through some of its value being provided remotely by the supplier to the intermediary's customer. Websites such as those of car manufacturers may build a brand and provide customer information while pointing customers to traditional outlets for actual purchase. This is the model adopted by a card manufacturer we studied in its relationship with retailers, where its website is supplementing its agent network rather than replacing it.

5 *Media switching/addition.* Finally, the organizations which form the various steps in the chain to the consumer may remain the same, but communication between them may be partially or fully switched from one medium to another. The many examples of this, the simplest type of transformation of the market map, include Dell's addition of the Internet to its other means of communicating with customers, and electronic components distributor RS Components, which has similarly added a Web channel to its dominant telephone sales model, while still selling to the same customers.

Predicting what reintermediation will occur is particularly difficult, as the possibilities are numerous. Will a given relationship – say, between CTN (confectioners, tobacconists and newsagents) stores and the manufacturers of the goods they sell – be a direct one? If so, will the shops buy from a range of suppliers' websites, or will the suppliers respond to tender requests provided electronically by shops? Or will there be a new intermediary acting as a marketplace between the two? As shown in Figure 3.8, the various possibilities can be placed in an approximate order, from a supplier's website (such as Japan Airlines, which puts out open invitations to tender to suppliers), at one extreme, to a vendor's website (such as the Consumers' Association, which provides an electronic version of its *Which?* magazine at a cost) at the other.

Neutral marketplaces are midway between the two. An example is an auction site, which is tied neither to the buyer nor to the seller. Somewhat closer to the vendors are intermediaries such as Auto-By-Tel, which passes on leads to a local dealer (though it has also more recently added a direct sales operation). A more buyer-oriented intermediary is TPN Register, which we discussed earlier: set up by a consortium of buyers, it acts to ensure that they gain low prices through economies of scale, as well as gaining efficiencies in processing costs.

Which of these possibilities becomes the dominant trading mechanism in a given relationship depends on the number of vendors and buyers, and their

Which type of
intermediary
becomes the
dominant trading
mechanism
depends on the
number of vendors
and buyers, and
their relative
power

Types of intermediaries		
Vendor controlled	Vendor website	Ernst & Young, HBR
Vendor oriented	Vendor run community Consortium distributor Vendor's agent Lead generator Audience broker	Cambridge Information Network thetrainline Tesco financial services Auto-By-Tel DoubleClick
Neutral	Market maker Shop Mall	eBay RS Components, wellbeing msn.com
Buyer oriented	Purchaser's agent Purchasing aggregator	comparenet Covisint
Buyer controlled	Buyer website	Japan Airlines

Figure 3.8
Types of
intermediaries

relative power. Where there are few buyers and many suppliers, or buyer power is great, the market will tend towards either individual buyer websites or buyer-oriented intermediaries such as the Covisint exchange set up by several car manufacturers. Conversely, a small number of suppliers selling to large numbers of customers will have the power to control the market through their own websites or through supplier-oriented consortiums. Large numbers of both suppliers and buyers will tend to use a neutral marketplace to reduce the search and transaction costs of both parties, though a supplier with a particularly strong brand and/or product differentiation, such as *Harvard Business Review* or the medical journal *The Lancet*, may choose not to participate in such marketplaces.

To reconfigure the market map, therefore, one needs to consider the potential effect of each of our five broad changes in turn. In each case, one needs to:

➡ sketch the effect of the change on the market map, indicating who will now provide the various aspects of value previously received by the end customer;

➡ consider whether the value received by the end customer, in benefits minus costs, is greater with the new structure (for each segment);

➡ if the effect is positive for some segments, incorporate the transformation in a revised market map.

Whether one regards the effect on customer value as positive depends on the organization's positioning within the relevant market. In terms of Michael Porter's three generic strategies this will imply:

→ for low-cost strategies, an approximate parity needs to be ensured on non-price buying criteria, while beating the competition on price;

→ for differentiation strategies, excellence needs to be ensured on one or more value-related criteria, while ensuring approximate parity on others;

→ for niche strategies, strength needs to be high on criteria important to the target niches.

Table 3.2 contains some additional questions for disintermediation, partial channel substitution and media switching/addition.

This process may seem complicated, but in practice it is possible to develop a good enough future market map in a couple of workshops. A summarized example from a UK groceries company is shown in Figure 3.9.

The current market structure (shaded boxes) involves manufacturers reaching consumers via a combination of the major multiple supermarkets, independent stores and CTN stores. The manufacturers participating in the workshop took the view that because the major multiples are few in number and hold considerable buying power, their relationship with manufacturers will either continue to be a direct one, using purchasing systems dictated by the multiples,

Table 3.2 Evaluating potential changes to the market map/value chain

Disintermediation	Does the removal of an intermediary improve physical flows?
	If so, can information flows or other value-adding services provided by the intermediary be as effectively handled by others in the chain?
	Can the flow improvements be translated into enhanced value for the end customers?
Partial channel substitution	Does the addition of an Internet communication channel improve information flows (e.g. cheaper communication with customer)?
	Can relationship with intermediary be redefined to deliver mutual benefit?
Media switching/addition	Within the current structure, can the Internet reduce costs or add value for some communications? Consider the e-marketing mix.

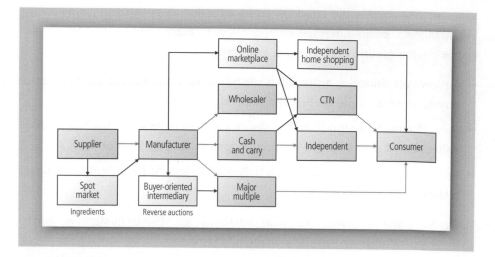

Figure 3.9
Current and
future market
maps: groceries

or will be mediated by a buyer-oriented intermediary, as shown in the potential future structure shown by the unshaded boxes.

The many-to-many relationship between manufacturers and independents or CTNs, though, needs a more neutral intermediary, such as is provided currently by wholesalers. The workshop predicted a similarly neutral online intermediary succeeding here, either through a new entrant start-up or through media addition by a wholesaler. Likewise, the relationship between manufacturers and suppliers is likely to include a neutral spot market for commodity ingredients. These predictions appear consistent with industry developments to date.

Towards a future market map in financial services

As another example, Figure 3.10 shows a current market map for retail financial services, developed by a panel of financial services strategists during a Cranfield workshop. Although the workshop did not get as far as a full future market map, the circled annotations suggest ways in which the map might change in the future as a result of e-commerce, according to the panel.

The changes they predicted were:

1 *Fund managers go direct.* Fund managers may find that e-commerce makes it easier to sell their products directly to customers. The simplification and transparency of pricing being encouraged throughout the industry should help customers feel more comfortable buying products directly: in fact they may

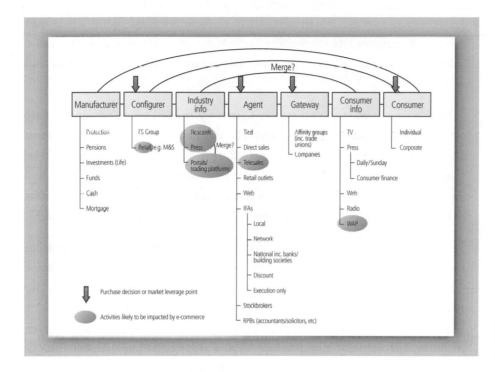

Figure 3.10
Long-term
investment:
future market

prefer this route since they may be wary of an agent who is receiving a large commission for his or her advice. The ability for fund managers to present clear and easy-to-understand information about their products and their performance online should encourage such direct sales.

2 *The customer becomes the configurer.* Using e-commerce, customers may be able to configure their own investment products from manufacturers. Currently this would be time-consuming and configurers have the significant amount of regulatory knowledge which is necessary to undertake this function. However, e-commerce applications that contain this regulatory knowledge as 'rules' could allow customers to undertake this function themselves.

3 *There is a blurring of industry and consumer information.* Currently information provided to agents and other professional advisers in the market is quite distinct from that provided to consumers. The former is more detailed and may require specialist knowledge to understand. However, there are already signs of distinction blurring, with insurance exchanges that have traditionally been wholesale or trade exchanges now providing e-commerce routes to end consumers.

4 *Affinity groups may become trusted portals.* Consumers in the online world may join communities of interest, such as ThirdAge.com, a community for over-60s. These communities may be the route that many choose to buy goods and services online.

5 *There is a 'dumbing down' of advice.* Currently many people wishing to buy investment products turn to a trained, regulated financial adviser. With e-commerce a rise of electronic agents offering advice is likely. These will be rule-based algorithms that base product recommendations on the answers to a few simple questions. There is a chance that such systems will miss subtleties in the client's situation, and hence result in the wrong product being bought.

6 *E-commerce results in greater product switching.* The ease of purchasing products via e-commerce, particularly with interactive TV that provides for flow-through sales, may lead to greater impulse buying and hence greater switching as consumers gain in confidence and perceive switching as easier. While sophisticated customers may gain, others could lose financially if they withdraw prematurely from products aimed at long-term investment. Suppliers will need to streamline administration to cope.

7 *E-commerce may cause cycles in consumer's buying patterns.* A pattern was observed in the US whereby many consumers transferred to no-load (no up-front fee) funds via telephone and Internet sales channels. As the value of their investment increased, many were turning back to personal advice on how to protect their investment. Similar cycles of consumer habits may occur in the future. Market conditions may add to cyclicality of consumers' buying patterns, bear markets tending to reduce investors' confidence to act without advice.

8 *Smaller players are more nimble.* Evidence of this in the investments market is already being seen with small IFAs adopting e-commerce services ahead of larger chains.

9 *E-commerce encourages customers to serve themselves but does not remove face-to-face contact.* By encouraging consumers to register changes of address or premium amounts online, the agent or manufacturer is outsourcing some of the administration to the consumer. But many consumers will continue to wish to combine electronic communication with face-to-face contact with advisers, particularly for more complex products.

Whatever the specifics for one's own industry, it is clearly sensible to come to a view on the future shape of the market before taking decisions on which channels to use for what purpose. Worksheet 3.1 at the end of this chapter suggests some steps for doing this in your own organization.

Multi-channel integration: channel chains

Once the future shape of the industry structure has been predicted, the organization at least knows who its customers will be in the future – an important step which is omitted from numerous standard strategy processes. The next step is to segment these customers into groups with similar buying behaviour.

As we have discussed in Chapter 2, this involves determining the buying factors, or critical success factors, which represent the main benefits customers use to decide between suppliers, and establishing their relative importance, or weighting, to the customer. Customers with similar buying factors and weights can then be grouped into clusters, or segments. An example was shown in Table 2.4 in Chapter 2.

Another example is the buying factors and weights listed at the bottom of Figure 3.12, for a hypothetical segment of the books market. These customers are most interested in the cost they pay – the price plus any other charges such as delivery – but are also concerned with such factors as convenience of purchase and the ability to browse for the book they want. We will return to this figure later.

We also need to know what channels each segment uses to buy currently, and what channels will be available to them in the future. Here, though, there is a complicating factor. In many markets, customers do not use a single channel. Rather, they use a number of channels in combination to meet their needs at different stages of their relationship with the supplier. To represent the current channel use, we therefore suggest the use of a new tool, channel chain analysis, which we illustrate in Figure 3.11.

Channel chain analysis involves describing which channels are used at which stages of the purchasing process. The stages of the process are listed on the left of the diagram. We have used our revised sales process from Chapter 1, but you can use whatever stages make most sense in your industry. The channels used to accomplish the stage are listed against each stage. The channel used for one stage will often affect which channel is likely to be used at the next stage, so the relevant boxes are joined with a line.

> In many markets, customers do not use a single channel. Rather, they use a number of channels in combination to meet their needs at different stages of their relationship with the supplier

> Channel chain analysis involves describing which channels are used at which stages of the purchasing process

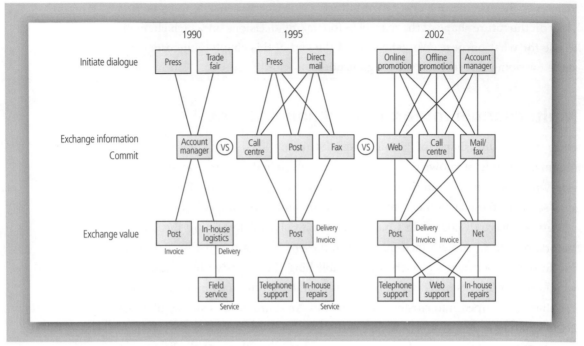

Figure 3.11 Channel chains – examples from the PC market

In this example from the business-to-business PC market, three of the common channel combinations are illustrated. The channel chain on the left shows the traditional account management approach, as exemplified by most of the large computer companies until the start of the 1990s, when most of the sales process was handled face-to-face by account managers. Still a model used for larger computers or major contracts, it has tended, though, to be supplanted by other channel chains which offer better channel economics for smaller deals.

The first of these new channel chains was the direct model pioneered by Dell, illustrated in the middle of the figure. Here, press advertising formed the dominant marketing tool, with further information provided by product brochures and call centre staff. The actual order could be placed by a number of means – often a traditional fax or order sent by post by the accounts department.

More recently, Dell and its competitors have added the Internet to the channel mix, as illustrated on the right. But Dell is far from a pure-play Internet provider. It has account managers for major accounts, who build relationships and negotiate discount levels. The account managers are freed from the details of product configuration and pricing by the website, while the order itself is as likely to be placed by fax or post as it is on the Web.

Different channels, then, are needed at different points in the sales cycle, and different competitors may adopt different approaches. The trick is to offer a channel chain that is appropriate to the differing needs of a company's target segments. It is easy to imagine a fourth, pure-play channel chain which has a low cost structure and is appropriate to certain price-sensitive segments – and, indeed, competitors adopting this approach exist.

> The trick is to offer a channel chain that is appropriate to the differing needs of a company's target segments

Having drawn the channel chains in current use, the next step is to consider possible future channel chains. This requires experimentation with channel chain diagrams to think through not just how the sale is to be made, but also how every other aspect of the customer's needs will be satisfied. Will a mobile phone purchaser buying over the Web be able to return a faulty phone to a nearby store? Will an e-hub be able to handle not just price negotiations, but also information flows on stock levels, complaints, returns and product development – and if not, what additional channels will be needed?

As with the industry restructuring which we considered earlier, the acid test as to whether these new channel chains will flourish is whether they represent a better value proposition to the customer: we will return to this topic below.

There is a timing issue to be considered as well. Even if a channel chain offers a theoretically better proposition to customers, they may not yet be ready for it. A channel chain innovation, like a product innovation, is likely to proceed along the lines of the diffusion of innovation curve we discussed in Chapter 1. If one hopes to convert customers to the Internet, for example, it is clearly necessary to consider what proportion of the customer base has Internet access and how mature their use of it is. We recall one department store which wasted millions on an aborted Web service in the mid 1990s because it was simply too far ahead of its market.

As a slightly different alternative approach, Worksheet 3.2 at the end of this chapter suggests some steps for considering how channels combine to meet customer needs in your own organization.

Channel choice: the channel curve

Channel chain analysis may generate numerous possible bases of channel competition. In a reasonably pure market, i.e. one which is not too skewed by regulation or monopolistic dominance, successful channel chains will be those which offer the best value proposition to the customer. At this stage, we need to compare the value proposition across the various potential channel combinations we have identified.

For this purpose, we recommend drawing up a chart as shown in Figure 3.12, which we call a 'channel curve'. For each segment, the buying factors and weights indicating their relative importance to the customer are listed. The ability of each channel, or channel chain, to deliver against each factor is then assessed judgementally on a 1–10 basis: the higher the score, the better this channel meets this buying factor.

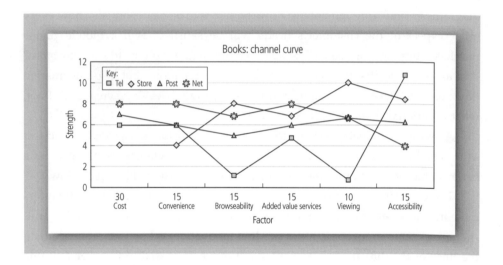

Figure 3.12
The channel curve: books example

In this hypothetical example, the various means by which a book can be purchased are compared. It can be seen that, taking all the factors together, the Internet and physical stores have the best matches to this particular segment. In reality, different segments of the book market are clearly best matched to different channels, which would show up clearly if the channel curve was drawn for each segment's differing buying criteria.

Another simplification of this example is that, as we have seen, it is often channel chains which compete rather than individual channels. In these cases, the various possible channel chains would each be compared against the buying criteria – so the channel chains would be listed in the key on the left, rather than individual channels.

Other than looking at the lines by eye to decide which offers the best match to customer needs, how can one determine which channel 'wins'? An alternative

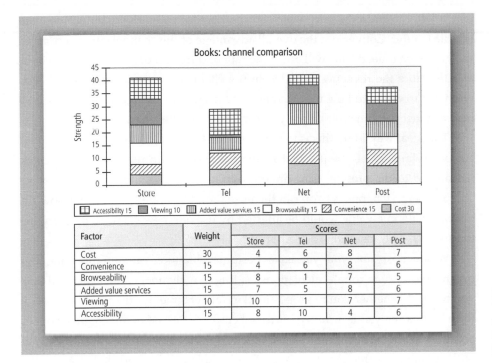

Factor	Weight	Scores			
		Store	Tel	Net	Post
Cost	30	4	6	8	7
Convenience	15	4	6	8	6
Browseability	15	8	1	7	5
Added value services	15	7	5	8	6
Viewing	10	10	1	7	7
Accessibility	15	8	10	4	6

Figure 3.13
The channel curve: an alternative presentation

way of presenting the same information makes this clearer. In Figure 3.13, the same underlying data – shown in the table – is presented in a stacked bar chart. The height of each segment of the bar is proportional to the score of a factor multiplied by its weight. So the overall height of the bar gives an approximate measure of how well, taking one thing with another, the channel meets customer needs. As with all analyses, though, management judgement should be exercised in its interpretation.

Both forms of presentation have their advantages, and you can use either or both. (This bar chart presentation was in fact the form we used when we first proposed this tool as the 'channel matrix',[6] but we then took the idea of the graphical presentation from Kim and Mauborgne in their 'value curve',[7] which however compared competitors rather than channels.) The main point is, one way or another, to assess channels not against whether we happen to like them, but against which will ultimately win out in the eyes of customers.

Our interests do, though, come into the analysis when it comes to price. The score of a channel chain against price-related factors, such as 'cost' in this example – the total cost including delivery – will be affected by the channel economics,

The main point is to assess channels not against whether we happen to like them, but against which will ultimately win out in the eyes of customers which will constrain the price which any competitor using the channel chain will be able to offer. Conversely, the overall advantage of the channel curve compared with other channel chains will affect the rate of diffusion of a new channel chain, and therefore the revenues included in the channel economics analysis. So you will need to estimate how much higher, or lower, your costs will be if you use a new channel combination before you can complete this chart.

The ideal way to do this is to work out the Current Lifetime Value (CLV) for customers in each segment – that is, the value of future revenues minus costs, discounted to the present using an appropriate cost of capital. (We will discuss CLV further in Chapter 5.) You can then use the CLV model to work out how the customer lifetime value would be affected by use of a new channel, by changing inputs such as transaction costs appropriately.

Whether or not you yet have customer lifetime value figures in your organization, some rough calculations leading to a channel curve chart will help you to check whether you're proposing the right channel for the right purpose. A form for this analysis is included in Worksheet 3.3 at the end of this chapter. For key accounts in business-to-business markets, it is useful to supplement this analysis with an internal value chain analysis. This is explained in Worksheet 3.4.

The prioritization matrix: defining channel strategy

As a result of the previous stages, the organization will have a list of possible channel innovations, and an assessment of the strength of each potential channel combination's value proposition to customers. All sorts of exciting possible strategies typically emerge by this point. But as one always has a limited budget and limited management time, it is now necessary to prioritize between the options available.

Our research, along with that of colleagues such as Cranfield's Professor Adrian Payne, suggests that in broad terms companies tend to adopt one of the following approaches to channel strategy:

➡ A *single channel provider* provides at least the bulk of its customer service through one channel. Direct Line and First Direct both started as more or less pure telephone operations, while in the Internet world the approach is referred to as 'pure play', and represented by Amazon, eBay and so on.

➡ A *channel migrator* started with one single channel, but is attempting to migrate its customer base onto another channel on the grounds of increased value or reduced cost. EasyJet initially sold tickets by phone, but now provides financial incentives to its price-sensitive customers to buy online, where the great majority of its tickets are now purchased.

➡ An *activity-based strategy* uses different channels in combination to provide different tasks in the customer experience – that is, a channel chain involving different channels at different points in the buying cycle. For example, a major corporate foreign exchange business uses the Internet to generate leads, a direct sales force to sign up new clients, and a call centre or the Internet to take orders.

➡ An *integrated multi-channel* approach involves offering different channels to the customer without attempts to influence which the customer uses. First Direct provides both telephone and Internet banking as an integrated service. While the Internet service has much lower unit costs and also has proved better for cross-selling, First Direct chooses to position itself on customer service and accept the higher costs from those customers who primarily use the telephone without penalizing them or rewarding Internet users.

➡ A *needs-based segmentation strategy* involves offering different channels to different customer groups to meet their varying needs. Each of these routes to market may use the same brand name, or different names. The insurer Zurich's multiple brands, including Allied Dunbar, Zurich and Eagle Star, tend to concentrate on different routes to market – direct sales force, IFAs, company pension schemes – in order to serve customer groups with differing needs and attitudes. Zurich has begun to rationalize this set of brands, though, to achieve economies of scale across Europe and concentrate on the brands with the best brand values.

➡ A *graduated customer value strategy* uses high-cost channels such as account managers for high-value customers, and steers lower-value customers to lower-cost channels such as the Internet, call centres or value-added resellers. The IT industry has long made use of this approach. The UK's clearing banks, though, are in danger of doing the precise opposite, offering the high-cost branch network to the lower-value customers who prefer not to bank by phone or Internet.

How are we to choose between these approaches? Although the channel curve will determine which approaches are likely to succeed in the market as a whole, an organization will typically not have the resources to pursue all viable options – some of which may, in any case, deliver little value to shareholders, despite being accepted by the market. It is this dimension of attractiveness to the organization which we have not yet considered fully. The answer is to use a portfolio matrix which looks both at the attractiveness of an offering to the customer, and its attractiveness to us.

The directional policy matrix, an elaboration of the earlier Boston matrix, has long been used to provide a rational basis for resource allocation between different product-market combinations, or product-markets. It is illustrated in Figure 3.14.

The matrix compares different product-markets within an organization or business unit, each represented by a circle. The product-markets are compared against three criteria:

➡ *Relative business strength.* How good the company is at satisfying customers, compared to the competition. Using a list of the customers' key buying criteria, as we did in the channel curve above, you score yourself and leading competitors against each criterion on a judgemental 1–10 basis, then compare the total of the company's scores against the total of the best competitor's. The

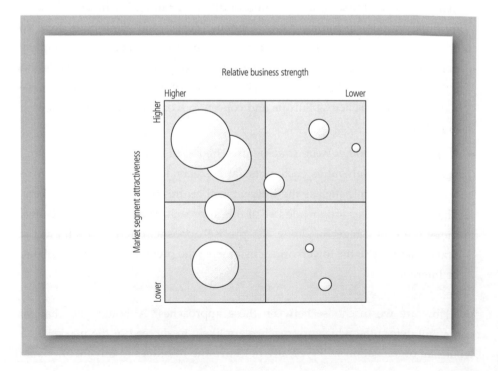

Figure 3.14
Directional policy
matrix

scores should be weighted against the relative importance of the various criteria to the customer.

➡ *Market attractiveness.* How attractive the product-market is compared with others. This uses a similar multi-factor calculation, but here using criteria such as market size, growth and profitability to compare the attractiveness of the various opportunities.

➡ *Revenue* from the product-market at present, which is reflected in the circle size.

All other things being equal, a product-market in the *top left* of the matrix should be invested in to grow the market share. The value of a high share in a fast-growing market will be even greater in the future, when the market is larger, than it is now, so it makes sense to invest for the future. In the *bottom left*, the market position should typically be maintained: these product-markets can be a good source of cash to fund the sources of future growth, so should be looked after though not excessively 'milked' or, on the other hand, invested in too heavily. The *bottom right* quadrant should be managed for cash, which may involve cessation or divestment, or just profit-taking. The *top right* quadrant involves selective investment in those product-markets where the company judges that it can move the position leftwards.

When working with companies on their e-commerce strategy, we have found difficulties with using the directional policy matrix in this form. However much we encourage managers to be future-oriented in their scoring, and to look for potential for profit growth rather than current profitability, the tool is most naturally suited to businesses where many, at least, of the product-markets to be plotted are up and running. In contexts such as e-commerce, though, the market may not even exist yet. So identifying the leading competitors may be meaningless, as may be trying to score our performance against the customers' buying criteria.

This is a real problem, as e-commerce and other new routes to market provide a myriad of opportunities which managers really need help in prioritizing. Various authors have proposed ways round this difficulty, an example being Cisco's eBusiness value matrix.[8] Another, specifically designed for e-commerce portfolios, has been proposed by Tjan.[9] He plots the viability, or potential pay-off, of each current or proposed e-project against its fit – its potential to dovetail with a company's existing processes, capabilities and culture. The

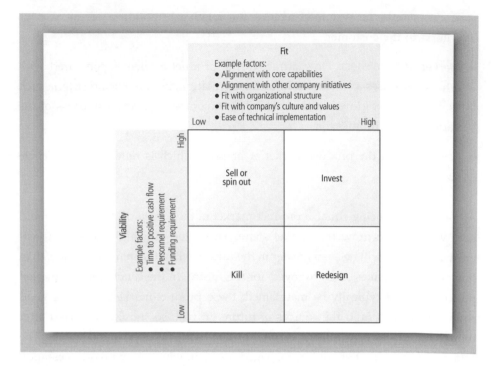

Figure 3.15
Tjan's Internet
Portfolio Map

proposed initiatives can then be plotted on a map, which suggests whether each should be invested in, redesigned, spun out or killed off – see Figure 3.15.

While these approaches have considerable merits, a disadvantage they share is that while they assess the attractiveness of an opportunity to the company, they do not measure its attractiveness to customers – clearly equally critical if the figures in the business plan are to be achieved.

Along with our colleague Dr Liz Daniel and the innovative marketers at Skandia, we have therefore developed a variant on these approaches, termed the prioritization matrix, which we explain in full in Worksheet 3.3 at the end of this chapter. It is summarized in Figure 3.16.

In this prioritization matrix we compare not rival competitors but rival business models

In brief, this approach compares opportunities such as e-commerce projects against two dimensions: attractiveness to us and attractiveness to the customer. In many ways it is just like the directional policy matrix. But in assessing the horizontal axis – attractiveness to the customer – we compare not rival competitors but rival business models. In other words, if we are considering selling via a Web/call centre combination rather than a direct sales force, how would this business model compare in the customer's eyes with their current way of doing business?

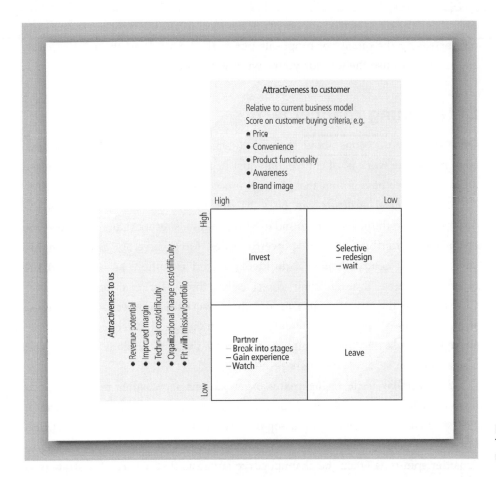

Figure 3.16
The prioritization matrix

You may have spotted that we have already done much of the work to fill in this matrix in previous tools. The rival business models are often different channels, or channel combinations, which we have identified in the 'channel chains' tool. We have compared these against customer needs using the 'channel curve'. So the horizontal axis simply corresponds to the position of the proposed way of doing business on the channel curve compared with the alternatives. A better curve than the alternatives will correspond to a position well to the left of the matrix. In fact, the position on the horizontal axis can be determined mathematically by comparing the height of the bar chart for our proposed channel, in the alternative presentation shown in Figure 3.13, with the highest of the alternative channels.

We have found that using this tool provides a welcome structure to the board's decision-making debate and rapidly sorts out which projects are the top

The prioritization matrix rapidly sorts out which projects are the top priorities

priorities. It also forces the proponents of a project to ask the right questions early on, increasing the quality of proposals put to the board. Worksheet 3.3 explains exactly how to use the tool for your own organization.

Determining channel tactics

Once strategic decisions about channel choice and channel combinations have been made, the work is, of course, only just beginning. Here are just some of the areas where we have found that channel innovations can go wrong in practice.

Organizational structure can be a barrier to change if it encourages the organization to think and act around existing channels rather than new ones. One organization told us how its powerful sales force directors gave a highly successful call centre channel a decidedly mixed reception, as it reduced the business coming through their direct sales force. Turkeys rarely vote for Christmas, so the structure may need radical overhaul to reflect a new channel strategy. Sales directors, incidentally, often make good directors of Internet strategy, because they are thoroughly unimpressed with technology and fads, and concentrate on serving customers profitably.

A particular issue facing many organizations is whether to 'spin out' a business using a new channel. Much in vogue during the Internet euphoria of 1999 and early 2000, setting up a separate company to exploit the Internet or a 'direct' call centre business has had varying success. A logical approach is to consider spin-outs when the channel curve suggests that a pure-play strategy is appropriate to one or more customer segments. Where the customer need is for a hybrid model, though, innovation needs to be wedded with integration. Just as IBM initially set up its PC division with considerable autonomy, later 'roping it in' to exploit synergies with the rest of the business, so Gap initially set up its Web operations with highly independent departments which, however, were kept within the company in order to integrate them as time went on. Another successful example of melding independence with synergy is Thomas Cook, which has re-integrated ThomasCook.com Ltd back into the business. This hybrid, semi-detached approach seems appropriate for the many companies requiring a multi-channel model, particularly in the cases of an integrated multi-channel strategy or activity-based strategy which we discussed earlier.

As with organizational structure, *reward systems* can become tied to a particular channel, hence distorting behaviour in favour of maximizing returns from that channel. As profits ultimately come from satisfied customers, a more

Organizational structure can be a barrier to change if it encourages the organization to think and act around existing channels rather than new ones

reward systems can become tied to a particular channel, hence distorting behaviour in favour of maximizing returns from that channel

beneficial approach is to provide rewards based on customer profits or, ideally, customer lifetime value.

The chief executive of a major retailer's Web service found that store managers were not encouraging customers to visit a low-cost Web channel because they feared it would reduce their annual bonuses. He therefore worked with the store managers to define metrics which would estimate how much trade was generated by each store for the website, as well as measuring business passed in the other direction from the website to local stores. These metrics could then be used to reward managers to act in the best interests of the business.

Finally, *project management* for large IT-enabled projects is never easy. Evidence from an in-depth study we conducted of numerous projects suggests that the use of software packages, where these are available, not only reduces risk, but also acts to embed and encourage best practice. Channel innovators may well find, as with innovators in other IT-enabled areas, that packages are not yet sufficiently mature to meet the whole of their needs; but it is certainly worth making a thorough exploration of what is available. A staged approach to project management is also likely to reduce business and technical risk, as well as being more likely to keep the board on side through delivery of quick wins.

Implementation is never easy, and we will expand on these points in Chapter 6. But without a clear, customer-focused channel strategy, the smoothest implementation of the best CRM package will deliver limited value. Those organizations which develop their channel strategy by focusing on their customers, not their products or their cost base, will reap the rewards of high loyalty and high customer lifetime value.

Summary

The dotcom stock market bubble could not carry on indefinitely, and it duly burst early in 2000. With it, the prevailing attitude towards channel innovations using this high-profile channel also seemed to change. 1999s' 'just do it' rhetoric of first-mover advantage, Internet years and the new economy was supplemented by a rediscovery of the language of profit, customer satisfaction and return on investment, and a recognition of the need to safeguard hard-won brand values from being diluted by rushed channel initiatives.

If the stagnating dangers of planning based on extrapolation of the past are not to be replaced by fashion-led, highly expensive channel experiments, some kind of synthesis is needed, in a planning process which endeavours to allow for creativity and which is applied flexibly and without dogmatism. The process we have proposed to meet this need draws extensively on existing planning processes and tools, but differs from them particularly in the following respects:

➡ The emphasis on evolving industry structures. Many planning methods skip from an understanding of the industry's current structure, perhaps supplemented with PEST analysis and lists of opportunities and threats, to the issue of how the organization should position itself within that structure. Our industry structure analysis stage adds the important step of predicting how the industry structure itself is likely to be changed as a result of channel initiatives, quite independently of what position the planning organization takes towards potential new channels.

➡ The analysis of how channels combine to serve customers through their life cycle. Rather than simply looking up the relevant chapter of a marketing textbook corresponding to 'the channels we use in our industry', we advocate a creative analysis of how channels might be combined to add customer value, via the channel chain technique.

➡ The adaptation of critical success factor analysis to the problem of channel choice in the 'channel curve' provides an intuitively sensible 'acid test' as to whether a channel innovation will, in fact, succeed.

➡ Often it is not competitors which compete, but business models. And yet talk about business models can become an excuse for woolly thinking and endless losses. The variant on traditional prioritization matrices we have outlined allows the right business model to be chosen to best meet customer needs as well as the organization's objectives.

We do not pretend that combining market-focused planning and entrepreneurial innovation is easy. But we believe that it is, at least, better to use planning processes which do not constrain thinking within the current market structure, and which ask some of the right questions. The rest is up to your skill, intuition and imagination.

References

(1) Levitt, T. (1960) 'Marketing myopia', *Harvard Business Review*, July/August, 45–56.

(2) Chandler, A.D. (1962) *Strategy and Structure*, Boston, MA: MIT Press.

(3) Ansoff, I.H. (1965) *Corporate Strategy*, London: Penguin.

(4) Andrews, K.R. (1987) *The concept of Corporate Strategy*, 3rd ed., Homewood, IL: Irwin.

(5) Evans, P.B. and Wurster, T.S. (1997) 'Strategy and the new economics of information', *Harvard Business Review*, September–October, 71–82.

(6) McDonald, M. and Wilson, H. (1999) *E-marketing: Improving Marketing Effectiveness in a Digital World*, London: FT Prentice Hall.

(7) Kim, W.C. and Mauborgne, R. (1999) 'Creating new market space', *Harvard Business Review*, January–February, 83–93.

(8) Hartman, A. and Sifonis, J. (2000) *Net Ready*, New York: McGraw-Hill.

(9) Tjan, A.K. (2001) 'Finally, a way to put your Internet portfolio in order', *Harvard Business Review*, February, 76–87.

Worksheet 3.1 Future market mapping

1 Having drawn the current market map as described in Chapter 2, identify those points (junctions) where actual decisions are made about what is bought by the ultimate consumer/user and the percentage of total value/volume thus decided at each junction. In some cases, this point will be the ultimate consumer. In others, it may be a distributor or other influencer, such as an architect who, although not buying, say, radiators, decides for a builder what radiators should be bought.

2 Now do a buying factors analysis for each of these junctions, as follows:

(a) Name of decision-making junction, or segment	**(b)** List the most important buying factors considered by the members of this junction or segment	**(c)** State the relative importance of each of these factors to the buyers. Score out of 100.

	1	
	2	
	3	
	4	
	5	

Total 100

3 Using your analysis of competitive forces from Chapter 2, in what ways can these needs be better met through e-commerce or other new channels?

4 Now redraw the market map as it will be in, say, 3–5 years' time, given your knowledge about likely developments in the market, such as:

– new entrants

– new channels

– industry consolidation

– etc

5 OPPORTUNITIES

Draw up a list of opportunities for your organization.

Cost reduction		**Value creation**
1		
2		
3		
4		
5		

Worksheet 3.2 Channel combinations

1 For *each* major decision-making junction on the market map (see Worksheet 3.1), consider what different means of communication customers use, leading to the purchase they make. The following chart indicates (as column headings) the major steps in any purchase process. Against each step, indicate what means is used by the decision-maker to perform the step. Thus, in each vertical column, what percentage of this task is currently completed using this medium?

	Initiate dialogue	Exchange information	Negotiate/ tailor	Commit	Exchange value
Offline advertising (TV, press etc.)					
Direct mail					
Sales force/face-to-face contact					
Telephone					
Electronic					
Other (state)					

2 How, from the customer's point of view, could this sales process be improved? Reassess the percentages in these columns as they will be in, say, 3–5 years' time, taking account of e-commerce or other new media.

3 OPPORTUNITIES

In any rows where you envisage the percentages changing, list the opportunities for your organization.

Cost reduction		Value creation
1		
2		
3		
4		
5		

Worksheet 3.3 Prioritization matrix

When to use the tool

- To decide on the relative importance of a number of possible channel initiatives (e.g. e-commerce projects).
- First-cut prioritization: to decide which potential opportunities should be developed into a full proposal.
- Second-cut prioritization: to help the board to prioritize limited resources, taking into account 'soft' issues such as strategic fit as well as 'hard' financial issues.
- The tool is, though, no substitute for the development of carefully researched financials such as ROI calculations, which should be done in parallel and used to inform the vertical axis, particularly for a second-cut prioritization.
- The tool can help to depoliticize debates about prioritization, and to sell the conclusions reached.

A. Defining opportunities

1 Select a business unit whose opportunities you wish to prioritize. This may be the whole organization or part of it.

Business unit: _____

2 List below the channel-related opportunities (e.g. e-commerce projects) which you wish to prioritize. These may be projects in development, projects which have gone live or possible future projects.

Opportunity number	Opportunity name
1	
2	
3	
4	
5	
6	
7	
8	
9	
10	

B. Attractiveness to us

1 List a few opportunity attractiveness factors for your organization. In other words, what attracts you to one opportunity rather than another? For example: impact on revenue; impact on margins; fit with organization's mission; fit with organization's skills; IT difficulty; business change difficulty.

2 Indicate the relative importance of the factors to you when comparing opportunities by allocating weights out of 100.

3 List your opportunities below 'Opportunity 1' etc.

4 Score each opportunity out of 10 on each factor, where 10 is highly attractive.

5 Calculate a weighted average score for each opportunity. Multiply the weight by the score and divide by 100, then add up these weighted scores to arrive at a total between 0 and 10.

Attractiveness factor	Weight	Scores							
		Opportunity 1	Opportunity 2	Opportunity 3	Opportunity 4	Opportunity 5	Opportunity 6	Opportunity 7	Opportunity 8
Total score									

Notes

➡ Stick to three to six factors if possible for simplicity. Consider deleting factors with a weighting of less than 10, or combining them with other factors.

➡ The factors should not have anything to do with customer take-up, which is dealt with in the following analysis. So assume project success, from the point of view of the customers, in your scoring. In assessing, for example, 'impact on revenue' of a new website, assume that customers will like it and use it.

➡ Clear factors and weights on this axis with senior management before proceeding.

➡ Keep factors separate from each other.

➡ Research your financial scores as carefully as you can, particularly for a second-cut prioritization.

➡ If the results don't meet your intuition, consider whether you need to iterate, or whether your intuition needs updating!

C. Attractiveness to customers/stakeholders

Fill in the table below for each opportunity.

1 How do customers choose between rival suppliers in this opportunity's target market? List their few key factors under 'Buying factor'.

2 Indicate the relative importance of the factors to the customer by allocating weights out of 100.

3 The remaining column headings are for the different business models (e.g. different channels) by which you, or your competitors, can serve these customers. 'New model' is for the business model you are considering for this opportunity, e.g. selling a particular product set via a new website; or selling via a business-to-business exchange you're considering starting up. 'Current' is for your 'traditional' way of doing business, as currently done by your organization, e.g. selling via a direct sales force, or selling over the Web with your current site. If necessary, add other options (e.g. different business models used by competitors) as well under 'Other 1' etc., but for today it's generally best to leave these blank.

4 How would your customers score your proposed business model against its alternative(s) out of 10 on each of the buying factors? Enter the scores on the form.

5 Calculate a weighted average score for each business model. Multiply the weight by the score and divide by 100, then add up these weighted scores to arrive at a total between 0 and 10.

6 Subtract the 'current model' score from the 'new model' score to arrive at a number representing the 'attractiveness to customers'. Enter this at the bottom of the form.

Opportunity number: _____   Opportunity name: _____

Buying factor	Weight	Scores				
		New model	**Current model**	**Other 1**	**Other 2**	**Other 3**
Total score						

Attractiveness to customers (new model score minus best alternative score): _____

Opportunity number: _____ Opportunity name: _____

Buying factor	Weight	Scores				
		New model	**Current model**	**Other 1**	**Other 2**	**Other 3**
Total score						

Attractiveness to customers (new model score minus best alternative score): _____

Notes

➡ Research factors and weights. Where possible, ask customers, whether formally or informally. Otherwise, involve a small cross-functional team of those in your organization who are close to the customers. If you have completed the 'Future market mapping' worksheet (Worksheet 3.1) you can take the factors and weights from there.

➡ Factors and weights will vary by opportunity, unless two opportunities represent different means of targeting the same customer groups with the same need.

➡ Include all the main buying criteria, even if they are unaffected by the new business model you are proposing.

➡ If different segments are known to exist and buy on different criteria, the form should technically be filled in for each segment, but for simplicity you may choose to fill it in for a typical representative of the target market (i.e. a distributor, consumer, pensions decision-maker in a company, etc., depending on the opportunity).

➡ If the opportunity is targeted at a different stakeholder group, e.g. a supply-side system, modify these instructions to assess the attractiveness factors for this group. So a system for suppliers might be assessed, in their eyes, on: margin achieved; transaction costs; fit with organization's procedures; scope for building long-term relationship; etc. A recruitment site might be assessed on range of vacancies, ease of obtaining information, etc.

D. Prioritization matrix

1 Put a cross on the matrix below for each opportunity. Take its vertical position from the weighted average score at the bottom of form B. Take its horizontal position from its 'attractiveness to customers' at the bottom of form C. Label the cross with the opportunity name.

2 Consider the implications for the organization's resource allocation:
  – Where should the investment in money, management time etc. go?
  – For these high-priority opportunities, what needs to be done to ensure that your envisaged scores on the customers' buying factors are reached?

Notes

➡ Don't take cross-lines too literally! What matters is the relative position of your opportunities, not their absolute position on your grid.

➡ Consider interactions between opportunities. If you invest in one opportunity such as a direct sales channel, will that affect your revenue or profits through another, such as an agent network?

➡ However, you can't hold back the tide! If customers wish to switch to a new way of doing business (represented by a position towards the left of the matrix), 'cannibalization' of your traditional business may be necessary if you are not to leave a competitor to fill the gap.

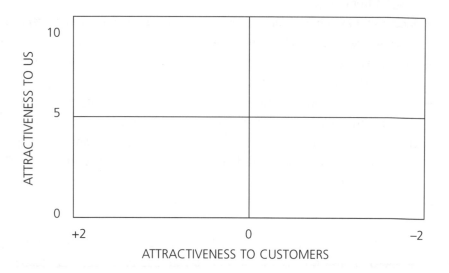

Worksheet 3.4 Internal value chain

Only for organizations for whom key accounts are of major significance. For each key account, list ways in which you improve the key account's value chain, by reducing their costs or creating value for their customers. Consider e-commerce, other new media or any other means of adding value to their business. (For service companies consider using the alternative version which follows.)

		REDUCING COST	CREATING VALUE
Infrastructure	– legal, accounting, financial management		
Human Resource Management	– personnel, pay, recruitment, training, manpower planning, etc.		
Product and Technology Development	– product and process design, production engineering, market testing, R&D, etc.		
Procurement	– supplier management, funding, subcontracting, specification		

INBOUND LOGISTICS	OPERATIONS	OUTBOUND LOGISTICS	SALES AND MARKETING	SERVICING	
e.g. quality control receiving raw material control etc.	e.g. manufacturing packaging production control quality control maintenance etc.	e.g. finishing goods order handling despatch delivery invoicing etc.	e.g. customer mgmt order taking promotion sales analysis market research etc.	e.g. warranty maintenance education/ training upgrade etc.	REDUCING COST
					CREATING VALUE

For service companies such as consultants this version may be more appropriate. For each key account, list ways in which you can improve the key account's value chain, by reducing their costs or creating value for their customers. Consider, for example, opportunities provided via the Internet or other new media.

	REDUCING COST	CREATING VALUE
Infrastructure – legal, accounting, financial management		
Human Resource Management – personnel, pay, recruitment, training, manpower planning, etc.		
Product and Technology Development – product and process design, production engineering, market testing, R&D, etc.		
Procurement – supplier management, funding, subcontracting, specification		

MARKETING THE CAPABILITY AND BUSINESS ACQUISITION	PROBLEM SPECIFICATION	KNOWLEDGE APPLICATION	RESOURCE ALLOCATION	CONFIGURE AND EXECUTE SOLUTION
REDUCING COST				
CREATING VALUE				

4

Making the future happen

Communicating and delivering value

➡ The e-marketing mix

➡ Towards the digital enterprise: a stage model

➡ IT at the customer interface: front-office CRM

Introduction

In the last chapter we described how to develop a marketing plan which takes account of today's changing channels to market. The purpose of this chapter is to explore how to implement the marketing plan – that is, how to communicate with customers and deliver the promised value to them, through the variety of media, frequently IT-enabled, which are likely to be involved. We are therefore dealing with the bottom box in the map of marketing we have used as the basis for this book (see Figure 4.1).

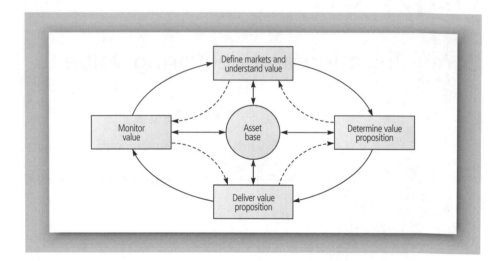

Figure 4.1
'Deliver value proposition' and the map of marketing

Making marketing plans work was never easy, but it used to bear at least some resemblance to the textbooks. You could look up chapters in many a thick volume on how to manage the sales force, how to brief an advertising agency or how to commission market research. These skills are still of course needed, but today's marketer is just as likely to be setting up call centres, negotiating with Yahoo! over banner advertisements, or obtaining customer feedback by e-mail questionnaire. And at the times when the beginning of a large customer database project seems long ago and the end is nowhere in sight, it can be difficult to see how this morass of meetings, specifications and schedules will ever deliver more value to customers.

So we will concentrate in this chapter on what's different about IT-enabled channels and how to manage them.

Fortunately, by this stage in the book, we have a vision to provide some light at the end of the tunnel. We know who our customers are, how they segment, what they want from us, and what channels they would prefer to use. And we have decided which of the resulting opportunities we want to prioritize. So we have a list of projects to deliver, and a clear idea of what customer needs each must meet.

Still, when the web designers start talking about hit rates and cookies, it is easy to lose one's way. They offer new ways of dealing with the customer that are rather different from those we're used to. Should we allow the customers to talk to each other through a chat facility? Do we want to tailor e-mails to them instead of sending all the same brochure-like mailing? And how about pricing?

Friction-free capitalism

We need some handle on what is different about IT-enabled marketing, and we will start with the Internet. Luckily, we were all told the answer some time ago, weren't we? Economists told us that the Internet would provide 'friction-free capitalism'. Typical was this quote from *Business Week* in 1998:

" The Internet is a nearly perfect market because information is instantaneous and buyers can compare the offerings of sellers worldwide. The result is fierce price competition, dwindling product differentiation, and vanishing brand loyalty. *"* [1]

So all we need to do is use the Internet to streamline everything and compete on price.

But it hasn't turned out that way. Most of us in practice don't shop around for the cheapest source of a CD or a Christmas present. Once we've found the one we want from a source we trust and whose prices we generally find respectable, we buy it. Only 16 per cent of us bother to look at more than one website when shopping for a toy, and only 11 per cent for a book.

Neither are we different as business buyers. Many of the business-to-business exchanges or e-hubs that tried to turn everything into a commodity to be traded purely on price have come unstuck. The early successes have concentrated instead on lowering transaction costs for both parties, improving information flows and building relationships, with reverse auctions and the like being a relatively minor part of the value that they add.

Achilles, the exchange that is making most mileage within the UK utilities sector at the time of writing, is a case in point. Formed by a company with a long history of vetting potential suppliers to help utilities form a purchasing shortlist, it understands well that business-to-business purchasing is about trust, reliability, service and relationship as much as it is about price.

> Many of the e-hubs that tried to turn everything into a commodity to be traded purely on price have come unstuck

So online or offline, price is just one of a number of buying criteria. Should this really surprise us? After all, even today orders are normally placed by people not computers, and they are still the same people who are buying online today who were buying offline yesterday. And as we saw in our discussion of the channel curve in the last chapter, our buying criteria remain fairly constant with time – it's just that the means of satisfying those needs and wants evolve. So if offline market research has suggested, over the years, that the price-sensitive segment of most markets is only around 10–15 per cent of the market, we should not be surprised to learn that only 8 per cent of Internet users are active bargain hunters.

So if, like easyJet, our whole business model is based on keeping costs down so as to target the more price-sensitive customers, then using the Internet to compete on price makes perfect sense. But most of us will have to look elsewhere for our primary source of advantage. Prices online may be lower in most product categories, and prices may be subject to much more frequent change as players use short-term price modifications to match supply and demand, but the price spreads between the lowest- and highest-priced offerings are just as great, showing you can compete successfully on other criteria.

> Price spreads between the lowest- and highest-priced offerings are just as great online as offline, showing you can compete successfully on other criteria

The three Cs of Internet marketing

So we need to differentiate ourselves through other means. A well-known checklist for doing this is the three Cs of Internet marketing: content, community and commerce. Attract customers to your site through rich content, provide community facilities such as online debates to ensure that the site is sufficiently 'sticky' that they hang around, and eventually if only to escape from your clutches they'll resort to placing an order.

As with the notion of friction-free capitalism, there's a grain of truth here. For some customers, some of the time, content and community facilities can add value for which they are prepared to pay. But most of the time, we go to a website for a particular purpose which we wish to fulfil as soon as we can. The idea that 'stickiness' is inherently a virtue is akin to McDonald's deciding to persuade its customers to stay in its stores all day long, even if they've only come in because it's cold and they have no desire to buy anything.

> The idea that 'stickiness' is inherently a virtue is absurd

What was missing in this early thinking about e-commerce? A grounding in the deep understanding of customer needs. And that's why, before looking at what's different about the Internet, we have spent half a book understanding the customer, what they want and whether they want to use the Internet anyway. With that understanding, we are able to apply the right acid test for any proposed IT-driven innovation: which customer need will be better served thereby, for which customer segments?

Having made that important warning, we will turn to a summary of what variables the marketer can manipulate in positioning online, or indeed using other IT-enabled channels such as call centres. For this purpose we will use our 'e-marketing mix' or 'Six Is' framework.

After that, we will deal with the difficult issue of phasing. Although IT-enabled marketing has vast potential, the development costs of IT-enabled channels can be prohibitively expensive. An important issue is therefore the order in which the relevant IT and process infrastructure should be put in place. Can one switch to a multi-channel, CRM-enabled business model in one go? Or if a phased approach is adopted, what order should be followed? While generalized answers to these questions are difficult, organizations typically follow a similar route to each other, which may provide at least one clear route through the future. A 'stage model' showing this route is the subject of the middle section of the chapter.

Finally, when talking to IT colleagues, marketers need at least an overview of the technology for supporting product/service delivery and what it can do. This is the legitimate domain of front-office CRM. We will provide an overview of front-office software at the end of the chapter.

The e-marketing mix

The six Is of the e-marketing mix show the levers that are available for the marketing manager to pull through the use of IT. Many of our examples will relate to the Internet, but the framework applies equally to other IT-enabled channels such as call centres, interactive TV, sales force automation and direct mail.

Like the classic four Ps of marketing, it does not follow that each of these levers must be fully pulled in every situation. In the same way that not every product requires a low price, it is clear that not every product requires information-enabled individualization, for example. These choices must depend, as always, on the needs of specific customer segments and their matching to the organization's capabilities and desires.

But a starting point is to be clear on what options are available, and this simple framework provides a structure for a brainstorming discussion between

> **Definition**
> e-marketing mix is the set of six major variables which the marketer can manipulate online, in addition to marketing's four Ps

technologists and their commercial colleagues in terms which both sides can understand. The framework is summarized in Figure 4.2, and we will discuss each of its elements in turn. Worksheet 4.1 at the end of the chapter can be used as a framework for your own organization if you wish.

Integration: know your customer

In the smallest organizations, customer information can be held on a few index cards. For the rest of us, if we are to manage customer relationships, we need systems which manage data about the customer, unifying this data throughout the customer life cycle, from initial contact, through configuration and sales, to delivery and post-sales service. Because the customer may contact us through a variety of channels, this data must also be integrated across communication mechanisms. That way, a call centre operator will know about a letter that was sent yesterday, and a field sales representative can call on information about previous purchases and customer profitability to assist judgements about discount levels.

> If we are to manage customer relationships, we need systems which manage customer data

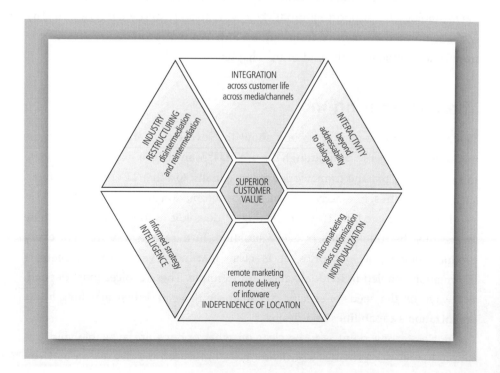

Figure 4.2
The e-marketing mix

This integration is as important with the Internet as with any other communication medium, a fact often lost on companies who delegate the website to enthusiasts in one corner of the organization, or outsource its development and operations with minimal provision for information transfer – hence repeating the mistakes often made in the early days of the call centre. As surveys continue to show, it is all too easy to advertise one's products on the Web with no attempt to gather vital customer information, obtain customer feedback, or utilize existing knowledge about the customer in the propositions put to them. And prospects are rarely impressed by such lack of care.

Not that integration is easy. Front-end website development is generally the tip of the iceberg of integrating with back-end systems. But the Internet manager of UK Internet pioneer RS Components, which distributes electrical components to engineers, said the best decision he ever took was to include the back-end integration from the first piloting of his online trading system. Hard as this was, it was the only route to genuine added value.

Interactivity: beyond addressability to dialogue

Knowing your customers means closing the loop between the messages you send to them and the messages they send back. Clearly, IT is supporting an increased use of interactive communication mechanisms, such as telephone and the Internet, to complement less interactive mechanisms such as mail or mass media advertisements. It has been said that this is the 'age of addressability', as organizations have endeavoured to communicate with individual customers through direct mail, e-mail or SMS. Interactivity goes one step further, supporting a dialogue rather than a one-way communication – although there will, of course, continue to be many occasions when the asynchronous interactivity of the reply coupon is sufficient and appropriate.

> It has been said that this is the 'age of addressability'. Interactivity goes one step further

Whatever the media used, interactive communication is essential if the aims of relationship marketing – a long-term relationship with customers, in which continually refreshed customer knowledge is used to ensure that their needs are met, leading to customer satisfaction, higher retention rates and enhanced lifetime customer value – are to be realized. The IT systems that underpin this relationship need to be accompanied, though, by a substantial shift in thinking about the nature of the sales process, and corresponding changes to internal processes.

Figure 4.3 illustrates traditional views of the sales and purchasing processes, with our revised interaction perspective between the two.

Supplier perspective		Interaction perspective		Buyer perspective	
Advertising	Selling	Marketing activity	Interaction	Decision theory	Consumer behaviour
		Define markets/ understand value		Problem recognition	Category need
		Create value proposition	Recognize exchange potential		
					Awareness
Brand awareness	Prospecting	Initiate dialogue			Attitude
Brand attitude	Provide information	Exchange information		Information search	
• Information re benefits					Information gathering and judgement
• brand image					
• feelings					
Trial inducement	Persuade	Negotiate/tailor		Evaluation of alternatives	
	Close sale	Commit		Choice/purchase	Purchase process
	Deliver	Exchange value ↓			
Reduce cognitive dissonance	Service		Monitor	Post-purchase behaviour	

Figure 4.3
An interaction perspective on the sales process

Traditional 'push-based' models of marketing, in which after the product is made, prospects are found and persuaded to buy the product, are illustrated on the left. The delivery and service that follow are operational functions with little relationship to marketing.

Traditional models of buyer behaviour, illustrated on the right of the figure, assume more rationality on the part of buyers, but underplay the importance of what the buyer says back to the seller. The seller's offer is assumed to be predetermined, rather than developed in conjunction with the buyer.

In today's world, we need to think of the sales process as something like the middle, interaction perspective:

➡ 'Recognize exchange potential' replaces 'Category need' or 'Problem recognition'. Both sides need to recognize the potential for a mutual exchange of value. For the selling organization, this is much of the purpose of the first two major processes in our model of marketing, 'Define value' and 'Determine value proposition'.

➡ 'Initiate dialogue' replaces 'Create awareness' or 'Prospecting'. The dialogue with an individual customer may be begun by either party. One feature of the

Web, for example, is that on many occasions new customers will approach the supplier rather than vice versa.

→ 'Exchange information' replaces 'Provide information'. If we are to serve the customer effectively, tailor our offerings and build a long-term relationship, we need to learn about the customer as much as the customer needs to learn about our products.

→ 'Negotiate/tailor' replaces 'Persuade'. Negotiation is a two-way process which may involve us modifying our offering in order better to meet the customer's needs. Persuading the customer instead that the square peg we happen to have in stock will fit their round hole is not likely to lead to a long and profitable relationship.

→ 'Commit' replaces 'Close sale'. Both sides need to commit to the transaction, or to a series of transactions forming the next stage in a relationship, a decision with implications for both sides.

→ 'Exchange value' replaces 'Deliver' and 'Post-sales service'. The 'post-sales service' may be an inherent part of the value being delivered, not simply a cost centre, as it is often still managed.

One-to-one communications and principles of relationship marketing, then, demand a radically different sales process from that traditionally practised. This point is far from academic, as an example will illustrate.

One-to-one communications and principles of relationship marketing demand a radically different sales process from that traditionally practised

The company in question provides business-to-business financial services. Its marketing managers relayed to us their early experience with a website which was enabling them to reach new customers considerably more cost-effectively than their traditional sales force. When the website was first launched, potential customers were finding the company on the Web, deciding the products were appropriate on the basis of the website, and sending an e-mail to ask to buy. So far, so good.

But stuck in a traditional model of the sales process, the company would allocate the 'lead' to a salesperson, who would phone up and make an appointment, perhaps three weeks hence. The customer would by now probably have moved on to another online supplier who could sell the product today, but those that remained were subjected to a sales pitch, complete with glossy materials, which was totally unnecessary, the customer having already decided to buy. Those that were not put off would proceed to be registered as able to buy over the Web, but the company had lost the opportunity to improve its margins by using the sales force more judiciously.

In time, the company realized its mistake, and changed its sales model and reward systems to something close to our 'interaction perspective' of Figure 4.3. Unlike those prospects which the company proactively identified and contacted, which might indeed need 'selling' to, many new Web customers were initiating the dialogue themselves, and simply required the company to respond effectively and rapidly. The sales force were increasingly freed up to concentrate on major clients and on relationship building.

Individualization: information-enabled tailoring

Having listened to the customer through interactivity and shared this knowledge through integration, the company is in a position to individualize the product or surrounding services where appropriate. The 'cooking' of CDs to order and the provision of tailored news e-mails are cases in point.

The example in Figures 4.4 and 4.5 documents a simple but effective move towards greater integration, interactivity and individualization in a company which provides an equipment maintenance service to consumers and, in some cases, corporate customers. It is instructive in that the changes the company made were incremental, moving from a situation which was not wholly wrong to one which was not wholly right, under the constraints of the complexities of IT development and the vast investment already made in 'legacy' systems – a situation common to many of the companies we talk to.

> Having listened to the customer the company is in a position to individualize the product/services

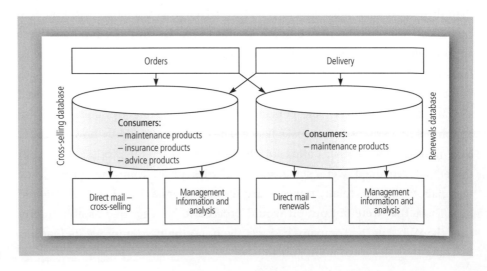

Figure 4.4
A consumer product maintenance company – previous situation

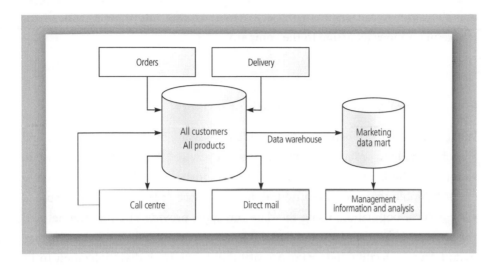

Figure 4.5
A product maintenance company – planned situation

Previously, the core maintenance services had their own renewals database, designed to increase the customer retention rate. A cross-selling database used much of the same information in order to generate business for related products such as insurance and advice services. Both databases were updated from the same operational systems dealing with order handling and delivery of the maintenance product through a field engineer force.

One problem with this situation was that the two activities are not co-ordinated: a customer might receive a renewal mailing just before a cross-selling mailing, and may object that his or her response to the first was not taken into account in the second. The data from the different systems could be difficult to analyse: names and addresses, for example, were duplicated, sometimes with minor differences, so that it was difficult to establish a complete view of the customer. And separate systems supported the corporate customers, so analysis by product type was difficult.

As shown in Figure 4.5, the company replaced the two marketing databases with an integrated data warehouse, which holds information about all customers and all products. Copies of parts of this data, carefully kept synchronized, are used for purposes such as a marketing data mart for marketing information and analysis, and an operational system for call centre support. Now a single mailing can encourage the customer to renew based on a bundled package with other related services, assessed according to all available information about the customer's needs, and priced according to an assessment of the customer's overall value. A call centre with access to the same information widens the marketing options available to the company.

Independence of location: the death of distance

What is the difference between shoes made to measure by the village cobbler and a kitchen made to order by an Internet design service? Both achieve individualization, but the latter combines it with post-industrial revolution economies of scale. It is able to do this because the design service can serve a widely-spread geographical population, using the data transport provided by the Internet and the physical transport of our industrial-age infrastructure, plus a database-driven manufacturing facility. Independence of location allows individualization to be achieved economically. Niche products can serve their target markets even if spread globally.

Being able to reach your customers wherever they are can also widen customer choice and extend customer power. As we discussed earlier, this can result in lower prices, as customers expect the savings made through the lack of location-based infrastructure to be passed on. Interestingly, prices are not always lowered online: a study of Japanese online car auctions,[2] for example, found that online prices were in this case higher, as sellers were able to reach a larger potential audience in the search for a buyer prepared to pay a given price. Similar cases of higher online prices are memorabilia and perishable goods such as concert tickets, where the geographically spread target market can be efficiently reached online.

Independence of location is a variable to be manipulated appropriately, not a 'good' in itself

Note that as with all the elements of the mix, independence of location is a variable to be manipulated appropriately, not a 'good' in itself. Plenty of successful businesses will continue to exploit physical locations as a fine means of meeting customer needs. While Cranfield University School of Management, for example, helps its MBA students to learn more routine material such as basic accounting remotely via the Internet, it believes that there is (currently at least) no equally effective substitute for the interactive and team-based learning that takes place in the same physical location, and which Cranfield regards as a key differentiator. So it is choosing an intermediate position on the variable of independence of location. For perfectly good reasons relating to their strengths and target segments, other competitors may take different positions.

Intelligence: informed strategy

Better customer data can also improve decisions on marketing strategy, such as which segments to prioritize. When a major computer manufacturer discovered that it could not measure its segment share of particular application areas such as accounting, personnel and stock control, it changed its order procedures to track the type of use to which the computer was being put on purchase. This information could then be aggregated to enable effective planning, as well as enabling initiatives to serve particular segments more effectively.

In this example of the use of customer information to provide intelligence for decision-making, the segments were predetermined. In other cases, the segmentation itself may be derived from the data that has been gathered. In the next chapter we will expand on IT support for segmentation and other analyses.

Industry restructuring: redrawing the market map

If the previous Is can be regarded as opportunities to change our marketing approach through the use of IT, this final category represents the observation that if we do not exploit these opportunities, someone else will. Viewed from outside the industry, the net effect of IT-enabled marketing will often be radical industry transformation. As we have seen in Chapter 3, many industries are already being restructured as organizations redefine themselves to take advantage of IT-enabled marketing, or are replaced by newcomers who operate according to the new rules. E-commerce expert Joe Peppard regards this as a 'third-order effect' in his discussion of the impact of IT on industry structures:

> The net effect of IT-enabled marketing is often radical industry transformation

II 'The first-order effect is a partial substitution of human co-ordination by IT. For example, the first-order data processing systems replaced some clerical jobs. If you take the analogy of transport, the first-order transport of the bicycle simply replaces walking by cycling the same journey. The second-order effect is of increased co-ordination. Just as people travelled more as railways were introduced, so with IT a travel agent can search for more flight options using a computer reservation system. A third-order effect is a shift towards more co-ordination-intensive structures, such as the virtual organization. This is analogous to the introduction of suburbs and satellite towns, as a structure that has evolved due to the greater transport capability. Nike are an example of a reconfigured organization. All they do is design and market. Manufacturing, distribution and sales are all outsourced. Now this isn't possible without the increased co-ordination capabilities of IT. Research has shown the average firm size to be getting smaller: one of the reasons might be the move towards the virtual organization. "

Joe Peppard (author interview)

Towards the digital enterprise: a stage model

The example of a consumer maintenance company showed how increasing one's 'score' on such dimensions as integration can be a massive task. Unless one has the luxury of a 'green-field' business, this cannot generally be tackled in a single phase. And yet some sense of direction is needed if today's decisions are not to constrain tomorrow's. As one war-worn marketing manager told us as he finally began to see customer benefits 18 months into a CRM project: 'You have to eat the elephant of CRM one bite at a time. But first choose the right elephant.'

You have to eat the elephant of CRM one bite at a time. But first choose the right elephant

We will therefore describe a stage model of the stages which organizations typically go through, and discuss the variations on this process seen within some of the companies we have studied. The model is summarized in Figure 4.6.

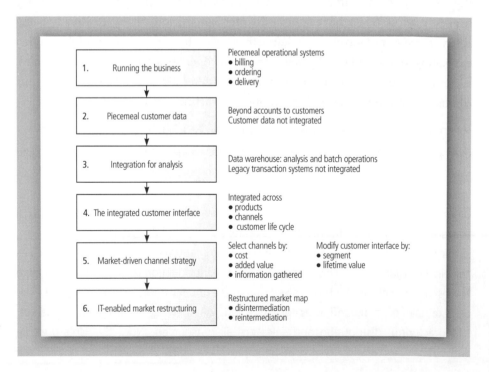

Figure 4.6
A stage model for IT-enabled marketing

Stage 1: running the business

IT began by supporting such functions as finance, payroll, logistics and production. If the customer came into systems at all, it was as an 'account' with a billing address, a list of orders and some delivery notes; but beyond the bare details necessary to support these transactions, the customer was otherwise faceless and anonymous. This situation represents low 'scores' on all six elements of the e-marketing mix of the six Is. Although numerous small businesses are still in this position, none of the larger companies we talked to are at stage 1.

Stage 2: piecemeal customer data

At this stage, endeavours have been made to support marketing activities by the construction of marketing databases that list customers, not just accounts, with at least some information which is added for purely marketing, rather than operational, purposes. Most larger companies have one or more customer databases, though companies with a chain to the end consumer have differing levels of sophistication of customer information at different points in the chain. But numerous organizations complain of a variety of customer databases developed for different purposes, with consequent restrictions in the co-ordination which is possible across product lines, functions and geography.

> Numerous organizations complain of a variety of customer databases that have been developed for different purposes

The difficulties that lack of integration can cause are illustrated by the case of Cranfield University School of Management itself, which until recently was at stage 2. Figure 4.7 illustrates the situation that had developed historically, concentrating on short courses for managers.

A 'client service' database supported the administration relating to delivering the product: taking orders for courses, sending out information beforehand, planning 'production' resources such as lecture rooms and catering, answering customer queries and providing financial management information.

A separate direct mail database, developed over several generations, supported the School's primary marketing medium, direct mail. This interfaced to the client service database, passing on information before the course, and taking a data feed in the opposite direction after the course had happened.

The relatively new marketing channel of the Web had its own database of product information, but did not as yet hold customer information. Through e-mail or by printing order forms, customers could then deal with the client service staff to make further enquiries or place an order.

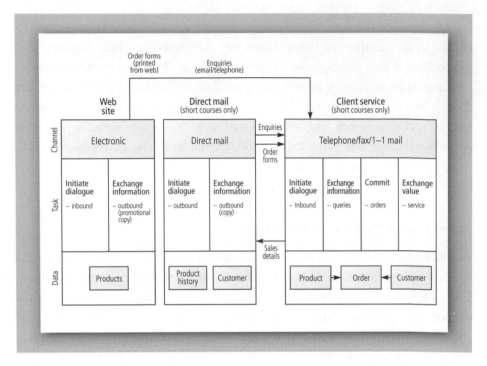

Figure 4.7
Typical difficulties
with integration –
a business school

As with many of our case studies, this situation was neither wholly good nor wholly bad. By the standards of its sector, the direct mail operation was reasonably sophisticated, and the website was proving a valuable resource for its customers. But the limited integration was posing some restrictions. For example, the website could not draw on customer information to suggest courses that build on others that the customer had attended or expressed interest in. The direct mail system had delayed information from the client service system, restricting the currency of information on course attendees. The fact that these systems covered only a part of the School's product range – due to separate systems for the MBA programme, for example – restricted the scope for specific targeting of courses, for example, of particular interest to those already holding MBAs. These and other restrictions are reasons why the School's CRM systems have recently been replaced.

A paper manufacturer we studied was also at this stage. It had developed databases for particular points in the sales cycle, so a marketing database could not make use of the sales force's knowledge when mailings were carried out, and the sales force did not know when samples had been requested. Its systems nevertheless provided a degree of integration, with some independence of

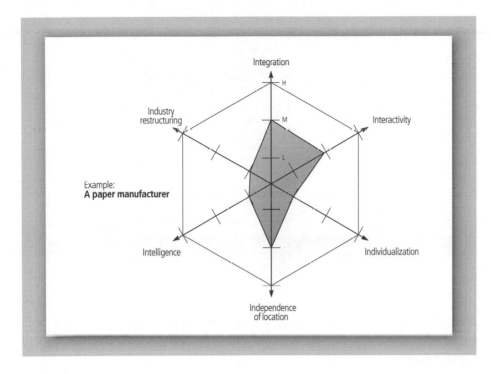

Figure 4.8
Stage 2 against the e-marketing mix

location provided by telemarketing facilities on top of the marketing database. Its positioning against the six Is is illustrated (with approximate judgement-based scores) in Figure 4.8. This company recognized that it could leverage much more value from its IT investments if they were conceived more holistically.

Stage 3: integration for analysis

"If someone queries their statement every month, they're probably in an anally retentive sector."

An interviewee illustrating segmentation from CRM data

Some companies tackle the problem of integrating data for the 'Understand value' tasks of marketing analysis before attempting to integrate the front-office transactional systems. An example is the utility illustrated in Figure 4.9.

This company defined a project to collect information from a variety of existing operational systems to form a marketing database, hence creating what has been described by data warehousing expert Sean Kelly as a 'first generation data warehouse'. As with many such systems, it could be used to understand the

First generation data warehouses lack the key link back to operational systems

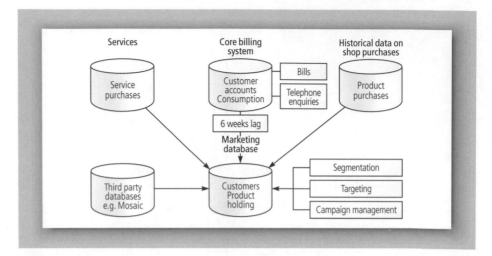

Figure 4.9
Integration for
analysis – a utility

customer base and generate mailing lists, but otherwise lacked the key link back
to the operational systems which characterizes his second generation, as we will
explore later.

The operational systems centre around the core billing system for home
consumption, which also provides a base for telephone enquiries. The information on customers – or, more correctly, on accounts – from this system is copied
into the marketing database, where it is joined by information on the customers'
purchases of related services. The resulting data can be used for such purposes as
segmentation (supplementing the internal data with third party information) and
targeting, evaluating customers for direct mailing lists and estimating response
rates.

Problems with this architecture include the time lag on getting information
into this analysis database – up to six weeks, depending on the information – and
the limited capacity of the database for holding past history. The operational
systems also differ in their view of the customer, making it difficult to gain an
integrated view of the product holdings of one individual, or to track the
individual when they move house. The lack of a clear view of customers also
prevents calculation of a customer's lifetime value to the organization, as a
marketing manager told us:

*We are shifting from volumes of customers to understanding the value of the
relationship. Depending on the differing value, one may be able for example to

reduce effort and expenditure on those who cannot be of great value to us. The problem is that our current systems do not allow us to deliver that because we are organized by product. We primarily provide a commodity which people consume, and all our systems are designed around billing and handling queries relating to that.*"*

Furthermore, the information flow into the marketing database is one way. It is difficult to feed back knowledge gained about customers into the operational systems, so as to affect such customer interactions as when the customer telephones.

These issues are being tackled, but the situation as it stands is a good example of stage 3. Its positioning against the six Is is illustrated in Figure 4.10. Customer intelligence is the main variable which is improved by the marketing database, enabling strategic segmentations to be developed for example, although this intelligence is limited by inconsistencies between the data sources. This intelligence enables individualization in direct mail communications, but not in other communications such as billing, handling telephone queries and so on.

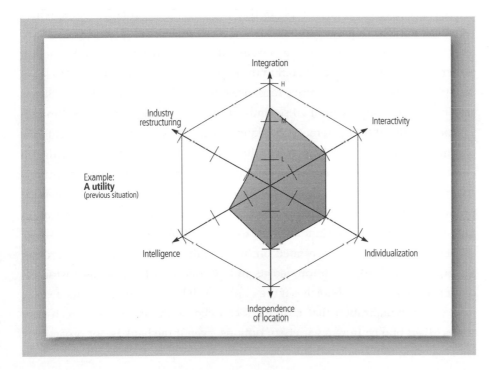

Figure 4.10
Stage 3 against the e-marketing mix

Stage 4: the integrated customer interface

We have seen, then, that the scope for tailoring all the activities of 'Deliver value proposition' to the needs of particular segments is limited if the customer interface is not integrated. While the main purpose of integration at the customer interface is to enable customized marketing strategies – stage 5 in our model – some organizations go through the intermediate stage of integrating the customer interface first, leaving issues of individualization to later projects.

Off-the-shelf CRM systems do not automatically deliver segment-driven marketing strategies

Consider the implementation of an off-the-shelf CRM system (these are described further later in this chapter). These systems ensure that everyone at the customer interface has access to common information, leading to efficiencies internally. This can avoid the disadvantage of annoyed customers who have to tell their change of address to several different parts of the organization, or lost sales opportunities because an enquiry is not passed on.

But of themselves these systems do not extend into the segmentation-driven marketing strategies that can make use of the resulting rich customer data, although they may provide an excellent platform for such work.

In other words, integration is necessary but not sufficient for individualization.

We illustrate with the example of the Netherlands-based Fortis Bank, which recently completed a project to outsource most of its incoming telephone calls to a digi-centre, as well as enquiries by fax, e-mail and the Web. Its aims were tactical rather than strategic: to free up staff in the expensive high street locations to serve face-to-face customers; to improve response rates to telephone calls (now at 80 per cent of calls answered within 20 seconds); to improve customer service through 24-hour availability of remote banking facilities; and to ensure that the organization speaks with 'one voice' through arming representatives with full customer information. These were laudable aims, and were achieved impressively quickly. But work on exploiting this information to proactively assess what products customers might actually need, rather than the industry's usual scatter-gun approach, was understandably left to a second phase.

Hence the project concentrated on the Is at the top of Figure 4.11. Through integration, the bank has improved its independence of location, as customers don't need to come into branches if they don't wish to. It has at least achieved the limited individualization that customers can choose the means by which they contact their branch from a variety of options, even if the bank is not proactively endeavouring to influence this.

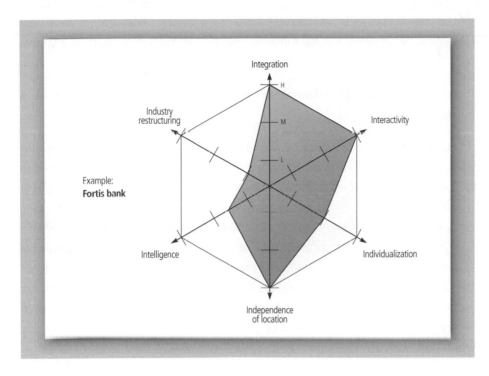

Figure 4.11
Stage 4 against
the e-marketing
mix

Stage 5: customized marketing strategy

" If a customer is high value, we give him a gold-plated proposal. If he's low value,
he gets a black and white bill proposal on toilet paper.*"*

Interviewee on customization

The next stage is to use the flexibility of an integrated CRM system to implement
customized strategies adapted to the needs of different segments. To illustrate, we
describe a bank in which the operational systems have already been integrated
with a unifying 'front-end' system. The bank is now grappling with how best to
use this infrastructure to define the operational implications for analyses such as
segmentation and customer value. In other words, how is the customer handled
differently as a result of the knowledge gained about him or her?

With an inheritance including a merger between a bank and a building
society, the organization has a wide range of products available, including
mortgages, bank accounts and credit cards, and high customer numbers. In using
this asset base, it described its strategy several years ago as:

*"*We are in business to create long-term profitable relationships with our customers, by providing the full range of financial products supported by a unique bank.*"*

What this emphasis on relationships means in practice was spelt out by a marketing manager.

*"*Fundamentally the difference between the relationship approach and our previous transaction approach is that previously it was all about selling the product. Servicing it afterwards was regarded as a cost and an annoyance. You were focused down in the product silos, and you tended to treat every customer exactly the same, working on averages on all the customer/product and profit data. The relationship approach is to recognize that not all customers are created equal. They differ in what they are looking for, in the way they use the product and how they deliver stability to us through their buying behaviour. It means dealing in smaller segments, so we now ask which customers we want to acquire, which give us a mix of short-term and long-term potential, and then which products should we focus on for that customer and which communication method is best, as well as how to retain them.*"*

The first piece of the IT strategy to support relationship management has been to integrate operational systems behind one common interface, providing a unified view of the customer to all staff. This allows implementation of the notion of seamlessly transferring the customer from wherever they are actually speaking to a centre of excellence where staff can deal with their needs, as opposed to trying to multi-skill everywhere. This unified customer-facing system is illustrated on the left of Figure 4.12.

The second major component of the IT strategy is an analysis database. Originally developed in order to generate direct mail, this database now also forms the basis for models which aim to understand the customer better, illustrated on the right of the figure. This customer understanding is not just of use in generating direct mail. The bank is now working out how analyses such as lifetime customer value should affect the handling of the individual customer interactions in the branch and on the telephone. Development into online banking, either through use of the Internet or interactive digital TV, is regarded as a natural extension to the approach.

Overall, the strategy can be summarized as recapturing the individual service of the old-fashioned bank manager without the prohibitive costs entailed. Its positioning against the six Is is illustrated in Figure 4.13.

> This bank's strategy is recapturing the individual service of the old-fashioned bank manager without prohibitive costs

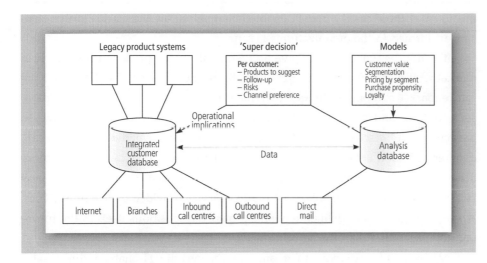

Figure 4.12
Customized marketing strategy – a bank

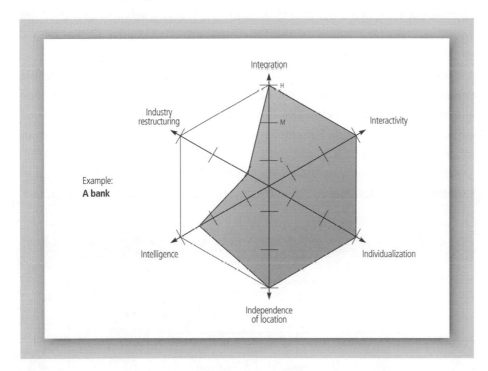

Figure 4.13
Stage 5 against the e-marketing mix

Stage 6: IT-enabled market restructuring

So far we have described how IT can enable a customer-driven strategy based on an understanding of customer needs and a translation of those needs into different organizational behaviour at every point of contact. Stage 6 goes beyond this to cover those cases where IT-enabled channels allow the market structure to be transformed in the organization's favour.

It would be wonderful to have a crystal ball which predicted how a given market would change in the future. In its absence, we described in Chapter 3 the future market mapping technique by which the organization can at least explore some options and come to its best guess as to how the future might look. In particular, we discussed disintermediation and reintermediation. To recap, disintermediation is the abolition of intermediaries, where IT can enable a more direct approach, while reintermediation refers to the appearance of new intermediaries such as the holidays-to-hotels service provided by lastminute.com. A stage 6 organization deliberately and proactively positions itself in the future market map rather than the current one.

We have referred more than once to the heavily IT-enabled direct sales approach of Dell, as it is interesting in many ways. It certainly changed the rules within its industry through the market restructuring it initiated. Dell's channel structure is summarized by Figure 4.14.

Dell began by selling personal computers 'off the page' in the computer press, using mail and the telephone to undercut dramatically its rivals with their expensive networks of field sales forces and shops – though as we discussed earlier, it has since added a small field sales force to concentrate on senior relationships within its largest clients.

Its experience in telephone selling gave it a natural head start in understanding how the Internet could be effectively added to the channel mix: indeed,

> A stage 6 organization deliberately and proactively positions itself in the future market map rather than the current one

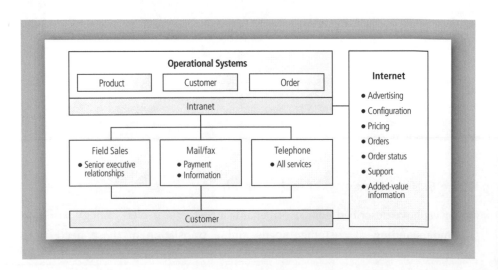

Figure 4.14
Dell's channel structure

the manager responsible for its website has claimed that 'If a company does not know anything about telemarketing, it must learn about it before developing an Internet strategy'.[3] For example, it had been forced from an early stage to collect and distribute integrated information about its customers and their purchases, so that any telephone operator could deal effectively with any call. When a website was added as an alternative route to purchase, it was linked into the same databases so that it could share the same information on products, customers and orders.

Dell's website provides all the same services that are available by telephone, plus some more. In addition to the usual 'brochure-ware' of words and pictures describing what products are available, and a standard ordering facility, the site includes:

➡ a configuration service that helps the user to tailor the computer they want, and calculates its price;

➡ information on the order's status, lead time and so on;

➡ automated customized pricing for its major 'platinum' customers;

➡ added-value services such as online support, information on future product releases and discussion forums for users to communicate with each other.

The high proportion of visitors to the site who ultimately place their order by other mechanisms such as the telephone is an important point which emphasizes that the impact of the Internet cannot be measured simply by measuring online sales, and more generally that IT-enabled channels are often complementary:

//We don't see Dell.com as a competing channel. We see it as a complementary channel. A lot of people visit Dell.com and then call us on the telephone and buy. Is that a bad thing? No, because it takes six to eight telephone calls to sell a computer, and we just made five of them go away, with a commensurate reduction in operating expenses. **//**(3)

Dell effectively uses all elements of the e-marketing mix, as shown in Figure 4.15.

By way of another example, a manufacturer we visited was initiating market transformation in its industry through e-commerce (Figure 4.16). Beginning gently with EDI-style automation of ordering, invoicing, sample requests, and product information, the more far-reaching potential included: more direct routes to market through disintermediation, allowing new market sectors to be

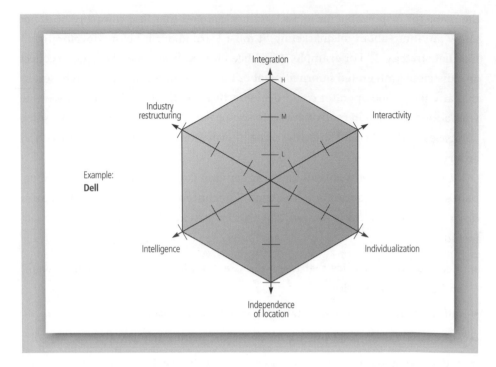

Figure 4.15
Stage 6 against
the e-marketing
mix

Independence of
location is the
variable which is
contributing most
frequently to
industry
restructuring

profitably addressed; radical improvements in stock control and hence return on capital through electronic integration with the supply chain; and more personalization of the product offering through just-in-time production.

Of the other five Is, independence of location is the variable which is contributing most frequently to industry restructuring. This is one lesson of the particularly high penetration of the Internet in sales of books, pre-recorded music and videos. The traditional market structure is dominated by local bookshops and other retail outlets. Telephone sales have had a relatively minor impact, as the customer needs to know exactly what item is required without further browsing. Mail order has carved out a number of niches, in which a limited catalogue sent by post has been sufficient to meet the browsing needs of, say, science fiction enthusiasts or keen gardeners. But Internet booksellers are proving a much more successful challenge to the local bookshop. Large catalogues can be provided online without the prohibitive expense of printing and mailing, while browsing can be enhanced by computer search facilities. The added value is accompanied by lower costs – low-unit cost transactions with a computer replace the high cost of shop assistants, and capital does not need to be tied up in moving books into

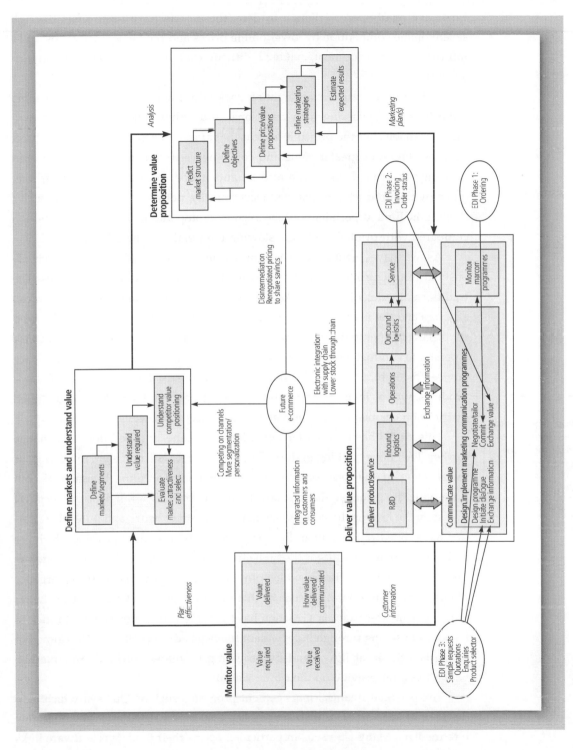

Figure 4.16 Market restructuring through e-commerce – a manufacturer

expensive retail space – though to date, these costs have been offset through severe online competition by lower online prices and the heavy capital cost of IT infrastructure development, making it difficult even for the market leader to turn a profit.

Naturally the retailers are fighting back with their own websites, and some publishers are bypassing both traditional and online retailers with their own direct channels, but the principle is clear that at least for many purchases a direct purchase provides greater value and convenience to the customer. A long-term challenge to printed books can also be anticipated from electronic publishing, whereby the product is distributed electronically, not just ordered electronically, though the limited portability of the average laptop and its low screen definition compared with printed books are slowing the uptake of the e-book.

As we have mentioned, an information-intensive industry in which IT-enabled restructuring is already well under way is retail financial services. The traditional model of local banks (as well as local insurance offices, financial advisers and the like) is based largely on information-processing needs: the need for pieces of paper to document transactions and to represent money; the need for a person to conduct a routine transaction (bank clerks) or to provide face-to-face advice (bank managers). The bank may outsource the origination of some products, such as investment products or mortgages, but it aims to act as a unified distribution channel for a wide range of products to the consumer.

The one-stop-shop' high street bank has been under threat for some time

This model has been under threat for some time, and will doubless change further. Telephone banking in the style of First Direct is a first step, involving the replacement of the local branch by the telephone for some transactions, but preserving the principle that a single 'bank' can provide a range of products. At first sight the Internet banking which many high street banks and pure-play start-ups have rolled out is similar. But new intermediaries are appearing which are making life more difficult for the high street providers, including portals such as The Motley Fool and FT.com, which provide financial advice, and the emergence of online fund supermarkets such as that provided by John Charcol. The always innovative insurer Skandia's reaction has been interesting: determined to stick to its policy of selling through independent financial advisers (IFAs), it has aimed to strengthen the local IFA's hand by providing a white-label fund supermarket, which IFAs can provide on their own website.

The personal financial management programs such as Quicken which help the user to keep track of their money can also be regarded as a potential new intermediary. Many US users, in particular, access their banks via software links to their financial management packages. But they are proving more loyal to their software packages than to their banks – a finding important for the power of the software provider.

Naturally this information-intensive industry is under particularly radical change. But every industry has a substantial information-processing component in the interaction with the customer. The changes we have described in such relatively physical industries as bookselling and sales of computers illustrate that no one can afford to ignore the potential impact on their market structure of IT-enabled customer communications.

Summary

The stage model provides a useful overall sense of direction for IT investments in marketing. Not surprisingly, the later stages show an increasingly integrated approach to the support of the marketing map which we are using as a structure for this book, as Figure 4.17 illustrates.

We have seen, though, some important variations in how organizations navigate through this model. In particular, achieving full integration at the

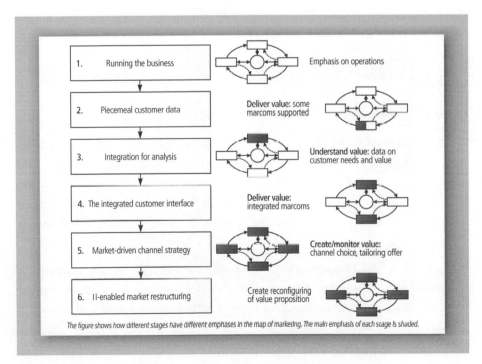

Figure 4.17
Stage model against value cycle

operational level (stage 4) is such a large elephant to eat that many organizations find it better to tackle just part of this meal at a time, and while digesting it add what value they can to customers through partial market-driven stagies (stage 5).

IT at the customer interface: front-office CRM

How will we communicate our offer to our customers? Previous chapters emphasized that it is only once we understand who our customers are and what they want from us, as well as which channels they prefer to use in communicating with us, that we are in a position to make sensible use of CRM technology in order to use the right medium for the right message in a co-ordinated way.

We have seen in this chapter, though, that we must also understand what the technology can do for us. We have looked at the e-marketing mix as a framework enabling a cross-functional debate about how best to use IT-enabled channels. We have also looked at the staging of IT/marketing developments. In this section we provide some more detail of the underlying technologies for those not familiar with marketing software. To do this, we build on the map of marketing by overlaying IT applications on to it. The result is an overview of the ways in which IT can support marketing processes, shown in Figure 4.18. The major IT application areas are shown in the ovals which are superimposed on the marketing map.

Overview

In brief, the main application areas are:

➡ *Enterprise Resource Planning (ERP) or Enterprise Systems (ES):* Under this heading comes the variety of operational systems that have been developed, often over a considerable period, to 'run the business'. These typically centre on the key operational tasks of Porter's value chain: inbound logistics, production/ operations, outbound logistics and service, as well as finance and human resources.

➡ *Operational EIS:* This operational data may be summarized for purposes of management information in an operational Executive Information System (EIS), which presents information in the form of charts, tables and reports.

➡ *CRM system:* The marketing equivalent of ERP are the systems, typically diverse, which support the customer-facing functions such as marketing, sales

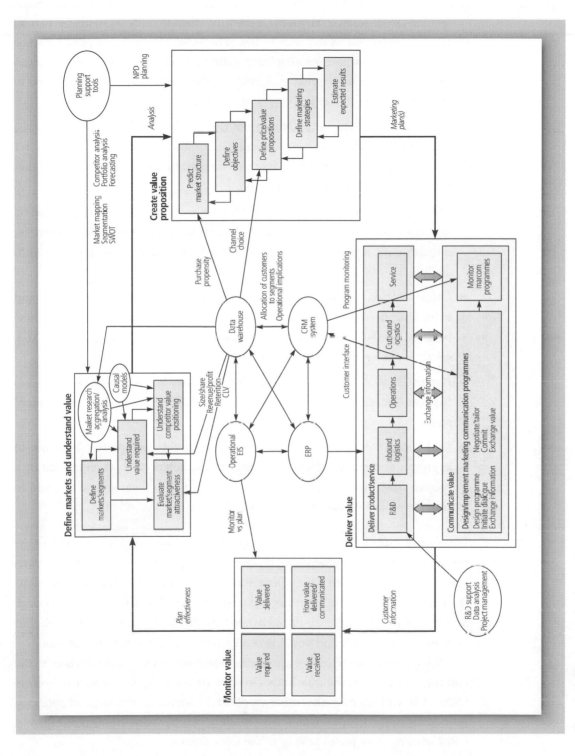

Figure 4.18 IT support for marketing

and customer service. These are generally labelled CRM systems. A variant also in current use is the term eCRM. The term 'eBusiness' is used by some vendors, but can be confusing. Depending on who is using it, it can mean anything from pure Internet marketing on the one hand to any application of IT in business on the other, with various shades in between.

➡ *Data warehouse:* The information from the CRM systems may be placed in a large analysis database, often combined with ERP data, as a basis for marketing decision-making. It may also be used for decision-making for other functions, which is outside our scope.

➡ *Market research aggregation/analysis:* Moving away from the data generated by the organization's operations, specific IT support may be provided for market research data, aggregating this across data sources and providing facilities to analyse it.

➡ *Causal models:* Another source of intelligence on customer needs and behaviour used by some organizations is causal models, which examine behavioural data to deduce such information as price sensitivity, advertising effectiveness and the impact of promotions.

➡ *Planning support tools:* A variety of other tools may be used to provide decision support for the 'Understand value' and 'Determine value proposition' stages.

➡ *R&D support:* Similarly, the R&D process may be supported by tools to aggregate and analyse data of relevance to marketers (such as on the status of projects, their market potential, risks associated with them and so on), and to provide project management support.

We should add a note on terminology. The IT industry likes to replace its terminology at least as often as we replace our computers or our cars, on the basis that we're more likely to pay for a new acronym than an old one, discredited as the latter is by the project overruns and underdelivered benefits last time around. So some of these terms may have changed by the time you read this book. But peer under the bonnet and you'll probably find the contents pretty similar.

We will describe below the application areas with immediate relevance to the current stage of 'Communicate and deliver value' – ERP systems and 'front-office' CRM. We will discuss the other application areas in the next chapter on measuring value. Readers who are thoroughly familiar with the current ERP and CRM markets may prefer to skip to the next chapter.

ERP systems

Although largely outside our scope, we will touch briefly on enterprise resource planning (ERP) systems as they relate to the customer interface. In some companies, core operations are performed through bespoke systems for areas such as finance, human resource, manufacturing and logistics, while in others the trend towards integrated packaged solutions has been followed, using software from suppliers such as SAP, the highly successful German vendor of integrated systems, which has led the market in ERP systems. These systems have become popular in large organizations, particularly manufacturing, despite the high cost and complexity of such ambitious projects, as they can in theory reduce the large costs and risks associated with integrating separate systems from separate vendors. Differing views remain, though, on whether it is best to implement a single integrated suite, or to buy and integrate 'best of breed' modules for different application areas.

The success of SAP, and rivals such as J.D. Edwards and Peoplesoft, and the annual growth rate through most of the 1990s of around 30 per cent in the ERP market as a whole, was not lost on software companies looking for sources of future growth, as they realized that there was (until recently, as discussed in the next section) no equivalent in sales and marketing. If the analogy was initially lost on the ERP suppliers themselves, they have wasted little time in catching up. SAP themselves, for example, have been buying into this market and rushing to improve their suite's capabilities at the customer interface, to offset their slowdown in profit growth at the beginning of the decade – itself attributed to the change in priority to use of IT at the customer interface, as well as to a lull in new projects as year 2000 implementations were completed.

It is interesting to note that another ERP supplier, Oracle, has been working at the component parts of its ERP solution since at least 1985, when one of the authors first examined it. Its vast investment, initially with scant returns, included the development of two parallel accounting systems over several years, one in the UK and one in the US, before standardizing on one and scrapping the considerable effort in the other. But as it now reaps the rewards of this investment, it has in turn invested in software to automate the customer interface. Venture capital has not been slow to follow the ERP example and provide a more rapid development path for integrated customer databases from suppliers such as E.piphany. Suppliers who already had products dealing with part of the problem, such as sales force automation, complaint handling or field service, have also

> The success of SAP was not lost on others as they realized there was no equivalent in marketing

been well-placed to move rapidly into the market for integrated systems by expanding their existing offerings.

Customer relationship management systems

IT in marketing is well behind other areas of business automation in its maturity. Most larger companies we studied in researching this book still have bespoke customer databases, or a mixture of bespoke and packaged solutions. It is illuminating, though, to look at the parallel developments in the packaged software markets, as the most mature packages available exemplify many aspects of best practice which the companies we studied, hampered as they are by complex legacy systems, are endeavouring to move towards. It is therefore worth looking at these packaged solutions more closely.

Automation of business areas tends to follow a common pattern. Early systems are developed bespoke, written from scratch for each organization. As the needs become better understood, suppliers look to leverage their experience by providing packaged solutions, and users seek to reduce their software development costs and risk by buying them. The market for packaged products starts with a large number of mostly small suppliers, selling limited solutions which need tailoring and integration with other systems. Over time, packages increase in scope, and a shakeout occurs as the few suppliers that can afford the now considerable product development costs compete for the now substantial market.

The market for packaged customer databases, or customer relationship management (CRM) systems, is following this model, and has until recently been at the intermediate stage with a multiplicity of small vendors. We can define the market roughly as systems, along with associated services, that incorporate both a customer file and also one or more of the operational areas that draw on this file to manage customer interaction. These operational areas include direct mail, telemarketing, campaign management, sales force automation, and more recently customer interaction via the Internet, mobile commerce and interactive TV. Commonly-provided functionality includes:

➡ *Sales force automation:* This can include sales force productivity tools such as contact management, order entry, checking inventory and order status, diary management, and reporting of expenses. Often now involving notebook computers used by the sales force in the field, the key facility is 'contact management' making all aspects of the contact with the customer available to the salesperson: notes of previous meetings, records of orders placed, notes on

Margin note: IT in marketing is well behind other areas of business automation in its maturity

service issues and complaints and so on. This is illustrated by the screen from the Oracle e-business suite (available from CRM Specialists Interchange Group, amongst others) shown in Figure 4.19. Integration with the Internet can include querying online databases to generate leads or find more information about a prospect, the Maximizer product for example allowing the Eagle online database of North American businesses to be searched by contact name, title and so on, as well as e-mail for the sales force to communicate with each other and with back-office staff. Benefits can include elimination of mistakes in pricing and configuration, and better inventory control. Features can also include management functions such as automated reports on staff perform ance, sales activity, forecasts versus actuals and so on.

➡ *Direct mailing:* One of the most mature areas of CRM, direct mail functions include selecting a subset of a mailing list, customizing letters and address labels, selecting appropriate literature, and tracking and forwarding leads. Management of lists can include facilities such as de-duplication, where two or more lists have been combined, and data quality reporting.

➡ *Telemarketing:* This typically includes management of call lists, scripting of the dialogue with the prospect, and tracking and forwarding leads for order entry. Again, data management of lists can form a major area of functionality.

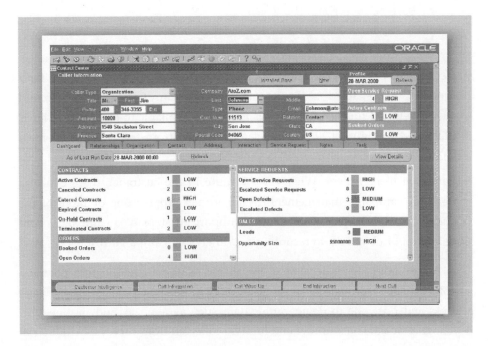

Figure 4.19
Tracking customer contacts in a CRM package

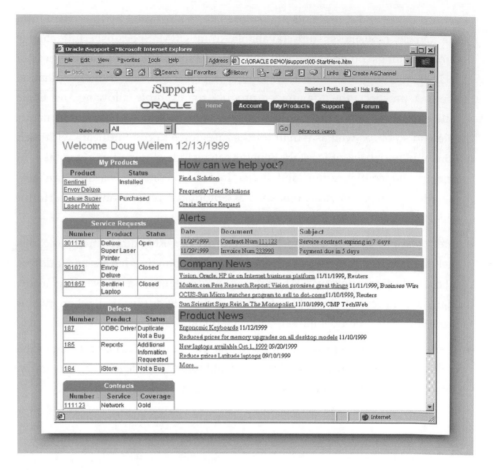

Figure 4.20
Making CRM data
available to
customers

➡ *Electronic commerce:* The CRM suppliers have worked hard to make their functions 'Web enabled', so that remote staff can use any CRM functionality, and so that selected functionality can also be made available to customers. This is illustrated in Figure 4.20, another sample screen from the Oracle e-business suite.

➡ *Campaign management:* Whatever the route to the customer, there is also a need for campaign management. Systems that support one or more of the above channels to the customer may support all steps of a campaign, from definition of objectives to recording and analysing campaign results.

This functionality is underpinned by shared data on actual and potential customers. The information can range from basic reference data such as name, address and postcode to demographic data such as age, sex and income, and psychographic data on attitudes and lifestyle collected from surveys. In industrial markets, information may be richer and more detailed about a smaller number of customers, covering for example organizational structure, key contacts and their roles, the customer's value chain and so on.

As well as details of customers' purchases from the organization, information may be held on their purchases from competitors. Information may relate to both direct and indirect customers, though typically it is weaker for the latter, and a similar range of information may be held for distributors and other relevant bodies or individuals such as influencers and sources of referrals.

Information is also typically held in marketing databases on the customer's involvement with the organization. Transaction data can include items such as what products have been purchased at what price, the buying channel used, purchasing frequency and account balance. The transaction data typically references product data, which includes product codes, pricing and in some cases information on costs, margins and promotions. Contact history information, such as sales contacts, mailings, complaints, service calls, and proposals may also be held. This may include soft data on why the customer did or did not buy, aiding analysis of market needs and the extent to which the organization is satisfying them at the aggregated, market level.

Developments in the packaged software market

Studies in the late 1980s and early 1990s showed a market for packaged marketing software still dominated by a myriad of small suppliers.[4][5][6] Mostly national rather than international, few had a turnover in excess of £10 million. The lion's share of live systems had been developed bespoke, either by internal IT departments or by software services companies, as larger organizations found the off-the-shelf solutions inadequate for their needs. Systems often focused on one means of customer interaction, such as direct mail or sales force automation. The small suppliers varied considerably in their ability to tackle the complex issues involved in successful implementation within the user organization, while user companies themselves as usual tended to look for quick fixes and to under-estimate the business re-engineering required. The result was high levels of customer dissatisfaction and the development of a series of piecemeal systems covering different aspects of the relationship with the customer.

Figure 4.21 suggests that the market for customer databases is now beginning to reach the shakeout stage as integrated, highly flexible packages are developed. These integrated systems potentially provide the crucial added value of

Company	2001 market share (%)
Siebel	22.7
SAP	6.1
Peoplesoft	5.2
Oracle	4.6
Vignette	3.8
Remedy	2.8
Broadvision	2.8
Dendrite	2.3
Microstrategy	2.1
Nortel/Clarify	2
ATG	1.6
E.piphany	1.6
Pega	1.1
Davox	1.1
Onyx	1.1
Interact	1.1
Chordiant	1
Kana	1
Trilogy	1
Pivotal	1
Firepond	0.7
Xchange	0.6
e-Gain	0.6
Applix	0.5
Point Information	0.4
Epicor	0.4
Open Market	0.4
Saratoga	0.3
Quintus	0.3
Total market value (2001, estimated): $7.8 bn	

Figure 4.21
The CRM software package market – global market share, 2001

Source: Hewson Group

integrating all the routes to the customer, whether via mail, telephone, face-to-face contact or the Internet. Hence contacts made by one route can draw on information collected by another route. This development of hybrid systems has broken down the previous division of the market between call centre systems, sales automation, direct mail and so on – although specialists in one or more of these areas are still likely to flourish if their offering is particularly strong, as illustrated on the left of Figure 4.22.

It should also be noted that products do not all attempt to do the same job, so some of the products listed in Figure 4.21 can co-exist in a client company rather than compete. Still, severe competition is taking place for the middle ground represented by Siebel's impressive market share. In the view of CRM analysts Hewson Group, the companies offering the 'forward integration' of both

Severe competition is taking place for the middle ground represented by Siebel's impressive market share

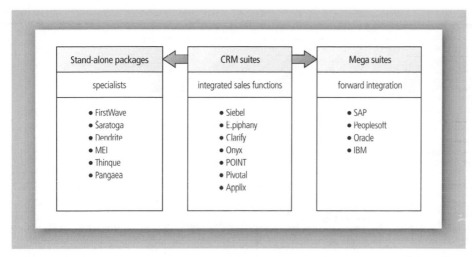

Figure 4.22
A categorization
of CRM suppliers

Source: Ovum

ERP and CRM software, such as Peoplesoft, SAP and Oracle, are likely to be particularly well placed at the time of writing to increase their share, as the boundary between ERP and CRM systems blurs.

Towards best practice in CRM software

These industry details are changing rapidly. But whether the enabling software for front-office CRM and ERP is bought from one source or several, our research suggests some enduring lessons about best practice in CRM design.

Task-independent data management

The market for integrated CRM systems has largely arisen out of the frustration of many companies with their multiple customer databases developed for different tasks. We have seen how many organizations are working towards a unified view of the customer, so that all aspects of the customer interface can be co-ordinated. In order to achieve this, systems need to manage customer data independently of the task being performed. For example, if a customer enters their name and address on a website, they do not wish to be asked the same information on the telephone. This requires all tasks to call on a single module which manages this customer data if a spaghetti-like set of system interconnections is not to result. We call this the principle of task-independent data management.

CRM systems need
to manage
customer data
independently of
the task being
performed if a
spaghetti-like set
of system
interconnections is
not to result

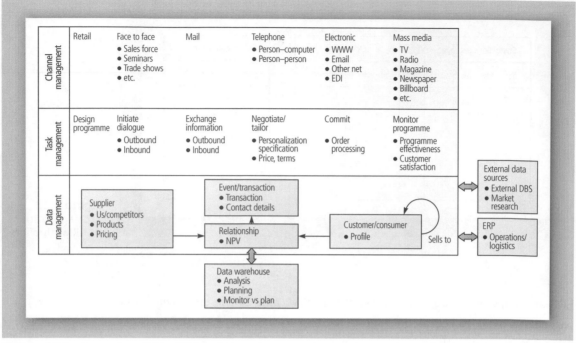

Figure 4.23 Towards a viable CRM architecture

This point can clearly be seen in Figure 4.23. The 'task management' layer needs to be separate from the 'data management' layer, rather than systems for each task endeavouring to manage parts of the customer data, as is still often the case.

Channel-independent task management

Another point which is clearly illustrated by Figure 4.23 is the importance of channel-independent task management. The 'channel management' layer of managing different channels or media is often bundled in with particular tasks. A 'direct mail system' will be *the* way in which the organization generates leads; an 'order processing system' will assume that orders come in to an order processing clerk (rather than, say, being made by a website); and so on. Such an architecture is inherently inflexible. An ideal CRM architecture separates the issue of managing the medium from that of managing the task.

An ideal CRM architecture separates the issue of managing the medium from that of managing the task

Design projects with both operational and strategic components

We were intrigued that most successful projects we have studied involve marketing tasks from diverse areas of the marketing map. In particular, all have elements taken from both the 'Deliver value proposition' stage and from the analysis and planning stages. We believe this to be for good reason. If projects concentrate entirely on 'Deliver value proposition', they may end up avoiding disadvantage through inefficient dealings with the customer; but without work on the analysis of the resulting data and planning as to how to use the new facilities, the project will probably not exploit its potential. Similarly, a project focused entirely on analysis or planning may suffer from a difficulty in having a significant impact on the company's operations where the real difference is made.

Summary

The front-office CRM technology with which we have ended this chapter can provide an excellent enabler for customer-focused strategies. We can draw several conclusions on how to bridge the gap between this CRM technology and the marketing strategy we discussed in Chapter 3:

➡ Delivering value optimally requires sophisticated use of the new options provided by IT-enabled channels. We do not advocate innovation for its own sake, but innovation which enhances the customer value offering. The e-marketing mix provides one means of generating ideas as to how the offer can best be enhanced.

➡ Building a multi-channel infrastructure to underpin value delivery takes time, and is generally best done in stages to reduce risk. Whether or not these stages follow those we have described, they need to add up to a truly market-driven channel strategy in which each interaction with the customer is carried out so as to maximize the value for both parties. It also helps if the staged plan can deliver some quick wins in earlier stages.

➡ The fact that one might decide to trade via an electronic channel doesn't change the customer. Prices may sometimes need to be different, but the proposition should still be based on a deep understanding of customer needs, which will vary by segment – so forget such mythical generalizations as the need for stickiness or the predominance of price competition, and concentrate on serving your target segments whose concerns, by definition, will be specific to that group.

References

(1) Kuttner, R. (1998) 'Friction-free capitalism', *Business Week*, 11 May.

(2) Lee, H.G. (1998) 'Do electronic marketplaces lower the price of goods?' *Communications of the AGM*, **41**(1), 73–80.

(3) Hill, K. (1997) 'Electronic marketing: the Dell Computer experience'. In Peterson, R.A. (ed.), *Electronic Marketing and the Consumer*. Thousand Oaks: Sage.

(4) Andersen Consulting (1989) *IT in Marketing and Sales '89*, London: Andersen Consulting.

(5) Shaw, R. (1994) *How to Transform Marketing Through IT*, London: Business Intelligence.

(6) Hewson, N. and Hewson, W. (1994) *The Impact of Computerised Sales and Marketing Systems in the UK*, 4th ed., Milton Keynes: HGC Publications.

Worksheet 4.1 The e-marketing mix

1 CURRENT POSITION

Locate your organisation on each of the six Is. Mark your location on the diagram below. Use the notes below to prompt you if you wish.

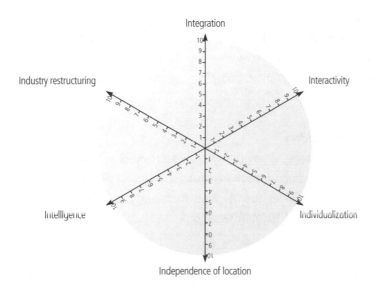

Notes on the six Is

Integration of customer data

Do you have detailed knowledge of individual customers, influencers or consumers?

Do you share this knowledge across all customer-facing parts of the business?

Interactivity

Do you use interactive media to allow your customers to communicate with you?

Do you listen to what they say and respond appropriately in a continuing dialogue?

Individualization

Do you use your customer knowledge to tailor products and services to the needs of particular individuals or segments?

Do you tailor all your communications to the characteristics of the recipients?

Independence of location

Do you exploit remote media such as mail, the telephone and the Internet to communicate with customers wherever they are in a cost-effective manner?

Do you exploit any opportunities to deliver information-based products and services electronically?

Intelligence

Do you inform your marketing strategy with intelligence gleaned from your operational systems at the customer interface? For example, through analysis of customer needs, segmentation, prioritizing segments according to customer lifetime value, etc.

Industry restructuring

Do you take advantage of any opportunities provided by new media to restructure your industry in favour of your eventual customers? For example, by bypassing unnecessary intermediaries (disintermediation), or providing added value through electronic intermediaries (reintermediation).

2 FUTURE OPPORTUNITIES

Fill in the form below to indicate how IT-enabled media (the Internet, mobile commerce etc.) might improve the position of competitors on the 6 Is, and how you might be able to exploit e-marketing yourselves.

	THREATS	E-OPPORTUNITIES	
		Cost reduction	**Customer value creating**
1 INTEGRATION			
2 INTERACTIVITY			
3 INDIVIDUALIZATION			
4 INDEPENDENCE OF LOCATION			
5 INTELLIGENCE			
6 INDUSTRY RESTRUCTURING			

5

Staying on track

Monitoring the value delivered

- ➡ Monitoring the value received
- ➡ Customer lifetime value
- ➡ Monitoring the value delivered
- ➡ Metrics for the sales process online
- ➡ Analytical CRM

Introduction

The purpose of this chapter is to discuss the 'Monitor Value' box in our map of marketing shown in Figure 5.1. The box is expanded on in Figure 5.2.

At this stage of the marketing process, we have developed a marketing plan and put it into action. But the process is a circular, not a linear one: we need to be continuously monitoring the marketplace for how customers are perceiving our offers, as well as looking out for changes in market needs, desires and buying patterns.

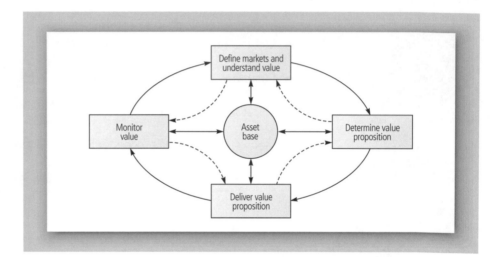

Figure 5.1
'Monitor value' and the map of marketing

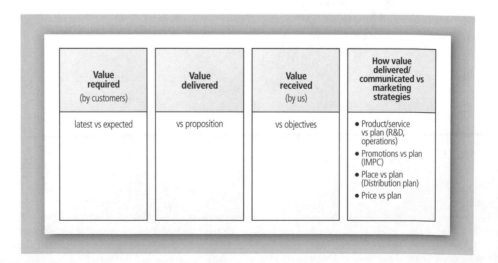

Figure 5.2
Monitor value

Fortunately, IT enables us to go far beyond the comparison of sales actuals against forecasts and look not just at what is going right and wrong, but why. The relevant area of IT can be termed analytical CRM, which we will describe later in this chapter.

But first, we will discuss what we are trying to measure in the first place.

Monitoring the value received

Of the four categories of measurement in Figure 5.2, most companies are best at the 'value received' box: what they receive – typically revenue and profit – in exchange for their goods or services.

The main complication is that accounting systems tend to be organized around products rather than markets. So if marketing objectives have been set in terms of market share, for example, it may not be trivial to monitor progress against them.

Does this matter? Consider the case of InterTech, a fictional company – albeit based on a real example – in Figure 5.3.

A glance at the figures suggests that all is well and the company has nothing to worry about. The company is growing its sales, profits and return on assets consistently. But what happens when we consider instead metrics based on the company's market position (Figure 5.4)?

It turns out that the company's sales growth is entirely attributable to growth in the overall market size. Indeed, the company has lost 5 per cent market share

Performance (£million)	Base year	1	2	3	4	5
Sales revenue	£254	£293	£318	£387	£431	£454
– cost of goods sold	135	152	167	201	224	236
Gross contribution	£119	£141	£151	£186	£207	£218
– manufacturing overhead	48	58	63	82	90	95
– marketing and sales	18	23	24	26	27	28
– research and development	22	23	23	25	24	24
Net profit	£16	£22	£26	£37	£50	£55
Return on sales (%)	6.3%	7.5%	8.2%	9.6%	11.6%	12.1%
Assets	£142	£162	£167	£194	£205	£206
Assets (% of sales)	56%	55%	53%	50%	48%	45%
Return on assets (%)	11.3%	13.5%	15.6%	19.1%	24.4%	26.7%

Source: The Marketing Process Company

Figure 5.3
InterTech's 5-year performance

Performance (£million)	Base year	1	2	3	4	5
Market growth	18.3%	23.4%	17.6%	34.4%	24.0%	17.9%
InterTech sales growth (%)	12.8%	17.4%	11.2%	27.1%	16.5%	10.9%
Market share (%)	20.3%	19.1%	18.4%	17.1%	16.3%	14.9%
Customer retention (%)	88.2%	87.1%	85.0%	82.2%	80.9%	80.0%
New customers (%)	11.7%	12.9%	14.9%	24.1%	22.5%	29.2%
% dissatisfied customers	13.6%	14.3%	16.1%	17.3%	18.9%	19.6%
Relative product quality	+10%	+8%	+5%	+3%	+1%	0%
Relative service quality	+0%	+0%	-20%	-3%	-5%	-8%
Relative new product sales	+8%	+8%	+7%	+5%	+1%	-4%

Figure 5.4
InterTech's 5-year market-based performance

Source: The Marketing Process Company

over the five-year period. Neither do things look set to get any better: customer satisfaction is falling, as is product quality, perceived service quality and the proportion of sales from new products.

It is plain that the company has much work to do if it is not to hit a crisis at the next sign of a downturn in this market, and these customer-focused metrics suggest clearly where this work will need to concentrate. But without this market-based view the company might be lulled into a false sense of security and do nothing until the crisis occurs.

So it is well worth monitoring sales by market or market segment as well as by product line or division. We suggest that one of the first tasks following a segmentation exercise is to revise internal systems so as to record sales according to the market segments. Allocating costs against markets so as to arrive at a profit or contribution figure by market or market segment is also highly beneficial, though rarely easy.

> One of the first tasks following a segmentation exercise is to revise internal systems so as to record sales according to the market segments

Customer lifetime value

A danger of the traditional approach to performance measurement is that it concentrates on the current time period, be it a month, quarter or year, which can encourage short-term thinking and discourage long-term investments. A useful antidote to this is the use of Customer Lifetime Value (CLV) as a key metric. Made possible by the profusion of customer data now available through CRM systems,

CLV looks not just at the profits from customers this year, but also at future anticipated profits. These are added together – discounted to the present to allow for the cost of capital – to give a single measure of the value of the customer. This can be calculated for the average customer in a segment, or even for individual customers.

Calculating CLV is a difficult exercise which will probably involve modifications to IT systems as well as the involvement of your accountants, but the general principles are illustrated in Figure 5.5.

● **Definition**
CLV: the financial value of a customer over the lifetime of the relationship, summing all revenues and costs, discounted to the present

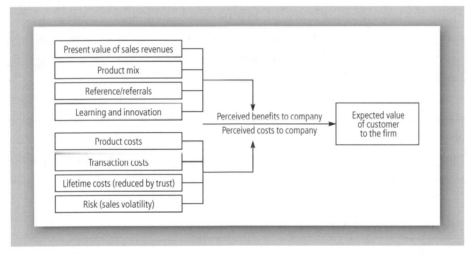

Figure 5.5
Calculating customer lifetime value

Source: Lynette Ryals, adapted from Earl Naumann, *Creating Customer Value*, Thomson Executive Press, 1995

The most obvious benefits to the organization from a customer relationship arise from future revenue flows, both from any existing products held by the customer and from any future ones they buy. But some customers may also be of significant value by acting as a reference customer: either you can put prospects in touch with them, or they refer their peers to you themselves. Other customers may be particularly valuable in the learning benefit which you gain from working with them. These indirect benefits can be estimated financially and included in the calculation.

Against these benefits, the various costs should be set, as well as risks such as the risk of losing the customer and hence the anticipated future revenue flows. As well as the cost of producing and delivering the product or service, you need to take account of transaction costs – how much it costs to take and process an order, for example – as well as lifetime costs such as the cost of acquiring and retaining the customer.

Much was made in the dotcom boom of the lower transaction costs which could be gained online. We were told that airline tickets cost $10 to sell through travel agents, versus $5 via call centres and $1 via the Web, with similar figures being widely quoted for the cost of bank transactions or the cost of share brokering. All true, and potentially invaluable. But the CLV calculation shows that transaction costs are not the only thing you have to watch. Often the cost-effectiveness of acquisition and retention runs in the opposite direction, with higher costs online. Many a dotcom has ignored to its peril statistics indicating that the average online retailer spends £66 to acquire a customer, against £13 offline.[1] They are also discovering that the scant attention to customer service and customer retention that leaves 25 per cent of e-mail queries entirely unanswered, and only 21 per cent answered within two days, has a high cost in low retention rates.[2]

> While the internet gives low transaction costs, often acquisition and retention costs are actually higher

This is one reason why we are increasingly seeing multi-channel strategies which use the different channels for different aspects of the relationship – acquiring the customer, perhaps, though the sales force and providing service through the Web and call centres, but with personal visits to handle complaints and ensure that the relationship is not damaged.

Monitoring the value delivered

The value we receive from the customer is only half the story. As the Intertech example illustrated with its dropping service quality and satisfaction levels, the value we are delivering in exchange is of course the root cause of our financial performance. And yet where do we concentrate our measurement efforts? How often do we measure customer satisfaction, or our performance compared with our competitors against the customers' buying criteria?

> Measuring the value delivered involves asking not our operational systems but our customers

Customers are mostly only too delighted to tell us what they think, as it enables them to get things off their chest, and helps them feel valued. But we will not generally get this kind of data for free from our operational systems, which, as we have observed, may record what the customers bought, but not why. If you have gone through the steps described in Chapter 2 to segment the market on the basis of buying criteria, you will now have this information on buying criteria at a particular point in time. But it will still need to be refreshed periodically to see whether your marketing strategies are working.

Let us illustrate the feedback loop between marketing strategies and what we then monitor with the example of a tyre company. In the country in question, the company sells imported, premium tyres for various purposes, such as earth-moving equipment, trucks and cars. The managing director felt he knew the business-to-business markets such as trucks well, and he felt able to plan for these markets on the basis of internal information and the judgement of the sales force. But although he felt that the company ought to be doing better in the car market, given the high quality of the product, he simply didn't know how the market segmented, which he recognized was a vital starting point. So he commissioned some market research along the lines of the segmentation process in Chapter 2, which led to the four segments illustrated in Figure 5.6.

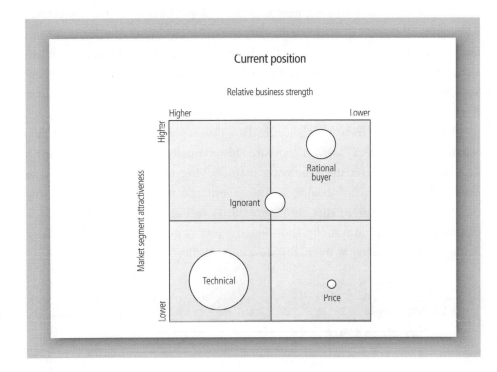

Figure 5.6
A tyre company –
directional policy
matrix

The figure shows the four segments on a Directional Policy Matrix (DPM), which compares their attractiveness on the vertical axis against the company's strength in each segment on the horizontal axis. We described this matrix in Chapter 3.

The price-sensitive segment was easily discounted. While amounting to about 20 per cent of the market, there was no way that the company's expensive imported tyres could compete here with the locally manufactured competition.

Neither would the managing director want to, as margins in this segment were wafer-thin or non-existent.

His strongest segment was the 'technical' buyers, who knew about cars, or at least thought they did. They recognized the superior quality of the company's product, and when they could afford it, they bought it. But this wasn't the most attractive segment to him. Far from brand loyal, these customers were as likely to buy from an obscure but good-quality competitor as from his well-known brand, and they were acutely aware of market prices.

The 'ignorant' segment was at least less price sensitive. These customers would buy primarily on brand image and on the recommendation of the dealer.

But the most attractive segment was the 'rational buyers'. In the UK market we would call these '*Which?* readers', after the consumer magazine. If they didn't know about tyres, they would quiz the dealer, read promotional materials or ask a friend in the trade, in an attempt to come to a reasonably informed decision. Typically middle class, they didn't mind paying a bit extra for a quality product. And yet they were not currently buying his product in great numbers.

How could he increase his share with this segment? The horizontal axis calculation in Figure 5.7, which compares his company's performance against a leading competitor on the segment's main buying criteria, showed what he needed to do. While he could do little about the high perceived price, the durability scores showed that customers didn't realize that the company's high quality led to a high durability and therefore just as good a price per mile. And neither had they taken in the high safety specification.

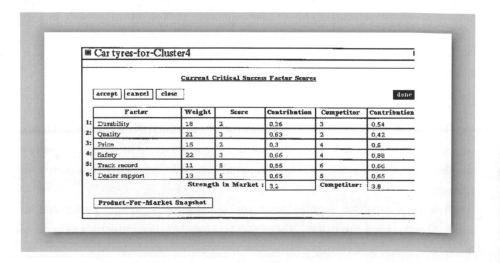

Figure 5.7
Measuring perceived performance against buying criteria

These perceptual issues were ideal targets for advertising. The managing director cancelled his current, technology-focused advertising campaign, and a few months later launched a new campaign focused at this target segment, and in particular at their perceptions of durability and safety.

What to monitor was now clear. He needed to poll the consumers again periodically, to check how consumer perceptions were changing, and what impact this was having on sales by segment. The strategy worked: overall car tyre sales duly went up, with a doubling of his market share over two years, as he succeeded in attracting more of the profitable 'rational buyers' without losing his share of the 'technical' segment.

Measuring the value we deliver, then, is just as important as measuring the value we receive in exchange. It is also worth remembering that as well as monitoring our perceived performance, the buying criteria themselves can change over time (the 'value required' box in Figure 5.2), though generally at a slower rate.

While this tyre company used market research to monitor the value it delivered, it is often possible in industrial markets to get good enough results through other means. A hotel chain we worked with asked some key travel agents to spend a day telling them about the product/service offering, using exactly the same kind of analysis of buying criteria to structure the discussion. A large computer company did the same with a handful of key customers. This kind of informal approach may not satisfy the statisticians, but it's better in our view to be approximately right than exactly wrong, and this kind of informal polling also helps to build relationships. What we guarantee is that if you ask even a few customers, you will receive some surprises in their answers.

> In business to business markets, informed alternatives to market research can work well

Metrics for the sales process online

The final box in Figure 5.2 is: 'How value delivered/communicated vs strategies'. The marketing plan may involve any number of specific marketing objectives and strategies to achieve them – the desired penetration of a new product, the extra sales from a pricing change, improved reach through new distribution, or the impact of a promotion – against which performance will need to be monitored. For most of these, standard metrics are available. But when it comes to the Internet, both theory and practice have yet to settle down, so the state of play in online sales metrics deserves some discussion.

The dotcom focus on registered customers was no substitute for metrics showing differential advantage

The rush of dotcom start-ups and spin-offs towards stock market IPOs did not help the development of rational, market-focused metrics. In the absence of significant sales, the number of registered customers was often picked on as some kind of indication of market interest. Unfortunately, that's all that it proved to be, not a substitute for a business model offering differential advantage against customer buying criteria. Examples abound of companies such as Excite which went under despite having millions of registered users, or of sites such as Lastminute which despite a high profile and a weekly e-mailing list of 3 million, had a 2001 turnover of less than the average supermarket. And more than one blue-chip has confessed to us that its priorities became seriously skewed for a while by the need to demonstrate a high number of registered users on its dotcom arm to shore up the share price. It is one thing to develop content which customers value enough to use, as American Greetings did with their electronic greetings cards – at one point, americangreetings.com was the seventh most visited commercial website. But as they discovered with their tiny subscription levels, it is quite another to persuade the customers to pay for the privilege, or to find sufficient advertisers to pay for the service indirectly.

How, then, can we ground our online metrics in offline best practice? A good start is the measurement of the value delivered and received with which we began this chapter, through metrics such as market share, customer lifetime value and customer satisfaction. But we also need to look at more detailed metrics for the sales process.

Marketers are used to measuring a promotion's success rate in generating prospects, and sales forces will often calculate their conversion rate of prospects into customers. Often the same metrics can be used online, which helps provide a crucial comparability between one medium and another, without which it is difficult to decide which medium to use for what purpose. But the Internet poses some particular problems in measurement, such as the difficulty in knowing anything about the surfer on a website until they choose to register, albeit balanced by opportunities such as the ability to try out and evaluate changes to the product, price or promotion rapidly.

Although companies vary in what is appropriate for them, a useful starting point for designing an appropriate set of measures for an online sales channel is shown in Figure 5.8 and explained below. Adapted from the pioneering model by Berthon et al.,[3] it focuses on transactional websites – not the whole of the Internet's commercial application, but a large part of it.

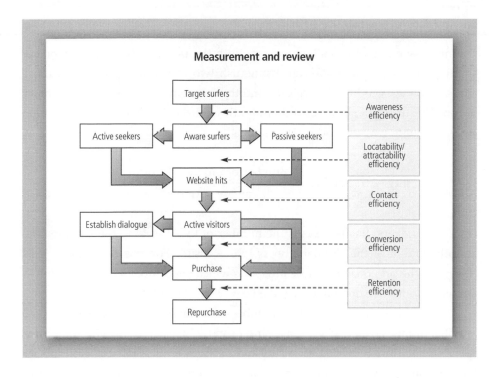

Figure 5.8
Metrics for online sales

Awareness efficiency

The first task is to make relevant potential customers aware of the website's existence. The first metric represents how well this task is being performed:

$$\text{Awareness efficiency} = \frac{\text{aware surfers}}{\text{target surfers}}$$

'Target surfers' are defined as the number of surfers who are potentially interested in the organization's products or service. This corresponds in traditional terminology to the size of the relevant product-market segment, or more precisely that proportion of the segment who use the Internet, as other members of the segment must be reached by other means or ignored. 'Aware surfers' are those who are aware of its website, without necessarily knowing its exact location (URL). The ratio corresponds reasonably closely to the traditional measurement of awareness as one measure of advertising effectiveness, where awareness is expressed as a percentage of the population (or the relevant segment).

Locatability/attractability efficiency

The next issue is that of making contact with the prospect through him or her 'landing on' the website. We can distinguish two categories of prospect: those who actively seek to find the website, and those 'passive seekers' whose primary purpose in surfing is not necessarily to hit the website. The meaning of this ratio varies for these two categories. The ratio is:

$$\text{Locatability/attractability} = \frac{\text{number of unique visitors}}{\text{aware surfers}}$$

For active seekers, this represents the number of those seeking the website who actually find it – the 'locatability' of the website. For passive seekers, this represents the proportion of those prospects which the company has succeeded in attracting to its website while they are browsing – its 'attractability'.

Note that we have used the 'number of unique visitors' rather than the 'number of hits' (which was the measure proposed by Berthon *et al.*). If a visitor spends some time browsing on a site, and perhaps returns later to gain further information, we want to count the visitor only once in this ratio. This kind of statistics collection is one good reason why most websites strongly encourage users to register (another being the ability to tailor the site as information about the user is collected).

Contact efficiency

A problem with measuring 'unique visitors' is that some of these will just be passing, looking at the home page and quickly deciding that this is not what they were looking for – rather like walking past a shop window. The next ratio therefore concerns the distinction between 'hitting' a website, perhaps in passing, and paying an active 'visit' with some serious intent and genuine interest.

$$\text{Contact efficiency} = \frac{\text{number of active visitors}}{\text{number of unique visitors}}$$

There are two ways of establishing whether a 'visit' has occurred: measuring the time spent on the website, and regarding a stay over, say, 2 minutes as a visit; and noting whether some interaction between the surfer and the website occurs, such as filling in a form.

Conversion efficiency

While not all websites aim to sell, for those that do, one can measure the percentage of visitors who purchase:

$$\text{Conversion efficiency} = \frac{\text{number of purchasers}}{\text{number of active visitors}}$$

A simplification for those who do not feel that the 'contact efficiency' measure is meaningful for them is to combine these two measures into a single measure of conversion efficiency, the number of purchasers divided by the number of unique visitors.

If the role of the website is to achieve some other transaction, for example, to ask the customer to fill in an enquiry form, then conversion efficiency can be adapted accordingly.

Retention efficiency

We can then measure the capability to turn purchasers into repeat purchasers:

$$\text{Retention efficiency} = \frac{\text{number of repurchasers}}{\text{number of purchasers}}$$

The model in practice

An example of the model in practice is shown in Table 5.1. This high-street retailer found that the cost of recruiting customers to its website via banner ads was £1,600 – hardly economic when the average purchase was perhaps £50! Clearly, much needed correcting. With some help from the Web designers and the search engine hosting the banner ads, it calculated these ratios to help it analyse what was going wrong.

The first problem was that click-through rates on banner ads have fallen sharply – from 2 per cent in 1997 to around 0.3 per cent in 2001 – as consumers lose their early interest in browsing out of curiosity, and concentrate on using their time online as efficiently as possible to achieve a focused purpose. The retailer found that more careful placing of advertisements, to attract surfers who were looking at related material, made some difference but not enough.

Click-through rates on banner ads have fallen sharply – from 2 per cent in 1997 to around 0.3 per cent in 2001

Table 5.1 Efficiency of a banner ad campaign

Ratio	Calculation	Notes
Awareness efficiency	$\dfrac{40,000}{200,000} = 20\%$	Banner ad campaign increased from 15% to 20%. Cost £50,000
Locatability/attractability	$\dfrac{3,000}{40,000} = 7.5\%$	3,000 unique visitors to Website during campaign (from 1 m page impressions). Cost per visitor £16
Contact efficiency	$\dfrac{600}{3,000} = 20\%$	600 visitors stayed beyond home page
Conversion efficiency	$\dfrac{30}{600} = 5\%$	30 purchases from click-throughs from banner ads. Cost per purchase £50,000/30 = £1,600
Retention efficiency	Not known	Not known at time of evaluation

The company decided, therefore, to experiment, starting with other online methods. It arranged a promotional e-mail to the customers of a related business – being careful to ensure that the e-mail came from the business on whose website the customers had already registered to avoid accusations of spamming. It made reciprocal arrangements with other online retailers with complementary product ranges, providing links to each other's sites in one case and a co-branded site in another.

While these methods offered much better economics, they did so on a fairly small scale. The company therefore also began to experiment with offline promotions. It made a big difference at virtually no cost – except considerable political perseverance by the Internet division's chief executive – through prominent displays of the website address on stationery, store signs, vehicles and so on. It tried handing out promotional leaflets in shopping centres, finding this a much more cost-efficient approach than banner ads. And it tried offline press advertising (with a promotional code offering a discount on first purchase, to ensure trackability). For the first time, it could compare advertising costs online and offline, as it had worked out the impact of its banner ads not just on sales but also on awareness levels. It found that offline ads were little better.

The company also paid attention to achieving a higher conversion rate once leads had been generated. Some simple changes to the home page improved the 'contact efficiency', while continuing usability testing ensured that customers weren't needlessly lost through user interface glitches.

The resulting strategy involved a mix of promotional approaches, and is constantly evolving. As a result of this careful attention to efficiency, the company's Internet sales are growing steadily, albeit less fast than had originally been planned, but the division has begun to turn in a profit, unlike its competitors.

Some of the morals of this tale are clear. The Web offers great scope for measuring response rates and modifying promotional strategy 'on the fly'. But an investment of management time, and a little effort from IT colleagues, is needed to ensure that the appropriate measures are in place.

Of course, for businesses with a different business model, the metrics may need adjusting from those we have given. This particularly applies with multi-channel business models. How much business is generated by a website for offline sales channels? How about leads generated offline? Not easy to measure, but vital if the board is to be able to make rational decisions on how much to spend on its online activities.

As for banner ads, they still have their place. And as the shakeout of dotcoms funded by venture capital and IPOs continues, prices may drop further. The key to their effectiveness is the relevance of the ad to the user at a particular place and time – 'contextual advertising' in the current jargon. A food advert may only be placed just before office closing time, to catch office workers wondering what to do for supper. A personal finance advert may be placed alongside personal finance editorial material on Yahoo! or FT.com.

> The key to banner-ad effectiveness is the relevance of the ad to the user at a particular place and time – 'contextual advertising'

The key aspect of relevance is illustrated by CNET.com, which provides an online source of reviews and information about electronics products. As people go to the site because they intend to buy something, they are receptive to advertisements about the relevant product category. So CNET.com generates more than $5 of advertising revenue per year per unique user, according to a McKinsey survey, much more than most such content sites.

This ability to target Internet advertising to the right people at the right time can only improve with technical innovations. Full-stream video of, say, sporting events would allow interposed adverts which would be tolerated for the same reasons that TV adverts are – the viewer is willing to wait for the video to continue. And mobile commerce offers, of course, the additional capability to provide offers relevant to the user's physical location.

Analytical CRM

We will now shift our focus from what is measured to how it is measured, and in particular, how IT can help.

In Chapter 4, we described how CRM systems can provide automated support for communication with the customer, through our discussion of the 'CRM system' and 'ERP' ovals in our map of IT in marketing, which we show again in Figure 5.9. We saw that CRM systems do this by drawing on a single repository of customer data. Our interest here is in 'analytical CRM': the analysis of this rich data to monitor how well we are delivering the value which our customers require, as well as what value we are receiving in exchange. We will organize this discussion around the various other ovals in the figure, beginning with data warehouses. The reader who is conversant with these topics may wish to move on to the next chapter.

Marketing data warehouses

Marketing data warehouses integrate customer-related data into a single database as a basis for analysis

Data warehouses aim to integrate data from all operational systems, such as order processing and billing, into one database using a single data model. That is, there is a single consistent view of such things as customers and products, so for example a customer's name and address will only be stored once, and all the products purchased by a customer can be readily ascertained. The data is refreshed regularly from the operational systems to keep it up to date – though we mentioned earlier the difficulties caused to one company by a six-weekly refreshment cycle, which meant that analysis was some weeks behind reality.

Data warehouses typically hold historical information, not just the current information needed for billing and so on. This has become possible due to the rapidly decreasing cost of computer power and storage, which also allows the information to be held at a fine level of detail. Information can be stored about individual purchases, even for mass consumer markets, over substantial periods.

Taken together, these developments provide a rich store of information which, at least potentially, integrates customer/product level data with aggregated data at the level of markets and product groups. A range of facilities for viewing and tabulating the information may be provided, such as the SQL query language, which allows data to be collected according to specified criteria, such as 'All customers with a salary of over £40,000 and an approaching renewal date who are

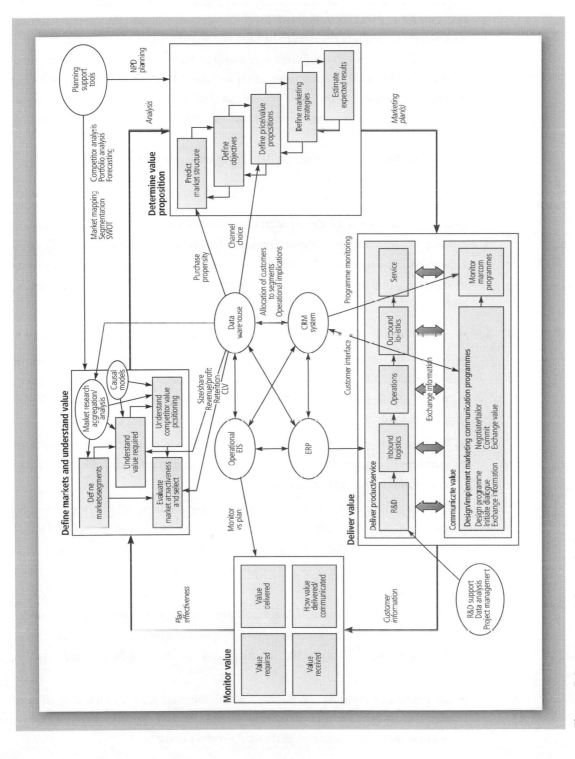

Figure 5.9 IT support for marketing

not currently using our highest level of service'. OLAP (OnLine Analytical Processing) tools allow the data to be browsed graphically and tabulated.

Some companies use different terminology for this repository of marketing-related data for analysis purposes, such as 'marketing database' or 'marketing datamart' (the latter being used where the data is itself extracted from a more comprehensive data warehouse which serves other functions, such as accounting and HR, as well).

The facilities for analysing the data bring us to our next buzzword.

Data mining

Definition ●

Data mining is the searching of internal databases for patterns and connections of commercial value

When mining, one may discover unexpected treasures – hence the term 'data mining' for searching for relevant patterns in data that had not necessarily been anticipated. The term tends, though, to be applied to most forms of data analysis using data warehouses. Some of the analyses of particular relevance to marketing are:

➡ *Segmentation*, such as clustering routines – discussed later in this chapter.

➡ *Evaluating segment attractiveness:* at the level of segments or indeed of individuals, the warehouse can be used to calculate aspects of segment attractiveness such as retention rates, customer profitability, and customer lifetime value.

➡ *Purchase propensity:* another powerful model is to predict the propensity of members of a segment to buy a particular product if offered – clearly valuable in planning cross-selling campaigns.

➡ *Channel choice:* we have discussed how customers increasingly demand to be able to choose the method by which they contact the organization. Channel choice models predict whether a customer is likely to prefer a particular channel, and whether it is in the interests of the organization to steer them towards a particular channel.

➡ *Causal, econometric or predictive modelling:* predicting the effect on, say, future sales based on predictions of various 'input variables' such as future price, advertising spend, competitor's price and so on, which we will discuss below.

➡ *Undirected searching for correlations:* asking the system to search for significant correlations between a large number of potentially connected variables, such as consumers' purchases of particular product lines.

The most famous example of undirected searching is from Wal-Mart, where a data mining tool discovered a connection between the sale of beer and nappies which was entirely unexpected. It transpired that a significant proportion of weekday sales were from men who just bought beer and nappies. On reflection Wal-Mart concluded that men who didn't normally shop would be asked by their partner to pop in and buy some nappies, and while they were about it they would buy some beer. So Wal-Mart put beer on display next to the nappies and claimed a $10 million dollar benefit.

One problem with such undirected searching is that it makes prior cost justification of the system difficult. Given that most data warehouses are in practice used more for directed searching than undirected, it seems sensible to identify in advance at least some major analyses which are likely to be of value. Warehousing consultant and author Sean Kelly provides an illuminating historical perspective:

// When we first put in a data warehouse in 1991, we delivered integrated data, and we had to then look for application areas that would deliver benefits. It was a huge risk for the early adopters. Today there's absolutely no excuse for taking that risk. We know exactly what the benefits are by vertical industry. In retail we can do basket analysis, we can do follow-on analysis to see if you buy x whether you buy y later on, customer value analysis to see who our best customers are, customer retention analysis to understand what are the attributes of customers who stay, margin analysis to understand the net margin, and ten other applications. Each can be looked at and cost justified on its merits.//

Sean Kelly (author interview)

Operational EIS

We distinguish the operational executive information system (EIS) from the marketing data warehouse. Most organizations have some kind of management information system drawing mainly on the operational ERP-type systems, whose purpose is largely to show progress against plan on financial criteria, though as with all the categories we are examining, terminology varies, with OLAP (online analytical processing) again being a common label.

EIS systems typically provide facilities for selecting the information required and displaying it in a variety of formats, such as tables and business graphics. They may provide additional support for management control such as data on

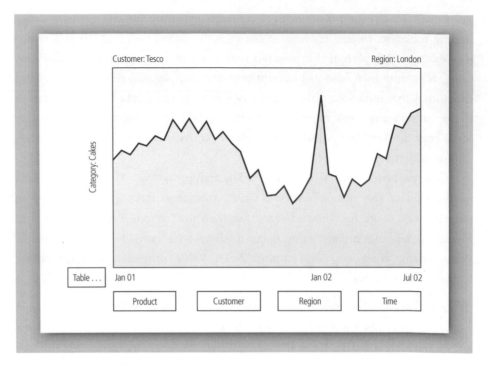

Figure 5.10
EIS in a food
products company

performance against plan by product, market, channel and so on, which may be tracked through simple graphical display, or through facilities such as exception reporting, where the system highlights areas where the divergence from plan is significant.

An example of a typical system is provided by Figure 5.10. The system allows sales information to be summarized according to a number of 'dimensions' such as product category, customer, region and time.

Market research applications

Market research largely draws on data at the level of whole segments, or random samples of customers, rather than each customer as in data warehouses. We have seen the importance of external data for ascertaining such information as customer needs. Some may be imported electronically from outside the organization, such as from market research (e.g. customer needs, customer product perceptions, relative market shares) and from external databases (e.g. market sizes, other market information). For consumer markets, a wealth of information can now be purchased on individuals from standard databases. In the UK, for example, the major types of information available are:

➡ *Geodemographic information:* Derived largely from census data, geodemographic information is so called because it combines geographical information on where a household is located with demographic information on the age, education, family composition, income, and so on of the residents. The census data itself is at the level of enumeration districts of about 200 households, which can be complemented by individual electoral roll data. The raw data can be analysed directly if the skills are available but, for many purposes, a standard classification such as ACORN is often used. CACI's ACORN, 'A Classification Of Residential Neighbourhoods', divides the UK into 17 major groups of neighbourhoods, such as 'wealthy achievers, suburban areas' and 'council estate residents, high unemployment', each of which can be further subdivided. Another such database is CCN's Mosaic, which illustrates the increasingly complex range of data sources combined by the information providers in that it also includes financial information gained from CCN's major business as a credit referencing agency.

➡ *Lifestyle information:* The household surveys that request information on what the household purchases in exchange for coupons have now reached a high proportion of households. The merging of two major players, CMT and NDL, allowed the launch of Claritas's Lifestyle Census product back in 1995, which includes data on an impressive 75 per cent of UK households. In Claritas's next-generation Universe database, launched in late 1997, data was guessed, or 'modelled', for the remaining 25 per cent, based on a variety of sources such as the electoral roll, share registers, County Court judgements, and NDL's ANNA system, which guesses a person's age based on their first name – girls called Agnes or Ethel being unusual in recent decades. Data can also be guessed based on data from neighbouring houses with the same postcode (Claritas's PAD, or Postcode Aggregated Data file).

➡ *Industrial markets:* Companies House is the main source of data on industrial firms. Private agencies offer alternative sources, sometimes with added details on job titles, department sizes and so on.

Data obtained externally may be used as it stands, to form a prospect list for example, or it may be integrated with internal information. Since 1986, for example, it has been possible to apply a neighbourhood classification code to your own customer data using Mosaic.

R&D support tools

Closely related to market research is IT support for R&D. This was a major focus in one company we studied, a drinks company, which illustrated the range of possibilities here with a variety of applications (shown against the marketing map in Figure 5.11):

➡ *Data aggregation and analysis tools:* Just as with market research, organizations can benefit from making data on R&D projects and ideas widely available. In this case, information on the status of R&D projects had previously been provided to marketing staff on a one-off basis at particular points in the project, rather than being available continuously to aid the communication between R&D and marketing. The current relationship between the departments was analogous more to a 'transactional' approach to marketing rather than a 'relationship' approach. IT was envisaged as an enabler to make the relationship closer and more productive.

➡ *Using the Internet to generate ideas:* A virtual (Internet-based) 'discussion café' was conceived, to provide an open forum for new product ideas originating from both employees and customers.

➡ *Planning support for R&D:* Planning tended to focus around existing products, with a plan for each. The company recognized the need to broaden the planning procedures to consider more creatively the range of possible product-market segments that could be addressed, and which of them were of sufficient attractiveness and a sufficient fit with the company's skills to be sensible targets. Although largely an issue of modifying business processes, it was recognized that IT support was also required.

An example of IT support for the R&D planning process from another organization we studied is illustrated in Figure 5.12. Developed by a pharmaceuticals company, it is designed to support the decision-making of a cross-functional group of managers about the vital issue of which R&D projects to back, in an industry where development costs are enormous and time to market can easily be a decade. A core analysis is the directional policy matrix, based on judgemental inputs gathered internationally in order to ensure buy-in to the results. This summarizes the potential of each project as well as the company's strength in the product area. Other analyses cover issues such as development risk and financial flows.

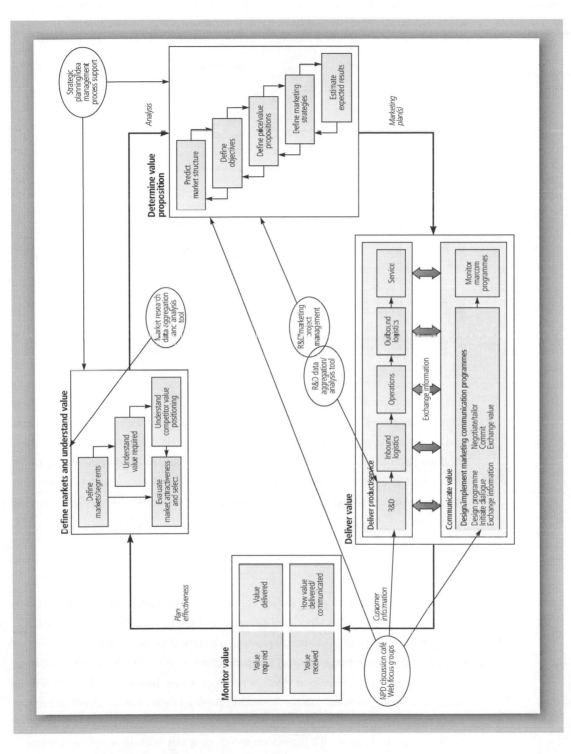

Figure 5.11 IT support for R&D – encouraging innovation

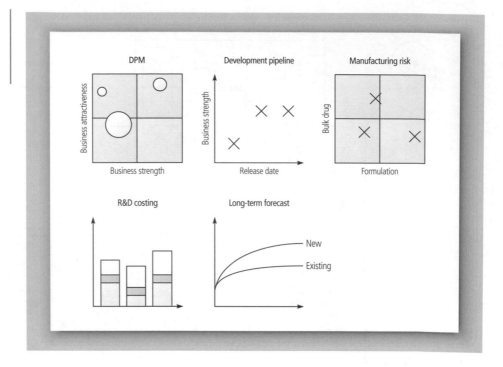

Figure 5.12
R&D planning
support in
pharmaceuticals

The main benefits reported by its users in the pharmaceutical company are greater consensus, due to a depoliticized debate around a common framework, and a better corporate memory of the basis on which decisions had been taken. Vital success factors in making this process work were the involvement of a range of business managers in the system's development, as well as in data input, and the definition of the right cross-functional team to debate the model and take the appropriate decisions.

Causal modelling

One way to understand a marketing variable of importance, such as market size or product sales, is to develop a causal model of the factors affecting the variable. This involves defining a mathematical relationship between a number of independent 'cause' variables and the dependent 'effect' variable whose variation is to be modelled. For example, a product sales model might include as independent variables consumer spending, product price, competitor's price, and advertising and promotion data. Or the dependent variable might be market size, as illustrated in Figure 5.13 (based on a real case but with invented numbers).

	Price	Promotion	Advertising	Consumer spending	BSE index	Market sales
Jan 95	2.11	10	45.1	121	12	1154
Jun 95	2.21	5	40.9	127	11	1213
Jan 96	1.97	15	35.1	131	35	950
Jun 96	1.80	20	50.4	133	32	920
Jan 97	2.05	15	48.3	137	12	1101
Dec 97	2.10	10	35.1	141	14	1081

- If prices drop by 10%, market sales will increase by 7%
- If a serious BSE scare occurs, sales will drop by 23%

Figure 5.13
Causal modelling in a meat products company

To take this example, all other things being equal, total market sales of, say, beef will go up in various circumstances: when the price goes down; when the producers advertise more heavily; and when there are fewer health scares (in this case measured by the number of press releases relating to BSE from the relevant ministry). Through the statistical technique of multiple regression (or various alternatives such as neural net algorithms), the relative importance of the 'cause' variables can be established by examining data from the past (illustrated by six rows in the figure, though in practice many more are required). This means that if the marketer can predict the future value of the 'cause' variables, the computer can predict the corresponding value of the 'output' variable. So the effect on sales of, say, a price war or a future health scare can be anticipated.

Several software routes are available for the construction of causal models. As well as general-purpose statistical packages such as SPSS, some specialist packages are available that specifically target the business modelling market, such as the 4Thought package.

The variable being studied does not necessarily vary with time. Cross-sectional analyses may be performed, for example, comparing the effectiveness of

A causal model can enable market size or share to be predicted and influenced with precision

distributors or stores, or the attractiveness of possible plan, warehouse or outlet locations.

Planning support tools

As shown in Figure 5.9, IT can support a number of marketing planning tasks. The previous section illustrated IT support for portfolio analysis, with particular reference to R&D. Another major area where our case studies encountered IT support was segmentation.

We saw in Chapter 2 that the process of segmentation is rarely straightforward. It is not too difficult to assess whether a segmentation, once proposed, is a good one: the segments will be of adequate size, members will be similar to each other but different from other segments, the segments will be reachable, and the criteria for describing the segments will be relevant to the purchase situation. But there are many possible variables to use in order to divide the potential market into these segments – demographic, geographic, psychographic (relating to attitudes, lifestyle and personality) and behavioural (relating to usage rate, loyalty, purchase patterns etc.). Which variables will relate most closely to the underlying needs-based segmentation is a major issue, but not fundamentally an IT one. IT is, however, relevant in supplying the raw information and providing analysis tools.

Data sources for segmentation

Internal systems mainly hold basic geographic and demographic data. The storage of behavioural data on customers' past usage is increasing, as loyalty cards, electronic point-of-sale systems and websites provide more raw information in consumer markets, and data warehouses allow large files of past behaviour to be economically stored. As we have discussed, though, the main disadvantage of segmenting on the basis of internal data is that information is typically only available on current customers (and possibly lapsed ones and current prospects). Hence the external data sources discussed earlier are often relevant. The uses and limitations of internal data for segmentation are summarized in Figure 5.14.

Profiling

Profiling is one means of combining this internal and external data for which IT support is available. Profiling involves seeing what the customers in the selected

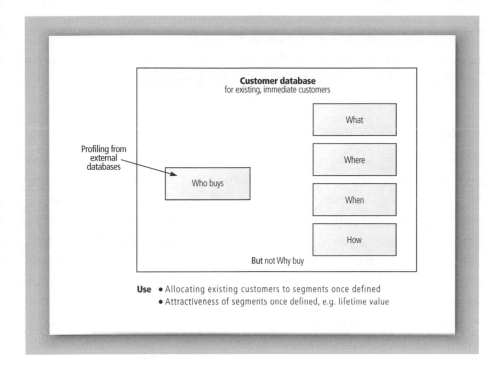

Figure 5.14
Customer
databases in
segmentation

segments have in common, typically based on internal data, and using these criteria to select likely candidates from wider lists. One can analyse, for example, the characteristics of customers who respond well to particular marketing tools, or who are loyal and profitable. The Scottish blood transfusion service, for example, used CACI software to analyse who has the greatest propensity to give blood, resulting in two segments – one an affluent group with high educational qualifications and professional or managerial jobs, and another less well-off group who are public spirited, live close to town centres and probably live alone. This information was used to seek new donors who fell into these segments.

Cluster analysis

IT support is also available to analyse market research data for segmentation purposes. We mentioned in Chapter 2 how cluster analysis can group the respondents into segments relevant to their purchase decisions. The tyre segmentation we described earlier in this chapter was based on a cluster analysis of respondents.

We saw in Chapter 3 that cluster analysis can also be used on internal data. A list of micro-segments can be developed based on numerous variables – who buys, what they buy, and why they buy. Clusters of micro-segments that share the same, or similar, needs are then grouped together to form viable segments.

Geographical information systems

Where geography is a major factor in segmentation, geographical information systems (GIS) may help by providing a graphical interface to the data using maps. Store location is a classic application of GIS, where a map interface may help to define an appropriate catchment area. Woolworth's, for example, used CACI's InSite system to understand the local market, providing information on local population characteristics within each store's catchment area as well as information on local competitors, highlighting the potential for particular products or promotions. This information was used to segment the stores as a basis for product selection and so on.

Segmenting purely on customer attractiveness

In the absence of data on customer needs as a basis for a needs-based segmentation, some companies conclude that to segment on customer attractiveness – the customer's lifetime value, for example – is at least better than purely undifferentiated treatment of all customers. One of the business-to-business companies we studied, for example, used data from a data warehouse to look at the penetration rates in different segments, penetration rate being measured by considering the number of companies in the segment who currently bought at least some products from the company, compared with the total number of companies in the segment. All other things being equal, a segment with a lower penetration rate was regarded as having higher growth potential than one with a very high penetration rate, particularly if experience in another country showed that the segment was potentially interested in the company's offerings.

Other companies similarly segment primarily on customer profitability, or lifetime value. We do not dispute that this can deliver some quick wins. However, we regard the most powerful combination as being a segmentation on different customer needs, combined with an analysis of the relative attractiveness of the resulting segments on financial criteria. If this is achieved, the company knows

Segment the market using customer needs, then profile segments for that attractiveness

not just which segments to address, but also how to address them in terms of the customers' buying criteria.

Conclusions

We have surveyed the multifarious collection of analyses which fall under the heading of 'analytic CRM'. Returning to their synthesis in the process model of Figure 5.9, we draw out here some overarching conclusions.

External view: market research, not just warehousing

The process map illustrates that marketing is quintessentially the function which matches customer needs to the organization's offerings. But we have seen how internal systems do not collect information on customer needs unless this is consciously attempted. External inputs are required, whether via market research, deliberate extensions to the minimum requirements of a transaction such as taking an order to collect further customer information, or otherwise.

> Internal systems do not collect information on customer needs unless this is consciously attempted

Monitor customer value, not just revenue

Just as segmentation and other tasks in the 'Deliver value proposition' stage suffer from a lack of external information, so the whole task of 'Monitor value' is seriously under-supported in many organizations, which myopically choose only to monitor what they receive, not what they give in return. Hence if sales go down the company has no idea why.

> Many organizations only monitor what they receive, not what they give in return

Need for processes for market-driven segmentation and planning

As well as making data available, market-driven segmentation and planning does not happen without processes being put in place. After 30 years of marketing planning theory, this may seem a strange point to make; but at least two of the companies we recently studied concluded that in order to exploit the possibilities for targeted communications offered by their CRM systems, they needed to call a pause in software development and revamp their planning procedures.

References

(1) Hayward, D. (2000) Leading article, *Computing*, 30 March, 24.

(2) Resource Marketing (2000) Quoted in IT-analysis.com newsletter, 4 April.

(3) Berthon, P., Lane, N., Pitt, L. and Watson, R.T. (1996) 'Marketing communications and the world wide web', *Business Horizons*, September–October, 24–32.

6

Avoiding pitfalls

Implementation issues

➡ Success factors in IT-enabled marketing projects

➡ Managing for results: the benefits dependency network

Introduction

We have completed our review of the marketing process. It will be clear by now, though, that today's marketer sometimes needs to step out of the day-job of following this process, and become involved in major IT-enabled business change projects – the commissioning of a website, the piloting of a mobile commerce facility, the development of an integrated customer database or a data warehouse. This chapter covers issues in successfully carrying through such projects.

Success factors in IT-enabled marketing projects

"Happy families are all alike; every unhappy family is unhappy in its own way."

Tolstoy, *Anna Karenina*

The history of IT is replete with failures

IT has a decidedly mixed track record at increasing the efficiency of white-collar work. The early emphasis on efficiency-based applications in such areas as finance, human resources and distribution has been replete with failures, whether measured by the proportion of projects which fail to meet their objectives, generally reported to be at least 70 per cent – even higher than today's divorce rates – or by IT's overall impact on productivity. To assess the latter, Morgan Stanley economist Stephen Roach[1] compared the productivity gains over a decade in the US service industry, which received about 80–85 per cent of IT investment, with those in US manufacturing, which spent the remaining 15–20 per cent. While service productivity might have been expected to increase more, gains were in fact less than 1 per cent a year, whereas the manufacturing sector managed over 3 per cent. Roach put what productivity gains there had been in services down to longer hours in the office – a far cry from the fears of excess leisure once computers did all the work. As with a family, plenty of things can go wrong in the relationship between the IT function and other areas of the business to cause these failures. Can we do better than Tolstoy and elucidate what these problems are and how to avoid them? A strong theme of research in information systems has been to identify these success factors, producing sizeable lists of such items as the support of senior management, the involvement of users in the design process and the need to adopt new business processes.

And yet despite this understanding, failure rates remain obstinately high.[2] One reason is that the target is a moving one, as the nature of IT projects changes. We have seen that there is a trend towards IT applications at the customer interface, the aim of which is as much to add value as to reduce costs. This change of emphasis from efficiency to effectiveness is a logical one, given that IT projects routinely overshoot their budgets, and that cutting costs alone is a perilous route to business success – none of the top ten discounters from 1962, the year in which Wal-Mart was born, being alive today.[3]

Do these effectiveness-based applications introduce new success factors? There is comparatively little emphasis in research into success factors on differences between application areas, most authors concentrating on developing generic factors independent of the purpose of the system. And yet one might expect the nature of marketing to produce quite different problems and solutions from those found with other functions:

➡ How can rational IT staff, used to automating a business function, deal with the paradoxical notion that marketing is inherently cross-functional, co-ordinating the organization's response to the external environment? Who is their customer?

➡ If the application is at the customer interface, involving the only partially predictable reaction of human beings to IT-enabled business changes, how can the project be thoroughly planned in advance, as IT managers like to do? How can the investment proposal be drawn up?

➡ IT professionals can readily see the similarity of CRM with enterprise resource planning (ERP) as another large integration project. Show a business analyst two computer systems and they will integrate them. But in the case of ERP, this process can take years – at the time of writing, the BBC are still struggling to complete the implementation of SAP which was begun in 1994. How can this be squared with the need to respond rapidly to market changes with new IT-enabled channels?

➡ IT staff like to ask 'the business' (whoever that is) for the 'business strategy' (whatever that is) – which they expect to be predetermined, formalized and explicit – so they can 'support it' by 'solving business problems'. How does this mindset relate to the notion that IT-enabled marketing channels raise strategic choices, such as whether to bypass intermediaries or whether to deliver product/service components remotely, which the board may not even be aware of as options?

➡ Business analysts work through a process of evolving specification documents. How can they work with marketers who by personality are intuitive doers, strong on creativity and weak on process definition?

To be fair, many of these issues are found in applications going back many years. But the continuing struggle of practising managers to deal with them is being brought into sharp focus within the domain of IT-enabled marketing. With CRM high on everyone's agenda, this has become even more of an issue. At the very least, we cannot assume that existing success factor research covers them adequately. In this chapter we therefore build on the relatively sparse previous work in this domain by reporting on the results on this topic from case studies which we have recently conducted.

A synthesis of previous research

In Table 6.1 we summarize previous research on success factors. Leverick *et al.* provide a wide-ranging review of success factor research with particular reference

Table 6.1 A summary of previous research on success factors

Factor	IT/marketing Leverick et al.[4]	CRM Ryals et al.[2]	Marketing decision support Wilson & McDonald[5]	E-commerce Dutta[6]
Determine INTENT				
Gain champion/sponsor	*	*	*	*
Ensure customer orientation		*	*	
Assess CONTEXT				
Identify need for system convergence/co-ordination	*	*		*
Organize round customer		*	*	*
Address culture change in project scope	*		*	
Describe CONTENT				
User involvement in system design	*		*	
Design for flexibility	*			
Manage IT infrastructure	*			*
See other applications	*		*	
Construct intervention PROCESS				
Rapid strategy/action loop			*	
Pilot testing/trial	*		*	
MANAGE intervention process				
Flexibility in project management	*			

to the marketing domain.[4] By way of more specific areas, CRM expert Lynette Ryals and her co-authors provide a comprehensive review of the CRM literature;[2] in Wilson and McDonald, the authors reviewed success factors for marketing decision support;[5] and INSEAD's Professor Dutta examines emerging success factors in e-commerce.[6]

We define success factors as issues influencing the success of an IT-enabled intervention which is designed to effect business change. The project, in other words, is trying to change business practice for the better, not just to introduce another piece of IT. It is sensible, therefore, to look at projects through the prism of change management. We have grouped the factors under headings from a model of IT-enabled change developed by Cranfield's Professor John Ward and Dr Roger Elvin from more generic change research.[7] Ward and Elvin's stages of the change process are as follows:

➡ *Determine the intent:* First, the organization determines why change is needed, sets expectations about potential outcomes and gains commitment to the intervention.

➡ *Assess the context:* An understanding is reached about the organizational and business context within which the intervention is to occur.

➡ *Specify the outcome:* The intent can be distinguished from a specification of the outcome of the intervention, in terms of the particular benefits which are desired.

➡ *Describe the content:* The content is what will change, under the two sub-headings of IT content and business content. These need to be defined and responsibilities assigned.

➡ *Construct the intervention process:* Here, the organization designs a process for implementing the content changes defined above, including a business case and plan.

➡ *Manage the intervention process:* The intervention process designed in the previous stage needs to be carried out, with modifications as necessary to ensure an outcome that satisfies the intent.

➡ *Assess satisfaction of the intent:* Finally, the degree to which the objectives of the intervention have been met, both in terms of content and outcome, can be assessed.

We have excluded two of these stages from our scope within this chapter, 'Specify outcome' and 'Assess satisfaction of intent'. The issue of the desired outcome varies substantially between different types of system, as we saw in Chapters 2 and 4, and we have dealt with the development of success measures in Chapter 5.

For simplicity we have omitted from Table 6.1 and subsequent consideration various well-established success factors for all IT projects on which we have little to add – but clearly these should not be forgotten. These are: the importance of clear and early definition of requirements; the need to link the IT system to business objectives; the need to have an adequate implementation plan; the need for adequate resources; the helpfulness of prior-user experience with IT and of support from any internal IT department; the importance of ease of use; and the need for adequate training.

We will discuss the factors of Table 6.1 briefly below.

Determine intent

As with other IT applications, top management sponsorship and the presence of a champion to drive the intervention are widely recognized as important. The potentially far-reaching effects of e-commerce lead Dutta to take the tough position that the Internet should be 'a top strategic priority for your CEO'. If the project's aim is to add to customer value, this needs to be complemented by a customer or market orientation – or at least by the perception of the need for it, in which case the project's scope should aim to increase it.

Assess context

The IT context of a project includes the existing set of systems. Leverick *et al.* emphasize the need for 'compatibility and integration with other marketing IT projects'. Ryals *et al.* go beyond this to the need for a plan for customer-facing systems to converge so as to give a single view of the customer or competitors. The wider organization also needs to be aligned around the customer, either through the organizational structure or through cross-functional teams. A further element of the context which has implications for the project scope is any adverse aspects of organizational culture, Wilson and McDonald, for example, identifying the need for systems to be 'perceived as empowering not controlling'.

Describe content

Successful system design depends on user involvement, which in this domain may need to be cross-functional. There is nevertheless an important role for the

IT function in ensuring that the IT infrastructure is managed appropriately to ensure synergies between projects and provide a platform for the future. As the customer interface is perhaps more susceptible than some internal applications to the need to respond rapidly to external changes, the need to design for flexibility is important. It may be helpful to see the proposed application in use elsewhere.

Construct intervention process

Dutta emphasizes the need to experiment in the marketplace with a 'rapid strategy/action loop' in order to 'compete in Internet time'. This goes beyond the need to conduct pilot tests.

Manage intervention process

Leverick *et al.* emphasize that project management needs to be flexible in order to respond to unexpected events during implementation and still deliver the desired outcome.

Success factors from case studies

How, then, has our research contrasted with these previous findings? We conducted case studies with five companies applying IT to marketing, to examine the factors which influenced the extent of project success, through 23 face-to-face interviews with IT and marketing managers. Table 6.2 shows the full list of success factors which resulted. New factors, or refinements of previously identified factors, are underlined.

Although we discussed some of these companies in earlier chapters, we briefly summarize the different applications here. Case A involved a project in which intelligence from a marketing database was being used to produce marketing communications targeted at particular segments – a significant step for a utility used to an operational focus in which all customers were treated in exactly the same way. Case B was the implementation of a second-generation sales force automation package within an electricity generator. Case C followed the progress of a business-to-business e-commerce project within a paper manufacturer. Case D involved rewriting a business school's direct mail application to ensure year 2000 compatibility, and simultaneously

Table 6.2 Findings on success factors for e-marketing projects

Factor	Full description
Determine the INTENT	
Gain champion/sponsor	A sponsor is needed, preferably at board level, to sell a proposed project and to build commitment across relevant functions. This may be a marketing, sales or IT director, but if cross-functional commitment is not gained, non-optimal 'silo' applications can result.
Ensure market orientation	The organization needs a market orientation, or at least the perception of the need for it, if an IT system is to be accompanied by the necessary business changes and deliver the intended benefits.
Define approval procedures which allow for uncertainty	Applications which aim to increase efficiency may be cost- justified precisely. But effectiveness-based applications are difficult to predict, even if the case is strong. Project approval procedures should recognize this. Otherwise project champions resort to spurious accuracy to gain project acceptance.
Gain board awareness of strategic potential of IT	If the board regards IT as merely a support function to keep the business running smoothly, ideas for major initiatives at the customer interface are unlikely to flourish.
Assess the CONTEXT	
Identify need for business system convergence internally and co-ordination externally	An explicit IT strategy for marketing should be developed to ensure that disparate projects can be integrated to deliver a single organizational view of the customer, product or competitors.
Organize round customer	As marketing becomes data-driven, its need to integrate closely with other functions increases. A joint sales/marketing director may be more conducive to IT-enabled marketing applications. Failing that, close teamwork on joint processes is necessary, such as with cross-functional process teams.
Address culture change in project scope	The project plan needs to address any requirement to change organizational culture, such as addressing staff willingness to share data, rather than leaving this issue until later or ignoring it.

Table 6.2 Continued

Factor	Full description
Describe CONTENT	
Involve users <u>interactively</u> in system design	Users of a system, or their representatives, need to be closely involved in such tasks as requirement specification. <u>This involvement works best if it is interactive: users may not have the skills to write requirements specifications, while they may not understand written specifications produced by IT staff.</u>
Design for flexibility	The difficulty in getting IT right first time, combined with the need to phase and a changing environment, necessitate the inclusion of flexibility as a key design constraint. Rapidly changing IT platforms and business needs require independence and generalizability of data models.
Manage IT infrastructure	While user departments may believe they have the skills to bypass the IT function, there is a need for co-ordination of IT infrastructure to ease future support and development, and to exploit the cross-functional and, indeed, inter-organizational nature of customer-facing processes.
<u>Leverage models of best practice</u>	Where available and suitable, the use of minimally tailored software packages can embed aspects of best marketing practice, as well as reducing development risks.
Construct intervention PROCESS	
Rapid strategy/action loop to experiment <u>and gain credibility</u>	Relaxed timescales render a project vulnerable due to loss of key sponsors, organizational restructuring, external events and so on. A phased approach can help to build the credibility of those driving the change through the visibility of early deliverables. 'Big-bang' approaches are more vulnerable to cancellation due to perceived lack of progress.
Prototype <u>new processes, not just IT</u>	Effectiveness-based marketing applications may have profound implications for internal or external processes and relationships. These need prototyping just as much as the IT; if left too late the IT will constrain necessary modifications to the initial plan.
MANAGE intervention process	
<u>Manage for delivery of benefits, not specification</u>	Documents such as requirement specifications may need refining during implementation, if the intended benefits are to be achieved. The implementation process needs to reflect this need for flexibility.

Note: Underlined text indicates new or modified factors compared with previous research

integrating the application with an order-handling system to provide a more flexible platform for the future. Case E covered the development and early use of a marketing analysis system which held statistics on sales and market size by product type and by market, using OLAP (online analytical processing) technology, in order to aid the identification of promising opportunities and the evaluation of campaigns in a business-to-business components distributor.

We will briefly discuss each factor, with particular emphasis on new and modified factors.

Gain champion/sponsor

Board-level backing was cited in all cases as crucial, with particularly strong evidence in the utility, in which a new marketing board member had proved essential to CRM initiatives. The dangers of championship from a limited range of functions was shown by the paper manufacturer, in which the aim of an integrated customer interface had in the past been hampered by differing views of different directors.

Define approval procedures which allow for uncertainty

This factor was introduced in Case B, in which the risk-averse culture of this electricity generator – a healthy and understandable attribute as far as its core operations were concerned – seemed to be a barrier to investment in sales automation, an area where a degree of risk about benefits is inevitable, customer behaviour being outside the direct control of the business. But not investing also had its dangers, in the view of one interviewee:

> *"* Did a better profile of customers arise from implementation of this IT, or from something that the account manager did differently, or from pure luck? Quantifying benefits is particularly hard in our business ... But sometimes you need the investment just to stay competitive in the marketplace. How do you quantify that? *"*

Clearly a degree of control is needed over the approval of capital-intensive projects from limited resources. The components distributor found a balance through flexible R&D budgets, which could be used to provide seedcorn funding until benefits could be better quantified.

A risk-averse culture needs to accept that CRM investments, however compelling, are inherently uncertain

Gain board awareness of strategic potential of IT

The business school showed the powerful shift from a costs focus to a benefits focus that could occur when the strategic nature of IT investments was recognized in board-level appointments.

Organize around the customer

Although the utility had an organization primarily around the product line, this was being successfully counterpointed by cross-functional teams to champion the customer perspective. The paper manufacturer showed the problems that can occur if marketing and sales departments are divorced under separate directors, with the two sometimes pulling in different directions.

Involve users interactively in system design

The utility case introduced the notion that user involvement in system design needs to be face-to-face, not just at a distance through the writing and review of specification documents. Here, as in other cases, business analysts reported that unlike users in domains such as finance, marketers were not necessarily skilled in the detailed process thinking needed for writing or reviewing specifications – a problem recognized by one marketer:

> *Marketers need to be involved face-to-face in design, not just sent specifications*

" We write things from a flowery marketing perspective. But our requirements specifications become tablets of stone. *"*

Furthermore, the nature of the domain required creativity in the definition of new processes, which was aided by the interactivity of face-to-face meetings. A workshop approach was proving productive in the electricity generator, in contrast to experience on a previous project which concentrated on written documents:

" The requirements specification was inches thick, and it still doesn't do what the users want. Because someone had to write out line by line what the system must do. That's extremely difficult for anyone, let alone the user who just wants the outputs, and doesn't wish to concern himself with inputs or processing. *"*

Design for flexibility

The importance of designing a system in such a way that it can readily be changed to meet future requirements was widely recognized. The electricity generator

provided a clear comparison between generations of the same system, the second generation being based closely on an off-the-shelf package to aid in future tailoring and support.

Rapid strategy/action loop

While the literature cites a changing competitive environment as the motivation for a rapid strategy/action loop, both the utility and the electricity generator added the problem of a changing internal environment. A long project may seem rational to the developers, but leaves it open to cancellation due to management changes, or a loss of faith from managers who do not understand the waterfall model of development and do not perceive progress until they see the resulting system. A clear vision, combined with short-term 'quick wins' which gain credibility, seemed the best approach for major projects.

Long projects, however rational, can suffer a loss of faith

Ensure market orientation

In the business school, in which the organization's culture and processes are focused strongly around understanding and responding to customer needs, these needs acted as a spur to enhance IT systems at the customer interface. In the utility and the components distributor, by contrast, a conscious perception that the organization needed to improve its customer focus was one of the motivations for IT developments to enable and embed corresponding process changes.

Need for IT convergence/co-ordination

In all but one of the cases, the project studied formed part of a longer-term initiative towards the development of an integrated customer repository, from which all customer-facing systems would draw. Limited benefits from the integration so far achieved were reported in the utility and the business school.

Address culture change in project scope

The argument that projects need to address the issue of cultural change was made by numerous interviewees, for example one in the utility:

❝ It's easier to move on the harder issues like technology than the softer ones. If you think about our interfaces [between parts of the organization], the biggest thing is culture. But we start with the hard systems first. ❞

Manage IT infrastructure

Past experience in the electricity generator and the business school supports the view that a danger of commercial functions taking on responsibility for IT systems is the lack of attention to IT infrastructure issues that can result. In both cases, the IT infrastructure is now more actively managed through stronger central control, although responsibility for specific applications is shared with user departments.

Leverage models of best practice

The electricity generator case introduced this widely-corroborated factor, through the observation that the second generation of the sales automation system benefited from being based more closely on an off-the-shelf package, which allowed the organization to benefit from the experience of others in refining best practice.

Prototype new processes, not just IT

This factor was introduced by the case of the paper manufacturer, in which the plans from the IT department for a new system did not seem to involve the testing of some plausible but far-reaching assumptions about the effect of EDI on both the organization and its customers. Although the case provided no evidence as to whether the authors' concerns over this were justified, the components distributor case showed the benefits which can occur when new processes are prototyped at an early stage. Here, the business case for further system development was clarified, as well as steering the system development in the light of the process prototyping.

Manage for delivery of benefits, not specification

This factor gave a more precise wording to the previously-identified factor of 'flexibility in project management'. There need to be limits to flexibility if projects are ever to complete, the electricity generator's project for example benefiting from a strict time limit. But limiting time or resources can backfire, as previous experience in the utility had shown:

> Project management must focus on whether the intended benefits are being achieved, not on the specification

"If you're not careful, your timescales become the drivers. You then come into descoping. Then what you get isn't what you really wanted. And having delivered to timescale, you spend the next six months sorting out the problems."

In this case, the need was identified to review requirements during the project to ensure that these were indeed adequate to deliver the required benefits:

" We need a review and challenge exercise six or eight weeks down the line, to say, 'do we still mean that'? It's all a matter of communication between owner and implementer. There's a steerage that's needed during implementation, to add clarity as to what needs delivering. "

Conclusions

Our results support various success factors identified by previous researchers: the importance to the success of IT/marketing initiatives of a market orientation; the need for business system convergence on a single view of customers and other entities such as competitors; the need to include cultural change issues within the project's scope; the need to design for flexibility; and the need to manage IT infrastructure.

Further light has been shed on certain other factors:

| A board-level champion is not enough. Genuine cross-functional commitment is needed

➡ We have seen that in this domain, the commonly-cited need to gain a board-level champion may not be enough. Commitment is often needed across numerous functions which deal with the customer: without such strong, genuine commitment, non-optimal 'silo' applications can result, in which the potential benefits of a single view of the customer in terms of understanding customer value, prioritizing resources on profitable customers, and understanding how to satisfy particular customer segments, cannot be fully realized.

| Separate directors for sales and marketing can be problematical

➡ A related point is that separate directorships for sales and marketing can be problematical. While a primary organizational structure around products can be effectively complemented by cross-functional teams focusing on the customer, the evidence we have seen strengthens the argument recently made by Hugh Davidson, author of *Even More Offensive Marketing*,[8] among others that organizations can best be viewed in the three major blocks of supply management, operations and demand management, which should arguably each have a single director responsible for them, or at the least should be designed coherently.

➡ We have added to the reasons for a 'rapid strategy/action loop' the observation that long-term projects seem particularly vulnerable to cancellation due to structural or personal changes, or simply due to perceived lack of progress, whether grounded in reality or not. This presents a problem given that implementing an integrated CRM suite or adding an Internet channel takes a great deal of work. The circle can be squared by defining 'quick wins' that collectively contribute to a long-term vision.

➡ Once a project is under way, effective communication between IT staff and their commercial counterparts is, as always, an issue, given the very different cultures they inhabit – as one interviewee put it, 'IT are from Mars, marketing are from Venus'. We have found that 'user involvement' needs to be interactive and face to face: sending specifications to each other for comment (whether on paper or electronically) simply doesn't seem to work. We recall the finding of Bartlett and Goshal that in many organizations disastrous consequences ensued when the generation and transmission of reports replaced direct communications from people representing their own ideas, analyses and proposals.[9] Instead, they advocated 'reinforcing the rope bridge of systems-based communication with the steel girders of frequent personal contact'. We have also found that personal contact needs to continue through the IT development cycle, rather than stopping once a specification is defined, if the project's benefits are to be realized.

> IT are from Mars, marketing are from Venus

➡ The IT itself is not the only area where iteration may be required before the right solution is found. We have also found that in this domain, in which IT is likely to be an enabler to radically different processes, those processes also benefit from being prototyped. As one successful implementer of an e-commerce channel argued to us, the best decision he took was to build a link to back-end fulfilment and finance processes into his very first pilot, as ironing out these processes was a key to success.

> Prototype new processes, not just new IT

We have also identified three success factors which were not present in the existing success factors research we surveyed:

➡ Leveraging a model of best practice embedded in an off-the-shelf system can, at least, reduce the risk involved in development of bespoke software. A CRM package can ensure that all customer-facing packages draw on a common data model, while a package for such management tasks as market segmentation, econometric modelling and marketing planning can implicitly provide a standardized process for these tasks.

➡ Given the strategic decisions implicit in CRM projects, it is not sufficient for the board to empower an IT director, or anyone else, to propose and develop systems. The board needs to be aware of IT's strategic capability, and actively involved in formulation of IT strategy.

➡ Rigid approval procedures for capital expenditure can act as a barrier to developments with a strong rationale but a degree of risk, favouring less important but more secure projects. Risk can be incorporated in the calculation of such measures as customer lifetime value, allowing risk to be taken account of without ruling out risky developments. Another loosening of traditional procedures we found effective was to set aside seedcorn funding in advance, which can be used to fund potentially important pilot projects quickly. Without such measures, project proponents will simply cook the books, underplaying risks and leaving the board in a worse position to manage those risks carefully.

> If marketing is still suffering from mid-life crisis, the younger discipline of IT is surely still suffering from adolescence

If marketing is still suffering from mid-life crisis, the younger discipline of IT is surely still suffering from adolescence, with all its attendant delusions of grandeur pierced by dramatic failures. The marriage of this undoubtedly talented couple may be no more troubled than most, but troubled it still is. The themes which need to be pursued in their joint therapy are at least becoming clearer.

Managing for results: the benefits dependency network

There are several threads which run through the chapter so far: the need for marketing personnel to work closely with their IT colleagues; the need for organizational change as well as IT change; the need for the large-scale projects which are so often a feature of today's marketing to be managed so as to deliver benefits to the business, not just an IT system on time and budget. All easier said than done. Fortunately, a project management tool has recently been developed at Cranfield which at least assists greatly with these tasks: the *Benefits Dependency Network* (BDN).[10] Instead of simply listing project elements and tracking their resourcing and timescales, this tool works backwards from the project's objectives to ensure that all necessary business changes are made, as well as any necessary IT developments completed. A simplified example from one project we studied, a gift manufacturer's extranet for retailers, is shown in Figure 6.1.

The main elements of the network are as follows:

➡ First, *drivers* of the project are defined, based on the nature of the opportunity in relation to the strategy from the application portfolio. A driver is a view by

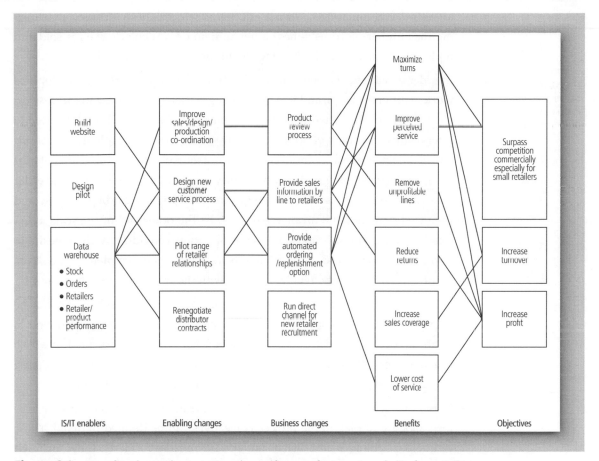

Figure 6.1 Benefits dependency network: a gift manufacturer's website for retailers

top managers as to what is important for the business, such that the business needs to change in response. In this case, the drivers (which are not shown in the figure) included the directors' desire to expand beyond their current profitable but small niche, and their recognition that this would imply reducing the organization's dependence on a small number of large retailers.

➡ The *investment objectives* are then a clear statement of how the project under consideration will contribute to achieving effective beneficial changes in relation to one or more of the drivers. In this example, the objectives related to turnover, profit, and market share of the small retailer segment.

➡ In order to achieve these objectives, some *benefits* will need to be delivered to different stakeholders, including customers. These are now explicitly identified and quantified. For the gift manufacturer, these included maximizing the number of 'turns' – how often an item on a retailer's shelf is sold and replenished each year; minimizing the number of returns; and so on.

➡ In order to achieve the benefits, it is necessary for organizations and people to work in different ways, and it is these changes that are captured in the *business changes* part of the network. In this case, business changes included the need to offer retailers a variety of options for how stocks would be replenished. At one end of the scale, a retailer could choose to 'outsource' much of the selling of gifts to a manufacturer-provided facility on the website, which could select and order gifts, keep them replenished, change the gift range according to past and predicted demand, and arrange payment. At the other end of the scale, other retailers could simply choose to use information provided by the website to inform their own decisions on what gifts to order, when to replenish and so on. By offering a choice, the retailer was left with the important sense of control.

➡ Other one-off changes may also be required before the technology can be implemented, for example to define new processes which are needed, and to establish organizational roles and skills sets. These are termed *enabling changes.* Here, these included the renegotiation of contracts for the existing agent network, and a piloting exercise with a handful of retailers.

➡ It is only when this analysis has been carried out that the specific role technology will play in the project's objectives can be defined in detail. These technology changes are listed under *IS/IT enablers.* Here, they included extensions to the company's core operational systems, as well as introduction of the website itself.

We have found that using this technique for e-commerce projects seems to require an iterative approach. In more traditional IT projects the network is used to ensure that the technology and business changes will deliver benefits required to meet the business drivers. Given the current stage of innovation with e-commerce, a further iteration starting with 'what can technology enable us to do?' is needed, to explore the potential changes and consequent benefits that could result. Balancing this more creative use of the BDN with the more outcome-focused, analytical use proved valuable both in uncovering new options and in realistically assessing what could be achieved.

We found that though time-consuming to apply – a thorough BDN typically taking two half-day workshops – this tool is invaluable for fleshing out the business changes which are needed to make the new use of technology effective if an e-commerce project is to succeed. This can also lead to more rational decisions on whether to proceed with a project: in one case, a forward-looking BDN brought to light such a scale of business transformation that the company decided it could not currently afford to proceed.

What was the result of the BDN's development in this gift company? It pointed out that many of the business changes relied on the managing director, clarifying the need for a new sales appointment, which was rapidly made. It also made clear that a pilot was needed to flesh out how retailers could best be supported online, as well as how the organization needed to adapt to complement the website itself. Most importantly, it convinced senior management that it needed to devote enough time to the relevant business changes and that this was not purely an IT exercise.

The company had experienced considerable difficulties in the past with new computer systems, due not to the system itself as much as the accompanying organizational changes which had not been fully thought through beforehand. The level of rigour demanded by the BDN was not universally popular – salespeople rarely welcome being hauled into meetings of any sort – but the company was left well placed to avoid a similar expensive mess.

The tool needs, though, to be used at the right point in the planning process. Notice that it is not possible to get as far as listing benefits which will be sufficient to achieve the intended objectives, let alone listing business changes, until the market is well understood and the strategic rationale for the proposed project is clear. That's why we have delayed covering this fine management tool until the end of Chapter 6! However, once a well-thought-through marketing strategy is defined, we believe the BDN to be a real contribution to the crucial issue of implementation.

> The benefits dependency network is invaluable for fleshing out the business changes which are needed if benefits are to be delivered

Summary

There are still some marketers for whom one quarter is much like the last. But such is the rate of business change, and the importance of IT-enabled routes to market, that most marketing practitioners need to develop project management skills to cope with large-scale business change projects.

In many ways, major marketing projects are no different from others: they need strong support from the top, close interactive involvement of business managers in the specification process for new IT systems, and forward planning of the business changes which will need to accompany these systems.

But we have identified some respects in which marketing projects can be a little different. Because marketing itself spans organizational boundaries, its projects tend to as well, necessitating cross-functional board support, process design and cultural change. And because marketing is about serving customers whose reactions to our change initiatives can never be predicted with certainty, there is a need to design and implement projects with flexibility, remembering that the objective is not simply to implement the original blueprint, but to deliver the intended benefits, even if that requires changes along the way.

In our experience, the benefits dependency network provides a valuable framework for addressing some of these issues, in particular ensuring that all the relevant aspects of business change are identified early on, and focusing the project firmly on its intended benefits.

References

(1) Griffith, V. (1997) 'Freedom fantasy: an interview with Stephen Roach', *Financial Times*, 13 August.

(2) Ryals, L., Knox, S. and Maklan, S. (2000) *Customer Relationship Management (CRM): Building the business case*. London: FT Prentice Hall.

(3) Kumar, N., Scheer, L. and Kotler, P. (2000) 'From market driven to market driving', *European Management Journal*, **18**(2), 129–42.

(4) Leverick, F., Littler, D., Bruce, M. and Wilson, D. (1998), 'Using information technology effectively: A study of marketing installations', *Journal of Marketing Management*, **14**, 927–62.

(5) Wilson, H.N. and McDonald, M.H.B. (1996) 'Computer aided marketing planning: The experience of early adopters', *Journal of Marketing Management*, **12**, 391–416.

(6) Dutta, S. (2000) *Success in Internet Time*, Working paper, Fontainebleau: INSEAD.

(7) Ward, J. and Elvin, R. (1999) 'A new framework for managing IT-enabled business change', *Information Systems Journal*, **9**, 197–221.

(8) Davidson, H. (1997) *Even More Offensive Marketing*. Penguin Books.

(9) Bartlett, C.A. and Goshal, S. (1995) 'Changing the role of top management: Beyond systems to people', *Harvard Business Review*, May–June, 132–42.

(10) Ward, J.M. and Murray, P. (2000) *Benefits Management Best Practice Guidelines*, Bedford: Cranfield University School of Management.

7

Focusing on tomorrow's customer

Future trends and the implications for marketing practice

➡ The changing customer

➡ Styles of planning in the digital age

➡ Measurement and accountability

➡ Marketing and organizational structure

The changing customer

We have presented a map of the marketing function, incorporating tools to position the organization in the market of tomorrow. But notwithstanding the loss of innocence in the Internet world, markets continue to change at a prodigious rate, providing powerful forces for change in every company. We end this book with some reflections on what the future might hold for marketing and its place within the organization.

Let us start with the customer. How are our customers changing their demands on us? Here are just a few examples:

> Customer expertise. sophistication and power is increasing in consumer and business markets alike

➡ *Trends in customer behaviour.* Today's first-world consumer is more highly educated, under higher stress, more specialized, living longer, and more influenced by global culture than those of the 1960s and 1970s when our view of marketing was formed. This is resulting in various changes to consumer behaviour, such as: an increased pressure on shopping time; a trend towards outsourcing by consumers, as in the increase in ready meals; increased consumer rationality; a fragmentation of consumer markets; and, overall, an increase in the consumer's power relative to the producer's. Nor are these trends specific to consumers. Customer expertise, sophistication and power is increasing likewise in industrial goods and services markets. This power shift stems partly from the concentration of buying into fewer hands, evident in many industries, and partly from the development of buyer groups, networks and alliances, all recent phenomena which have swung market control away from manufacturers.

➡ *The trend to consumer outsourcing.* The time spent by Americans in shopping malls has dropped from 30 hours per month to 7, partly due to longer working hours, but also due to the increased time spent in the IT-mediated worlds of the TV and Internet, the latter accounting for an hour a day among users. The numerous activities which are thus being squeezed, such as shopping and cooking, are increasingly being 'outsourced', only one meal in three being cooked in the home, with ready meals and meals out accounting for the other two-thirds. With an increased proportion of the workforce in self-employment, and many of the remainder being paid on deliverables rather than on time spent, the awareness of the opportunity cost of time is increasing.

➡ *Consolidation of e-shopping.* The mass of start-ups which occur in any new industry has certainly been seen with consumer websites. Between 1894 and

1903, 20,000 telephone companies were started in the US, eventually dropping to one. Of the 1,000 US car manufacturers in the 1920s and 1930s, only two survived. How many of our 20,000-odd e-tailers will still be there in ten years? If the experience in other industries is anything to go by, we will be left with some major players, plus a range of highly-targeted niche operators, like Simply Organic, the grocery store used by one of the authors, which sells products such as 'organic goat gouda with nettle and onion' to a sparse but profitable segment. The major players would, perhaps, number no more than one or two per major category. Contrary to popular belief, the argument of economies of scale certainly applies online, where the expense of serious website development and fulfilment is high and the marginal cost per new order relatively low. An examination of Amazon's quarterly accounts shows this clearly. Amazon's plans to reach profitability depend (among other factors) on reducing fulfilment costs from 15 per cent, on $2.5 billion of revenue in 2000, and the 13 per cent achieved by Q3 2001, to the 8–9 per cent which could be achieved, they believe, on revenues of $6 billion.

> Of the 1000 US car manufacturers in the 1920s and 1930s, only two survived

➡ *Home delivery.* Rationalization is inevitable in home delivery to cope with the increased demand and high service expectations of online consumers. Local drop-off points or boxes outside the home are being experimented with, for example, in Helsinki, and some such mechanism is sorely needed.

How can we make our organizations sufficiently responsive to cope with the high rate of change that this changing customer behaviour will engender? Part of the answer, we believe, is in the use of marketing planning tools which allow for rapid change, such as those we have outlined. But is the very concept of annual planning cycles too staid for today's markets?

Styles of planning in the digital age

Evolution and revolution

Strategy formation in practice is rarely the ordered, rational process of textbooks, in which a senior management team uses a predefined sequence of management tools to draw its conclusions, which are then scrupulously acted on over the forthcoming year. In some organizations, instead of this 'rational planning' approach, strategy is mainly the result of gut judgements made by the chief executive – a 'command' approach. In others, strategy evolves through a series of smaller decisions made on the problem of the moment – a 'rational incremental' approach. Most commonly, organizations actually adopt a mix of these various ingredients in differing proportions, so they can be regarded as 'dimensions' rather than exclusive alternatives.

After decades of inconclusive research endeavouring to find a link between a 'rational planning' style and better business results, strategy researchers now presume that the best approach will depend on circumstances – the nature of the industry, the positioning of the organization within it, the rate of change in the environment and so on. This is sometimes termed the 'congruence' between strategy formulation and the internal and external environment.

How, then, should one plan for e-commerce, m-commerce, interactive TV and so on? Should one plan at all, indeed, or just act? The mood of academic writings has followed that of the wider business community over the past two or three years. Before the technology crash of early 2000, revolution formed a dominant metaphor, with much emphasis on entrepreneurial management styles, experimentation and rapid change. While no one wants to go back to the excessively bureaucratic, inward-looking and unimaginative planning that formal strategy processes can so often result in, the aftermath of the crash has caused much reflection on how to achieve the best balance.

> While no-one wants to go back to bureaucratic, unimaginative planning, a balance is needed

The conventional wisdom that in the new economy time is too short for formal strategy exercises has been undermined by the recent fate of many of the dotcoms which had previously been lauded for their fleetness of foot. This new mood of 'more haste, less speed' has been typified by the already classic article by Porter, and is evident for example in his debunking of the 'myth of the first mover' which has motivated so much precipitate action.[1] There was, he argued, a

" general assumption that the deployment of the Internet would increase switching costs and create strong network effects, which would provide first movers with competitive advantages and robust profitability . . . This thinking does not, however, hold up to close examination . . . On the Internet, buyers can often switch suppliers with just a few mouse clicks. "

As for network effects:

" It is not enough for network effects to be present; to provide barriers to entry they also have to be proprietary to one company. The openness of the Internet, with its common standards and protocols and its ease of navigation, makes it difficult for a single company to capture the benefits of a network effect. America Online, which has managed to maintain borders around its online community, is an exception, not the rule. "

The costs of change

The change of mood is also reflected in the choices made by journal editors, the *Harvard Business Review* for example seeking out interviews with 'old economy' figureheads such as Nestlé's CEO Peter Brabeck, who argues that continuous improvement is just as successful an approach as radical change, and often a more appropriate one for long-established, broadly successful companies – and, indeed, Nestlé's $3 billion of annual profit is difficult to argue with.[2] His answer to the question 'What's wrong with radical change?' is simple: 'What's so good about it? Big, dramatic change is fine for a crisis. But not every company in the world is in crisis all the time.' But is there a price to pay for evolutionary change?

// 'Yes, you're unspectacular. There are certainly many companies out there that are very sexy, like a 20-year-old girl. Everyone wants to know about them. We are not that. We don't want to be. Our company is more like a 40-year-old, someone who is strong and trim, and who can easily run 10 miles without being pushed or pulled. *//*

The argument against unnecessary change 'to follow some sort of fad without logical thinking behind it', as Brabeck puts it, is much in evidence at present. Morgan laments how

// with all the transformation efforts going on these days, the workplace seems to have transmogrified into one continual change initiative. Maybe it's a relief to know that only a few of these efforts will actually be carried through to completion, but that knowledge doesn't do much for morale. Change fatigue is rampant, and it's exacerbated by a natural tendency to distrust change that's imposed from above. The remedy, say the experts, flies in the face of the revolutionary approach to change that reigned during the dotcom era's heyday: Pare down the number of initiatives. Be less preoccupied with large-scale transformation, and focus instead on small improve-ments. Above all, lose the notion that you need heroic leaders in order to have meaningful, sustained change. *//* [3]

The importance of ensuring that change initiatives are not imposed unnecessarily from above is taken up by Henry Mintzberg:

// The notion that change comes from the top is a fallacy driven by ego, the cult of heroic management, and the peculiarly American overemphasis on taking action. If companies in fact depended on dramatic, top-down change, few would survive.

Instead, most organizations succeed because of the small change efforts that begin in the middle or bottom of the company and are only belatedly recognized as successful by senior management.*'*

He therefore advocates that our notions of the role of the leader be modified to one rather like a queen bee, which 'does nothing but make babies and exude a chemical that keeps everything together' (Mintzberg, quoted in Morgan[3]).

What does this chemical glue need to achieve? One important role is to co-ordinate initiatives which may have been begun lower in the organization. As change expert Rosabeth Moss Kanter argues in her latest book *Evolve!*[4], innovative companies that once thrived on decentralization and internal entrepreneurship find that the Internet forces an unfamiliar degree of integration and knowledge sharing. But the CEO cannot achieve this co-ordination single-handedly: for the initiator of an idea, horizontal influencing skills within the organization are important, analogous to the intrigues within a court to develop court backers and supporters: the newer the idea, the more important this coalition building.

The role of strategy tools

| There are limits to how much change organizations can absorb at once

It is, perhaps, premature to endeavour to pull together this new mood into a consensus on the role of strategy and planning in e-commerce. But the common threads are, it seems, beginning to emerge: the leader as a co-ordinator of initiatives which originate from all levels; the limits to how much change organizations can absorb at once, and a recognition of the significant work involved in following through a change initiative; and the importance of careful rational thought, as exemplified in strategy tools and techniques, to validate ideas. Of the three styles of strategy formation with which we started this section, this amounts to something closest to the 'rational incremental' model.

| Strategy tools can help check out whether gut feel matches market reality

What is the role of strategy tools within this model? The tools will not of themselves generate strategy ideas, which can emerge from all sorts of chance discussions, experiments, or insights, by a sort of 'serendipity'.[5] But tools can provide a valuable prism through which to view and dissect new ideas, providing a rational means of checking out whether the gut feel of the idea's proponents matches the reality of the marketplace. Tools can also help with trade-offs between different options if, as Porter argues,[1] trade-offs are vital if companies are to focus on the few areas where they can genuinely achieve a competitive advantage. And they can help with change management, if strategy decisions are to be followed through successfully.

Strategy tools, then, will not necessarily be used only in the context of an annual planning process. Such a regular process may be of value in providing a basic framework for the firm's positioning within its industry, using tools such as five-forces analysis and market mapping. But other tools to assess market acceptance, such as the value curve, may be used within the development of major project proposals. Board evaluation of fully-developed proposals may use a rolling portfolio of current and future initiatives, evaluated under common criteria, such as the portfolio matrices we described earlier. And project implementation may be steered by change management tools such as the benefits dependency network.

Although there may, then, be a logic in continuing to present tools as part of an overall market-focused strategy development process, there can be no sense of failure if they are in fact used in a way more closely tailored to the needs and culture of the organization.

If marketing planning is changing, the role of the marketing function which co-ordinates it is also in flux. We will now turn to the future of the marketing function, how it is organized and how it measures effectiveness.

Marketing measurement and accountability

Business leaders are under intense pressure to deliver against stakeholder expectations: customers are demanding greater levels of customization, access, service and value; shareholders are expecting to see continuous growth in earnings per share and in the capital value of shares; pressure groups are demanding exemplary corporate citizenship.

Meanwhile, the rules of competition have changed The 'make and sell' model has been killed off by a new wave of entrepreneurial, technology-enabled competitors unfettered by the baggage of legacy bureaucracy, assets, cultures and behaviours. The processing of information about products has been separated from the products themselves and customers can now search for and evaluate them independently of those who have a vested interest in selling to them. Customers have as much information about suppliers as suppliers traditionally accumulated about customers, which has created a new dimension of competition based on who most effectively acts in the customers' interests.

On top of all of these pressures, business metrics such as shareholder value added and balanced scorecards, together with pressure from institutional shareholders to report meaningful facts about corporate performance rather than the traditional, high-level financial reporting that appears every year in corporate accounts, are forcing business leaders to re-examine tired corporate behaviours such as cost-cutting, mergers and downsizing as a route to profitability.

Accounts are measured because it is a legal requirement. But the marketing budget is a discretionary spend and historically has never been measured according to any universally accepted and systematic rules. Consequently, the marketing budget is often the first to be cut the moment profits come under pressure. This unprofessional approach, however, is changing rapidly as CEOs demand more accountability, hence measurability, from their marketing colleagues.

Chief executive officers should follow a number of principles when evaluating their organization's marketing processes.

> The marketing budget has never been measured according to any universally accepted and systematic rules

Objectivity

In marketing there are two basic kinds of data: hard data and judgemental data. Hard data measures outputs such as sales volume and value, market size, market share and profit margins. Judgemental data explains the reasons for the outputs. A SWOT analysis, for example, would normally seek to establish how well a particular organization meets the needs or requirements of a defined group of its customers. This presupposes that we actually know what these needs are, and herein lies perhaps the biggest problem of marketing – how to be sure.

Hard data is relatively easy to gather from external databases and most organizations have reasonably good measures of market size, total sales by product or service type and by application. Those which do not can commission such data relatively easily and cheaply from any good market research organization or consultancy. Figure 7.1 illustrates the types of data that all business leaders should ensure their organization has.

But marketing departments should not rely on their own internal database for such information, as this will typically hold data only on current and possibly lapsed customers.

The most important word missing from Figure 7.1 is 'why?' Why do customers and consumers behave the way they do? What motivates them to buy what they buy in the particular way they buy it?

Nearly every independent survey over the past 50 years has indicated a substantial gap between the rational views of suppliers and the real reasons for their customers' actual behaviour. But organizations persist in relying on the

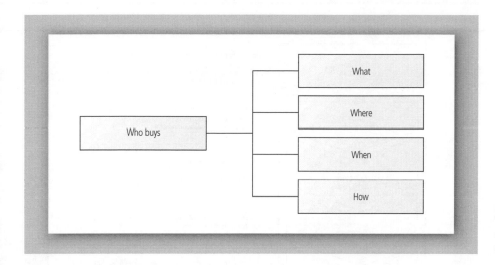

Figure 7.1
Types of data all organizations should have

views of their own managers – the sales force in particular. And more recent evidence indicates that attitudes are not always linked to behaviour: many people approve of a product or an organization, but do not necessarily use it. For example, a recent survey of corporate good citizenship by the Consumers' Association in Britain showed that the three highest-rated companies were performing badly on profits, while the three lowest rated were exceptionally profitable. Another survey showed that Peugeot 106 drivers rated their cars far more highly than Ford Fiesta drivers, though the latter were far more likely to repeat purchase. So business leaders should be careful to ascertain how their marketers gather the motivational information they use and how current it is.

Attitudes are not always linked to behaviour

Marketing metrics

Business leaders need to measure the effectiveness of their organization's marketing efforts. 'Marketing metrics' seek to measure and evaluate customer relationships. The 1980s saw the desktop personal computer explosion, followed by database building. The 1990s saw the customer service movement, sales automation, brand valuation and the balanced scorecard. The end of the twentieth century saw the advent of marketing metrics, partly because of a realization that marketing had never been truly accountable, and partly because technology now allowed senior managers to measure and evaluate customer relationships in a way never previously possible.

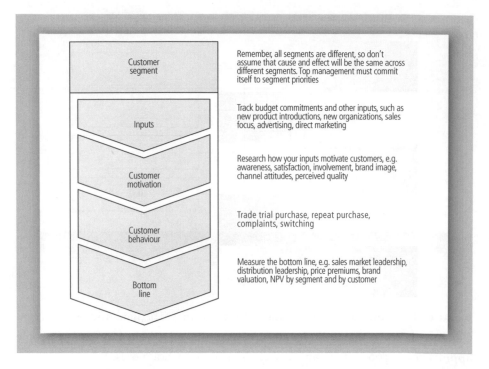

Figure 7.2
Marketing metrics
model

The general rule on marketing metrics should be: 'If you can't measure it, think carefully about whether you should do it.' The general model to follow should be as shown in Figure 7.2.

In the case of the strategic and tactical marketing plans, the major items listed in Table 7.1 need to be measured.

When selecting measures, check:

➡ Alignment – do the measures reflect the objectives and strategy, or are they disconnected?

➡ Actionable – are they directly actionable by someone?

➡ Predictive – can the measures provide early warning signals?

➡ Causal – do they indicate root causes, or are they merely symptoms?

➡ Necessary – will other measures suffice?

➡ Measurable – are they easy to measure and report?

The world's best companies are committed to marketing metrics. Those organizations that continue to ignore the legitimate demands of financial

> If you can't measure it, think carefully about whether you should do it

Table 7.1 Major marketing plan items to be measured

Marketing plans	Measurement
➡ Market segment attractiveness	Track the important factors that make markets more, or less, attractive
➡ SWOT analyses	Measure real strengths and weaknesses, against properly researched customer attitudes and behaviour. Also measure key external indicators
➡ Key issues to be addressed	Track whether key issues have been addressed
➡ Assumptions	Record and track what actually happens
➡ Strategic marketing objectives	Track key success indicators
➡ Strategies, programmes and budgets	Track progress on strategies, programmes and their outcomes

investors for better information about the return on marketing investments are doomed to failure.

Organizational issues and the future of marketing

Given all the principles outlined above, it is nonetheless fundamental that customers are indifferent to any supplier's organizational structure. All they want is the delivery of perfect products or services, on time, in full, whenever and wherever they want them and preferably at the same price everywhere in the world where they operate.

Consider for a moment how difficult, if not impossible, this is for any company that organizes as follows:

1 Around 'production' units, such as factories. Each one will endeavour to optimize its profitability, justifiably making its profit from production rather than based on any market forces.

2 Around 'functions'. With each function attempting to achieve its own objectives, it is extremely difficult, if not impossible, for each department to take account of customer needs in any consistent or coherent way.

3 Around geographical groupings, such as the UK, France, Germany, etc. Here, country 'barons', each with their own profit and loss account, frequently relegate the needs of global customers and markets below their own narrow profit-maximizing motives.

There are, of course, many other possible combinations, none of which will be perfect. No one particular organizational form can be recommended, common sense and market needs being the final arbiters. However, the following factors always need to be considered:

➡ marketing 'centres of gravity'

➡ interface areas (e.g. present/future; salespeople/drawing office; etc.)

➡ authority and responsibility

➡ ease of communication

➡ co-ordination

➡ flexibility

➡ human factors

> It is generally best to organize round customer groups, rather than products, functions or geography

Wherever practicable, however, it appears to be sensible to try to organize around customer groups, or markets, rather than around products, functions or geography. Increasingly, firms are organizing themselves around customers or around processes, such as product development. Quite a large 'industry', known as Business Process Redesign (BPR), grew up around this issue. The Cranfield/Chartered Institute of Marketing research study into the future of marketing has clearly demonstrated that the world's leading companies now organize themselves around customer groups and processes rather than around products. AT&T for example, organize around end-use markets and appoint multi-disciplinary teams to focus their attention on their specific needs. The result is personnel, accounting, production, distribution and sales policies that are tailored specifically to a unique set of market needs.

> The best marketing plans emerge from an inclusive cross-functional process

Finally, in our experience, the very best marketing plans emerge from an *inclusive* process. Fundamentally, marketing planning is simply a process, with a set of underlying tools and techniques, for understanding markets and for quantifying the present and future value required by the different groups of customers within these markets – what marketers refer to as segments. It is a strictly specialist function, just like accountancy or engineering, which is proscribed, researched, developed and examined by professional bodies such as the Chartered Institute of Marketing in Europe and Asia and the American Marketing Association in the USA. Sometimes customer-facing activities such as customer service, selling, product development and public relations are controlled by the marketing function, but often they are not, even though many of them are included in the academic marketing curriculum.

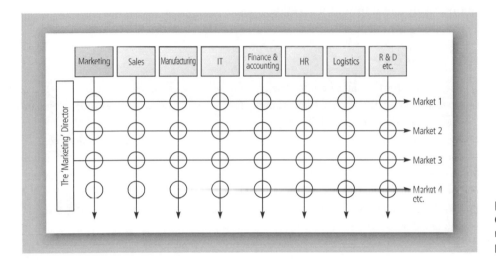

Figure 7.3
Organizing for marketing planning

In the model in Figure 7.3, representatives from appropriate functions are members of market planning teams, with the main body of work being done by the marketing representative who has the professional skills to accomplish the more technical tasks of data and information gathering and market analysis. The team might also include a representative from product development, brand managers, key account managers and so on, depending on circumstances.

The advantages of this approach are as follows:

1 Any plans emerging are based on a deep understanding of the organization's asset base and capabilities.

2 Members of the team 'own' the plan, thus preventing implementation problems later on.

3 The marketing director, or whoever is responsible to the board for integrating and co-ordinating all the plans emanating from this process, can be sure that he or she is not foisting unwanted plans onto reluctant functional heads.

4 Any strategic functional plans, such as IT, logistics, purchasing, R&D and so on, will be genuinely market driven or customer-needs driven rather than production driven.

5 Any business or corporate plans that emerge at a higher level will also be market driven.

This customer-driven process represents the best current practice and is undoubtedly the future of marketing.

References

(1) Porter, M.E. (2001) 'Strategy and the Internet', *Harvard Business Review*, March, 63–78.

(2) Wetlaufer, S. (2001) 'Nestlé's Peter Brabeck: The business case against revolution', *Harvard Business Review*, February, 112–21.

(3) Morgan, N. (2001) 'How to overcome change fatigue', *Burning Questions 2001 Conference*, 1–3, Harvard Business School Publishing.

(4) Moss Kanter, R. (2001) *Evolve! Succeeding in the Digital Culture of Tomorrow*. Harvard Business School Press.

(5) Oke, A. (2001) 'Managing innovation in the service sector', *Management Focus*, **16**, Summer, Bedford: Cranfield University School of Management.

Index

Accountability of marketing *see*
    Marketing measurement and
    accountability
Achiles (financial exchange
    organization), 117
American Marketing Association, 221
Analysis of industry structure *see*
    Market mapping/industry
    structure analysis
Analytical Customer Relationship
    Management (CRM), 174–87
  causal modelling, 182–4
  cluster analysis, 185
  data mining, 176–7
  geodemographic information, 179
  geographical information systems,
      186
  industrial markets information, 179
  lifestyle information, 179
  market research applications, 178
  marketing data warehouses, 174–6
  OnLine Analytical Processing
      (OLAP), 176
  operational Executive Information
      Systems (EIS), 177–8
  planning support tools, 184–7
  profiling, 184–5
  R&D support tools, 180–2
  segmentation on customer
      attractiveness, 186–7
  segmentation data sources, 184
Applix system for CRM, 149–50

Assets, tangible and goodwill, 74–5
Awareness (online) efficiency, 169, 172

Balanced scorecards, 27
Banks, marketing problems, 28, 29
Banner ads, 173
Benchmarking, 73
    see also Marketing measurement and
        accountability
Benefits Dependency Network (BDN),
    204–7
  business changes, 206
  enabling changes, 206
  investment objectives, 205
  project drivers, 204–5
  stakeholder benefits, 205–6
Benefits versus features, 62–3
Brady and Davis, *McKinsey Quarterly*
    1993 article, 2
Brand differentiation, 42
Budgets, marketing, justification
    problems, 2
Business Process Re-engineering (BPR),
    27
Business strategies, and marketing
    departments, 30
Buyers, technical, ignorant and rational,
    165–6

Call centres, 120–1
Campaign management, 150
Car retailing market map, 83–4

Causal models/modelling, 182–4
and IT, 146
Champions/sponsors, 198
Change *see* Marketing strategy and
planning
Channel chain analysis, 91–6
book example, 94–5
channel choice/the channel curve,
93–6
current Lifetime value (CLV), 96
Dell example, 92–3
value curve, Kim and Mauborgne, 95
Channel combinations worksheet, 107
Channel strategy and tactics, 96–103
activity based strategy, 97
channel migrators, 96–7
Cisco's eBusiness value matrix,
99–100
directional policy matrix, 98–9
graduated customer value strategy, 97
integrated multi-channel approach, 97
needs-based segmentation strategy, 97
organizational structure problems, 102
prioritization matrix, 100
project management difficulties, 103
reward systems approach, 102–3
single channel providers, 96
spinning out with new channels, 102
Tjan's Internet Portfolio Map, 99–100
Channel-independent task management,
and CRM, 154
Chartered Institute of Marketing, 221
Cisco's eBusiness value matrix, 99–100
Cluster analysis, 185
CLV (Customer/Current Lifetime
Value), 96, 162–4
Communicating the offer, 20

Competitive forces analysis, 42–9
dimensions of competence, 44–6
e-commerce/IT forces, 43–4
Computer industry, marketing
problems, 28
Consumer outsourcing, 210
Contact (online) efficiency, 170, 172
Conversion (online) efficiency, 171, 172
Core billing systems, 132
Cranfield University School of
Management, 129–30
Critical success factor, 14
CRM *see* Customer Relationship
Management
Current/Customer Lifetime value
(CLV), 96, 162–4
Customer aspects:
behaviour trends, 8, 210
the changing customer, 210–11
and consumer outsourcing, 210
customer intimacy, 45
customer retention, and CRM, 48
customer-centric focus, 51
customer-focused metrics, 162
customized marketing strategy, 135–7
e-shopping consolidation, 210–11
home delivery, 211
needs of and exerting influence on,
2–4
Customer Relationship Management
(CRM):
argument for, 6–8
and brand differentiation, 42
and competitive advantage, 39
CRM audit, 47
and customer requirements, 41–2
and customer retention, 48

definitions, 36–8

and dimensions of competence, 44–6

features, 38

management considerations, 48–9

potential benefits, 40

promised benefits, 38–9

railway equivalencies, 39–40

relationship marketing, 6, 123

and relationships, 48

and segmentation, 41

and targeting, 42

see also Analytical Customer
    Relationship Management
    (CRM)

Customer Relationship Management
    (CRM) systems, 144–55

campaign management, 150

channel-independent task
    management, 154

direct mailing, 149

electronic commerce, 150

Enterprise resource planning (ERP)
    systems, 147–8

packaged software market
    developments, 151–2

sales force automation, 148–9

and software best practice, 153–4

task-independent data management,
    153

telemarketing, 150

Customer/Current lifetime value
    (CLV), 96, 162–4

Data mining, 176–7

Data warehouses, 125, 146

  marketing data warehouses, 174–6

Database technology/application:

analysis databases, 136–7

influence of, 5

integrated data warehouses, 125

integration for analysis, 131–3

and piecemeal customer data, 129–31

see also IT-enabled marketing

Decision maker's identification, and
    market mapping, 53, 56–7

Define markets and understand value
    process, 13–15

Definitions of marketing, 2–4

  new marketing, 10–12

Deliver value proposition process,
    19–20

Dell:

  and channel chains, 92–3

  IT-enabled direct selling, 138–9

  promotion channels, 17–18

Determine value proposition processes,
    12–13, 15–17

  see also Market mapping/industry
    structure analysis

Develop value proposition, 21

Differential/differentiation advantage,
    73, 74

Differentiation strategies, 87

Diffusion of innovation, Everet Rogers,
    22–4

  curve for, 23–4

  rate of diffusion, 23

Digital enterprise, a stage model *see*
    IT-enabled marketing

Dimensions of competence, 44–6

  customer intimacy, 45

  and e-commerce, 46

  operational excellence, 45

  product leadership, 45

Direct mailing, 149
Directional Policy Matrix (DPM), 98–9, 165
Disintermediation, 84, 87
Distribution strategies, 18
Dotcom start-ups and spin-offs, 168
Drivers of change, 22–8

E-commerce/IT:
    Cisco's eBusiness value matrix, 99–100
    competitive forces, 43–4
    and dimensions of competence, 46
    innovators, 9
    see also Internet; IT
E-marketing mix (six Is of), 119–28
    independence of location (death of distance), 126
    individualization, 124–6
    industry restructuring, 127–8
    integration, 120–1
    intelligence, 127
    interactivity, 121–4
    worksheet, 157–8
E-shopping consolidation, 210–11
Egg (finance organization), 9
Electronic commerce, 150
Enterprise Resource Planning (ERP)/Enterprise Systems (ES), 144, 147–8
Evolution see Market maturity and evolution over time
Executive Information Systems (EIS), 144
    operational EIS, 177–8

Faddism, 27
Failure factors/rates see IT success/failure factors/rates

Financial husbandry, and market evolution, 26
Financial services:
    financial services market map, 88–91
    and IT enabled selling, 142
Fortis Bank (Netherlands based), 134
Four Cs, Cost, Convenience, Communications, Consumer wants/needs, 16
Friction-free capitalism, 117–18
Future market mapping worksheet, 106

GAP (clothes retailers), 9
Geodemographic information, 179
Geographical information systems, 186
Goodwill assets, 74–5
Grindley, Professor K.:
    on discipline of IT, 7–8
    on the IT marketing interface, 5–6

Home delivery, 211

Individualization, information-enabled tailoring, 124–6
Industrial market information, 179
Industry structure analysis see Market mapping/industry structure analysis
Innovation, responding to, 81–2
Integrated data warehouses, 125
Integrated marketing communications process, 17–19
Integration, know your customer, 120–1
Interactive communication, 121–4
Internal competence dimensions worksheet, 69
Internal value chain worksheet, 113–14

Internet:
  e-commerce innovators, 9
  and friction-free capitalism, 117–18
  and marketing strategy, 8–10
  on-line prices, 118
  see also E-commerce/IT; IT
Internet booksellers, 140–2
Internet marketing, three Cs, content, community and commerce, 118
IT:
  and database technology, 5
  and planning and innovation, 82
  as a strategy driver, 4–6
  see also E-commerce/IT; Internet
IT success/failure factors/rates, 190–204
  approval procedures definition, 198
  benefit rather than specification delivery, 201–2
  board awareness, 199
  case study findings, 195–7
  champion/sponsor backing, 198
  content describing, 197
  context assessment, 196
  convergence/co-ordination need, 200
  culture change aspects, 200
  designing for flexibility, 199–200
  efficiency and effectiveness, 191
  infrastructure management, 201
  intent determination, 196
  intervention construction and management, 197
  market orientation considerations, 200
  marketing considerations, 191–2
  organizing around the customer, 199
  previous research synthesis, 192–5
  process prototyping, 201
  success factor issues, 190–202
  US service industry, 190
  user interactive involvement, 199
IT-enabled marketing, 128–44
  stage 1: running the business, 129
  stage 2: piecemeal customer data, 129–31
  stage 3: integration for analysis, 131–3
  stage 4: integrated customer interface, 134–5
  stage 5: customized marketing strategy, 135–7
  stage 6: market restructuring, 137–43
IT/customer interface, 144–55
IT/marketing interface, 5–6

Key Discriminating Features (KDFs), 58–61

Lifestyle information, 179
Locatability/attractability (online) efficiency, 170, 172
Low-cost strategies, 87

Managing for results see Benefits Dependency Network (BDN)
Market definition, 49–50
  see also Market segmentation
Market leadership, and dimensions of competence, 44–5
Market mapping/industry structure analysis, 53–7, 83–91
  car dealer example, 83–4
  channel chain analysis, 91–6

Market mapping/industry structure
analysis (*continued*)
differentiation strategies, 87
disintermediation approach, 84, 87
financial services, 88–91
intermediaries, 85–6
low-cost strategies, 87
media switching/addition approach,
85, 87
multi-channel integration/channel
chains, 91–3
niche strategies, 87
partial channel substitution
approach, 85, 87
reintermediation approach, 84
substitute/reconfigured product
approach, 84
Market maturity and evolution over
time, 24–6
Market segmentation, 6–7, 9–10, 49–67
benefits versus features, 62–3
and CRM, 41
on customer attractiveness, 186–7
and customer segmentation/
customer groups, 50–1
and customer-centric focus, 51
customers and transactions, 57–61
data sources for, 184
and decision maker's identification,
53, 56–7
formation of segments, 64–5
growth and decline of segments,
66–7
Key Discriminating Features (KDFs),
58–61
market mapping, 53–7
micro-segments, 61–2, 64

purpose, 51–2
segment checklist, 64–6
Marketing data warehouses, 174–6
Marketing definitions, 2–4
new marketing, 10–11
Marketing function/departments:
banks, 28, 29
board of director relations, 30
budget justification problems, 2, 7
and business strategies, 30
computer industry, 28
marketing map concept, 30–2
organizational issues, 219–22
prerequisites for success, 28–30
strategic marketing planning, 75–81
and tactical marketing, 30
Marketing measurement and
accountability, 215–19
benchmarking, 73
marketing metrics, 217–19
objectivity considerations, 216–17
Marketing Myopia, Levitt, T., 41
Marketing strategy and planning,
73–81
assets, tangible and goodwill, 74–5
and benchmarking, 73
costs of change, 213–14
desired outcomes, 75
differential advantage, 73
differentiation, 74
evolution and revolution, 211–12
innovation, responding to, 81–2
and the Internet, 8–10
IT planning support tools, 146
IT, responding to, 82
IT as a strategy driver, 4–6
mission statements, 78

nine generic properties of good
strategy, 76
planning process, 77–81
planning styles, 211–15
planning timetable, 79–81
products and markets, 73
the strategic marketing plan, 78–9, 80
strategy tools, 214–15
sustainable competitive advantage, 74
SWOT analysis, 79
the tactical marketing plan, 78, 79, 80
see also Channel strategy and tactics;
New marketing
Marketing/IT interface, 5–6
Marks & Spencer (M&S), and financial
husbandry, 26
Measurement of marketing see
Marketing measurement and
accountability
Micro-segments, 61–2, 64
Mintzberg, H., on change, 213–14
Mission statements, 78
Monitor value process, 21–2, 159–87
awareness (online) efficiency, 169, 172
contact (online) efficiency, 170, 172
conversion (online) efficiency, 171, 172
Customer Lifetime Value (CLV),
162–4
locatability/attractability (online)
efficiency, 170, 172
retention (online) efficiency, 171
sales process (online) metrics, 167–73
target surfers, 169
value delivered monitoring, 164–7
value received monitoring, 161–2
see also Analytical Customer
Relationship Management (CRM)

Multi-channel integration/channel
chains, 91–3

'Need to be market driven', 22
New marketing:
definition, 10–11
process overview, 12–22
New media and industry competition
worksheet, 70
Niche strategies, 87

Offline promotions/press advertising,
172
One-to-one marketing see Segmentation
OnLine Analytical Processing (OLAP),
176
Operational excellence, 45
Operational Executive Information
Systems (EIS), 144, 177–8
Oracle, and ERP, 147

Packaged software market
developments, 151–2
Partial channel substitution, 85, 87
Pharmaceuticals, IT support for R&D,
180–2
Planning see Marketing strategy and
planning
Porter:
five forces model, 14–15
three generic strategies, 87
value chain, 19–20
Predict industry structure process, 16
Prioritization matrix, 96–102
worksheets, 108–12
Prioritization of target markets, 15
Product leadership, 45
Production, and market evolution, 25–6

Products and markets, 73
Profiling, 184–5
Promotion:
    Dell promotion channels, 17–18
    and market evolution, 26
    Offline promotions/press
        advertising, 172
Promotion strategies, 17
    see also Integrated marketing
        communications process

R&D support, with IT, 146, 180–2
Relationship marketing, 6, 123
    see also Customer Relationship
        Management
Relationship techniques, 27
Retention (online) efficiency, 171

Sales force automation, 148–9
Sales process (online) metrics, 167–73
SAP (German vendor of integrated
    systems), and ERP, 147
Segmentation see Market segmentation
Software best practice, and CRM, 153–4
Spamming, 172
Strategic marketing planning see
        Determine value proposition
        processes; Market mapping/
        industry structure analysis;
        Marketing strategy and planning
Strategy tools, 214–15
Success factors/rates see IT
        success/failure factors/rates
Sustainable competitive advantage, 74
SWOT analysis, and the strategic
        marketing plan, 79

Tactical marketing, and marketing
        departments, 30

Tailored specialization, 5
Tangible assets, 74
Target surfers, 169
Task-independent data management,
        and CRM, 153
Technical buyers, 166
Technology, and market evolution, 24–5
Telemarketing, 149
Tjan's Internet Portfolio Map, 99–100

Understand competitor value
        positioning, 14
Understand value process see Define
        markets and understand value
        process
Undirected searching with data mining,
        176–7

Value chain, Porter, 19–20
    Value chain management, 7
Value curve, Kim and Mauborgne, 95
Value delivered measurement, 168
Value delivered monitoring, 164–7
Value proposition delivering processes,
        12–13
Value received monitoring, 161–2

Wal-Mart, undirected searching
        example, 177
Worksheets:
    Channel combinations, 107
    the e-marketing mix, 157–8
    future market mapping, 106
    internal competence dimensions, 69
    internal value chain, 113–14
    new media and industry
        competition, 70
    prioritization matrix, 108–12

Marketing titles from Butterworth-Heinemann

Student List

Creating Powerful Brands (second edition), Leslie de Chernatony and Malcolm McDonald
Direct Marketing in Practice, Brian Thomas and Matthew Housden
eMarketing eXcellence, PR Smith and Dave Chaffey
Fashion Marketing, Margaret Bruce and Tony Hines
Innovation in Marketing, Peter Doyle and Susan Bridgewater
Internal Marketing, Pervaiz Ahmed and Mohammed Rafiq
International Marketing (third edition), Stanley J. Paliwoda and Michael J. Thomas
Integrated Marketing Communications, Tony Yeshin
Key Customers, Malcolm McDonald, Beth Rogers, Diana Woodburn
Marketing Briefs, Sally Dibb and Lyndon Simkin
Marketing in Travel and Tourism (third edition), Victor T. C. Middleton with Jackie R. Clarke
Marketing Plans (fifth edition), Malcolm McDonald
Marketing: the One Semester Introduction, Geoff Lancaster and Paul Reynolds
Market-Led Strategic Change (third edition), Nigel F. Piercy
Relationship Marketing for Competitive Advantage, Adrian Payne, Martin Christopher, Moira Clark
    and Helen Peck
The New Marketing, Malcolm McDonald and Hugh Wilson
Relationship Marketing: Strategy & Implementation, Helen Peck, Adrian Payne, Martin Christopher
    and Moira Clark
Strategic Marketing Management (second edition), Richard M. S. Wilson and Colin Gilligan
Strategic Marketing: Planning and Control (second edition), Graeme Drummond and John Ensor
Successful Marketing Communications, Cathy Ace
Tales from the Market Place, Nigel Piercy
The CIM Handbook of Export Marketing, Chris Noonan
The Fundamentals of Advertising (second edition), John Wilmshurst, Adrian Mackay
Total Relationship Marketing (second edition), Evert Gummesson

Forthcoming

Marketing Logistics (second edition), Martin Christopher, Helen Peck
Marketing Research for Managers (third edition), Sunny Crouch and Matthew Housden
Marketing Strategy (third edition), Paul Fifield
Political Marketing, Phil Harris and Dominic Wring
Relationship Marketing (second edition), Martin Christopher, Adrian Payne and David Ballantyne
The Fundamentals and Practice of Marketing (fourth edition), John Wilmshurst and Adrian Mackay
The Marketing Book (fifth edition), Michael J. Baker (ed.)

Professional list

Cause Related Marketing, Sue Adkins
Creating Value, Shiv S. Mathur, Alfred Kenyon
Cybermarketing (second edition), Pauline Bickerton and Matthew Bickerton
Cyberstrategy, Pauline Bickerton, Matthew Bickerton and Kate Simpson-Holley
Direct Marketing in Practice, Brian Thomas and Matthew Housden
e-Business, J. A. Matthewson
Effective Promotional Practice for eBusiness, Cathy Ace
Excellence in Advertising (second edition), Leslie Butterfield
Fashion Marketing, Margaret Bruce and Tony Hines
Financial Services and the Multimedia Revolution, Paul Lucas, Rachel Kinniburgh, Donna Terp
From Brand Vision to Brand Evaluation, Leslie de Chernatony
Go-to-Market Strategy, Lawrence Friedman
Internal Marketing, Pervaiz Ahmed and Mohammed Rafiq
Marketing Made Simple, Geoff Lancaster and Paul Reynolds
Marketing Professional Services, Michael Roe
Marketing Strategy (second edition), Paul Fifield
Market-Led Strategic Change (third edition), Nigel F. Piercy
The New Marketing, Malcolm McDonald and Hugh Wilson
The Channel Advantage, Lawrence Friedman, Tim Furey
The CIM Handbook of Export Marketing, Chris Noonan
The Committed Enterprise, Hugh Davidson
The Fundamentals of Corporate Communications, Richard Dolphin
The Marketing Plan in Colour, Malcolm McDonald, Peter Morris

Forthcoming

Essential Law for Marketers, Ardi Kolah
Marketing Logistics (second edition), Martin Christopher, Helen Peck
Marketing Research for Managers (third edition), Sunny Crouch and Matthew Housden
Marketing Strategy (third edition), Paul Fifield
Political Marketing, Phil Harris and Dominic Wring

For more information on all these titles, as well as the ability to buy online,
please visit **www.bh.com/marketing**

Learning Resources
Centre